Integrity, Assessment, and Collaboration in the AI Classroom

Tendai Charles
https://orcid.org/0000-0002-0253-5960
The British University in Dubai, UAE

Christopher Hill
Canadian University in Dubai, UAE

IGI Global
Scientific Publishing
Publishing Tomorrow's Research Today

Vice President of Editorial	Melissa Wagner
Director of Acquisitions	Mikaela Felty
Director of Book Development	Jocelynn Hessler
Production Manager	Mike Brehm
Cover Design	Jose Rosado

Published in the United States of America by
IGI Global Scientific Publishing
701 East Chocolate Avenue
Hershey, PA, 17033, USA
Tel: 717-533-8845 | Fax: 717-533-7115
Website: https://www.igi-global.com E-mail: cust@igi-global.com

Library of Congress Cataloging-in-Publication Data

(CIP Data Pending)
ISBN13: 9798260003282
Isbn13Softcover: 9798260003299
EISBN13: 9798260003305
British Cataloguing in Publication Data
A Cataloguing in Publication record for this book is available from the British Library.

Table of Contents

Detailed Table of Contents

This qualitative study explores how faculty members in various universities in the United Arab Emirates (UAE) view the role of artificial intelligence (AI) in higher education in the country. Specifically, the study, using semi-structured interviews with nine professors across the UAE, aims to uncover how AI has transformed the way faculty teaches, conducts research, and uses AI for administrative purposes. The study also sheds light on the mixed emotions that faculty members experience considering the surge of AI use in their institutions and among their students. From viewing AI as a personal assistant that can streamline daily operations to sharing ethical concerns regarding assessment, academic integrity, and cultural bias, the findings reveal how the professional identities of faculty members are evolving in a time of change and uncertainty. These findings are timely in the context of the UAE, a nation that is positioned as an AI leader not only in the region but also globally through its UAE National AI Strategy 2031 and Centennial 2071 Vision. The study offers recommendations for ethical and transformative integration of AI in higher education through focusing on AI literacy, upskilling faculty, and developing policy frameworks that can enhance AI integration in the UAE and beyond.

Integrating Artificial Intelligence (AI) into education transforms how teaching and learning are conducted. AI technologies, such as adaptive learning platforms and intelligent tutoring systems, offer the potential to personalize instruction, provide real-time feedback, and optimize administrative tasks. However, alongside these benefits come challenges related to bias, fairness, transparency, and the need for human oversight. This chapter explores the role of AI in education, emphasizing the critical digital competencies that educators and students must develop to collaborate effectively with AI. It also addresses the ethical considerations associated with AI, including bias mitigation and the promotion of equity. Furthermore, the chapter discusses the challenges and opportunities of incorporating AI into curricula and lifelong learning, highlighting the need for investment in teacher training, equitable access to technology, and robust ethical frameworks to guide AI's responsible use in education. The future of AI in education hinges on fostering both technical and ethical literacy, ensuring that students are proficient in AI technologies and capable of shaping a more just and sustainable digital future.

Education is undergoing a profound transformation thanks to artificial intelligence. AI has reshaped collaborative learning. In Arabic language education, AI stands out as a solution to morphological, semantic, and dialectal challenges. Initiatives such as the Sird Scale, the Zay Scale, and the Tal'a and Mubkar tests are pioneering Arabic models that use artificial intelligence for personalization and motivation. Despite these developments, issues of privacy, algorithmic bias, and cultural sensitivity remain central, with the teacher continuing to play a key role as the designer of learning. The future trend confirms that successful smart education is based on a balance between technology and human vision.

This paper presents a comprehensive review of the recent published literature on the uses of Artificial Intelligence in English Language Teaching, its benefits and challenges. The qualitative, narrative literature review design was employed to identify and analyze the articles published in the last five years on this topic. The researcher used most popular academic databases, namely Google Scholar, and screened the vast published literature between 2020 and 2025. Most studies that were searched presented systematic literature reviews; the researcher identified around 25 relevant papers on AI in ELT. The investigation of the literature has answered the three research questions on the topic of AI in ELT. Recent papers highlighted the benefits and useful application of AI tools in language education. While some papers revealed challenges and limitation of implementing AI in teaching and learning English Language. The researcher concludes the review by providing recommendations for future research.

Generative AI has entered MENA classrooms faster than institutional cultures and regulations can catch up. This chapter examines how tools that can instantly generate essays, solutions, and code unsettle long-standing ideas of originality, authorship, and effort. It maps the emerging risk landscape—from invisible outsourcing of assignments to the gradual erosion of students' confidence in their own thinking—while situating these dynamics within the socio-economic pressures and exam-centred traditions of MENA education systems. Rather than framing AI only as a threat, the chapter explores how universities and schools can respond through coherent policy, imaginative assessment design, and sustained staff and student development. Drawing on regional examples, it argues for a shift from policing misconduct to cultivating a shared culture of integrity, where AI is used transparently, critically, and in ways that deepen, rather than replace, human learning.

Artificial Intelligence (AI) is rapidly transforming higher education, reshaping pedagogical practices, administrative operations, and institutional strategies. This literature review synthesizes recent scholarship (2023–2025) to examine how AI, particularly generative tools such as ChatGPT, is being integrated across global higher education contexts. Findings highlight dual pathways of adoption: pedagogically, AI supports personalized and adaptive learning, intelligent tutoring, content creation, and collaborative learning environments; administratively, it enables data-driven decision-making, resource optimization, and student lifecycle management. While offering significant opportunities, AI adoption raises critical ethical concerns, including academic integrity, data privacy, algorithmic bias, and risks to human development and social interaction. Institutional strategies for effective AI integration emphasize the importance of responsible leadership, robust governance frameworks, faculty development, and infrastructure investment. Student perspectives reveal widespread adoption of AI tools, driven by efficiency and workload pressures, but tempered by concerns about reliability, autonomy, and social consequences. Global analyses underscore disparities in adoption across regions, with most research originating from high-income countries, leaving gaps in understanding cross-cultural and equity-focused implications. The review concludes that AI in higher education is not merely a technological shift but a systemic transformation requiring balanced

work offers practical guidance for institutions striving to promote fairness, originality, and trust in an AI-driven educational landscape.

Preface

The rapid integration of artificial intelligence into education has ushered in a moment of profound transformation. Across classrooms, lecture halls, and institutional boardrooms, AI is no longer a speculative innovation, it is a lived reality. From generative tools capable of producing essays and code to adaptive platforms that personalize learning in real time, the educational landscape is being reshaped at an unprecedented pace.

Nowhere is this transformation more visible than in the United Arab Emirates and the wider MENA region, where ambitious national AI strategies intersect with dynamic and rapidly expanding education systems. Institutions are navigating not only the technical adoption of AI, but also deeper questions about academic integrity, assessment, pedagogy, professional identity, and human collaboration.

Integrity, Assessment, and Collaboration in the AI Classroom brings together scholars and practitioners from across the region to examine these challenges and opportunities through empirical research, theoretical reflection, and practical frameworks. The contributors approach AI neither as an unquestioned solution nor as an existential threat. Instead, they situate AI within the broader human mission of education: cultivating critical thinking, ethical awareness, creativity, and authentic learning.

Together, these chapters argue that the future of education lies not in replacing human expertise with automation, but in thoughtfully integrating AI to enhance learning while safeguarding ethical principles. The work presented here offers timely guidance for educators, policymakers, researchers, and institutional leaders seeking to balance innovation with responsibility.

This volume ultimately affirms that the most powerful educational technologies are those guided by human judgment, cultural awareness, and a commitment to integrity. In the AI classroom, collaboration must define the path forward.

Collectively, these chapters demonstrate that AI's role in education is not merely technological but fundamentally human. The central challenge is not whether AI will shape education—it already does—but how institutions, educators, and students will shape AI's role in return.

By foregrounding integrity, assessment reform, collaboration, and ethical governance, this volume contributes to a growing body of scholarship dedicated to ensuring that AI strengthens the core values of education rather than diluting them. Below is a chapter-by-chapter summary to supplement your reading.

CHAPTER 1

"We All Need a Personal Assistant": Exploring Faculty Perceptions about the Role of AI in Higher Education in the UAE

This qualitative study investigates how faculty members across UAE universities perceive AI's role in teaching, research, and administrative work. Through semi-structured interviews with nine professors, the authors reveal that many educators view AI as a "personal assistant" that streamlines daily tasks such as content preparation, grading, and research support.

However, alongside optimism, faculty express concerns about academic integrity, cultural bias, overreliance on automation, and the erosion of authentic assessment. The chapter highlights how AI is reshaping professional identities and calls for structured AI literacy initiatives, upskilling programs, and coherent institutional policies to guide ethical integration.

CHAPTER 2

Human Collaboration in the Age of AI: Building Responsible Digital Competencies in Education

This chapter explores how AI technologies, such as adaptive learning systems and intelligent tutoring platforms, can personalize learning and improve administrative efficiency. Yet it emphasizes that effective AI integration depends on developing robust digital competencies among educators and students.

The authors discuss ethical concerns including bias, transparency, and fairness, arguing for human oversight as central to responsible AI use. The chapter calls for curriculum redesign, teacher training, equitable access to technology, and long-term investment in ethical frameworks to ensure AI enhances rather than undermines educational equity.

CHAPTER 3

AI-Enhanced Educational Motivation in Collaborative Learning Environments

Focusing on Arabic language education, this chapter examines how AI supports collaborative and motivational learning models. It discusses innovative Arabic AI-driven initiatives such as the Sird Scale, the Zay Scale, and the Tal'a and Mubkar assessments, which address morphological and dialectal complexities in Arabic learning.

Despite these advancements, the author underscores concerns about privacy, algorithmic bias, and cultural sensitivity. The teacher remains central, not as a passive user of AI, but as a designer and ethical mediator of learning experiences. The chapter concludes that sustainable smart education requires balance between technological innovation and human pedagogical vision.

CHAPTER 4

A Review of the Uses of Artificial Intelligence in English Language Teaching: Benefits and Challenges

This narrative literature review synthesizes research published between 2020 and 2025 on AI applications in English Language Teaching (ELT). Drawing from approximately 25 key studies, the chapter identifies major benefits of AI tools, including personalized feedback, language practice automation, enhanced engagement, and accessibility.

However, it also addresses limitations such as reliability concerns, overdependence, teacher preparedness, and infrastructural constraints. The chapter concludes with recommendations for future research and emphasizes the importance of balanced implementation that supports, rather than replaces, pedagogical expertise.

CHAPTER 5

Academic Integrity in the Age of Generative AI: Risks and Institutional Responses

This chapter analyzes how generative AI tools disrupt traditional concepts of authorship, originality, and effort, particularly within MENA educational systems. It maps risks such as invisible outsourcing of assignments, diminished student confidence in independent thinking, and policy gaps in fast-changing institutional environments.

Rather than advocating punitive approaches, the chapter proposes a cultural shift toward shared responsibility. It calls for imaginative assessment design, coherent institutional policy, and comprehensive staff and student development programs that promote transparent, ethical AI use.

CHAPTER 6

Artificial Intelligence in Higher Education: Applications, Ethical Challenges, and Strategic Pathways for Institutional Transformation

Synthesizing recent global scholarship (2023–2025), this chapter reviews AI integration across higher education systems. It identifies two primary adoption pathways: Pedagogical integration, including adaptive learning, intelligent tutoring, content generation, and collaborative tools, and administrative integration, such as predictive analytics, student lifecycle management, and resource optimization.

The chapter emphasizes ethical challenges, data privacy, governance, transparency, and bias, and outlines strategic pathways for institutional transformation. It advocates for long-term planning, interdisciplinary collaboration, and responsible governance structures to ensure sustainable AI integration.

CHAPTER 7

Evaluating the Efficacy of AI-Based Formative Assessment in Promoting Student Learning in Secondary Education

Grounded in Constructivist Learning Theory (Vygotsky and Piaget) and Feedback Theory (Hattie & Timperley), this empirical study compares AI-based formative assessments with traditional approaches in secondary education.

Findings indicate that AI-driven tools, such as interactive quizzes and LMS-based assessments, offer real-time, adaptive feedback, increased motivation, and personalized learning pathways. However, challenges include teacher readiness, technological infrastructure, and equitable access.

The chapter recommends professional development, infrastructural investment, and balanced integration strategies to maximize learning benefits while maintaining pedagogical integrity.

CHAPTER 8

Rethinking Student Assessment in the Age of AI: Insights and Framework Proposals from a Gulf-Based Educational Program

Based on qualitative observations from a high-stakes professional program in the Gulf region, this chapter examines the intersection of AI detection tools, institutional compliance, and student behavior. It reveals inconsistencies in detection outputs and widespread uncertainty among both students and faculty. In response, the author proposes a four-pillar framework: Early AI orientation for students, AI-resistant assessment design, diagnostic (not punitive) use of detection tools, and AI-aware rubrics.

Practical strategies such as oral examinations, staged submissions, and project-based assessments are recommended to enhance authenticity and trust. The chapter offers actionable guidance for institutions seeking fairness and transparency in AI-influenced evaluation systems.

Chapter 1
"We All Need a Personal Assistant": Exploring Faculty Perceptions About the Role of AI in Higher Education in the UAE

Salma Waly
http://orcid.org/0009-0008-2001-9872
Sharjah Education Academy, UAE

Maram Al Aqra
http://orcid.org/0000-0002-1889-7659
Sharjah Education Academy, UAE

ABSTRACT

This qualitative study explores how faculty members in various universities in the United Arab Emirates (UAE) view the role of artificial intelligence (AI) in higher education in the country. Specifically, the study, using semi-structured interviews with nine professors across the UAE, aims to uncover how AI has transformed the way faculty teaches, conducts research, and uses AI for administrative purposes. The study also sheds light on the mixed emotions that faculty members experience considering the surge of AI use in their institutions and among their students. From viewing AI as a personal assistant that can streamline daily operations to sharing ethical concerns regarding assessment, academic integrity, and cultural bias, the findings reveal how the professional identities of faculty members are evolving in a time of change and uncertainty. These findings are timely in the context of the UAE, a nation that is positioned as an AI leader not only in the region but also globally through its UAE National AI Strategy 2031 and Centennial 2071 Vision. The study

DOI: 10.4018/979-8-2600-0328-2.ch001

offers recommendations for ethical and transformative integration of AI in higher education through focusing on AI literacy, upskilling faculty, and developing policy frameworks that can enhance AI integration in the UAE and beyond.

INTRODUCTION

Background and Importance

In this chapter, we use the term artificial intelligence (AI) to mainly refer to generative AI tools and large language models (LLMs). We focus on how faculty members use generative AI and LLM-based tools for planning, material design, feedback, assessment tasks, research support, and administrative work. We realize the powerful role of AI is reshaping and transforming the way learning and teaching occur not only in K-12 settings but also in higher education. This transformation is rapidly changing roles and responsibilities among educators and learners alike. Recently, most research has focused on the impact of AI on K-12 education (Holmes, Bialik, & Fadel, 2019; Luckin et al., 2016; Chen, Chen, & Lin, 2020). While there are some studies that look at the perceptions of university professors in the age of AI, there seems to still be a void that needs to be filled to fully uncover how AI is changing the landscape of teaching in higher education. There is also limited work that focuses on the GCC as a geographical region that is at the crossroads of AI integration and innovation. Therefore, the importance of this study is attributed to the fact that research on AI in higher education, as opposed to K-12 systems, is scarce. The context in which the study is conducted, the UAE, is also a unique one given its position as a multicultural and global hub and its status in innovation and technology.

The study aims to explore the impact of AI on higher education by examining the perspectives of faculty members in the UAE. The goal is to provide guidelines for ethical, effective, and culturally responsive AI use. This will be done by looking at the process of transformational learning that faculty members are experiencing in order to construct an understanding of the role AI plays in their classrooms (Mezirow, 1991). The study also intends to offer recommendations that can help governments and institutions effectively integrate AI in teaching and learning while also supporting faculty members throughout the process.

Research Questions

The central research question driving this study is, how has AI impacted the roles and practices of university professors in higher education in the UAE? This question is supplemented by sub-questions exploring the specific benefits and challenges associated with AI in planning, content creation, research, and administration. The aim of these questions is to uncover the underlying mindset changes, new learnings, and professional identity shifts that accompany AI use and adoption. We anticipate that the findings of this study will guide future research on the role that AI plays in higher education institutions in the GCC, especially in areas of educator training and assessment in higher education. We also hope that the results of this study will inform policy recommendations for higher education institutions in the GCC and beyond. Overall, this chapter contributes an empirically grounded, theoretically informed account of how faculty in the UAE are reconstructing their professional identities and pedagogical dispositions in reaction to the adoption of generative AI in higher education.

LITERATURE REVIEW

Transformative Learning Theory as a Theoretical Framework

Given the exploratory nature of this study, we sought to use a theoretical framework that allows us to analyze how AI use is influencing the way professors think about their role and their practice. In their Transformative Learning Theory, Mezirow (1991) explains that learning and exposure are transformative when they result in a shift in one's perspective. This transformation in one's learning takes place through reflection and dialogue. The professors we interviewed came to our interviews with new learnings on the possibilities that AI can offer based on their experiences in the past few years. We also wanted our time with them to be one where they would feel at ease engaging in conversations that dig deeper into what they referred to as the "new normal." Because we share the same profession as our participants and understand the challenges they experience, our conversations with them were open, honest, and very reflective. Our understanding of the tenets of Mezirow's theory helped us capture instances of learning, relearning, and knowledge construction through our reflection and dialogue with fellow faculty members.

Mezirow explains that adults experience a process of transformational learning when they are faced with new situations or realities that challenge their previous understanding or perceived notions about their roles and responsibilities. When faced with big changes, they resort to questioning and self-examination to evaluate their current knowledge, skills, and attitudes. Dialogue with like-minded colleagues and critical self-reflection, as well as exposure to learning resources, can eventually help adults re-evaluate their roles and responsibilities and integrate new perspectives into their professional identities. Transformative Learning Theory is not about merely acquiring new knowledge. Instead, it is about constructing meanings. meaning. It also highlights the active role of the individual in adopting new understandings, adapting to fresh perspectives, and expanding their worldview so that they can make sense of and contribute to the world around them.

In the context of AI in higher education, faculty members are faced with the question of how their roles might shift and change as their institutions adopt multiple AI tools, and their students utilize AI for most of their work. Many faculty members are now grappling with the notion of how AI can be used to enhance their work, automate time-consuming and repetitive tasks, and allow them the time to work on impactful research projects. Despite the promise of AI and the excitement that usually accompanies its use and integration, faculty members, just like everyone else, are trying to adapt to and adopt these new technologies. This process can be very tense, especially when professors weigh efficiency gains against ethical concerns as well as the loss of professional authority. These instances of questioning, re-questioning, and reconstructing new understandings exemplify what Mezirow's theory is about: learning transformation that emerges from discomfort.

Recently, researchers have made direct connections between transformative learning and the use of AI in schools. For instance, King et al. (2022) explains that the use of AI in education requires teachers to go beyond simply learning how to use a tool to what they call *adaptive expertise*. That way, educators are not merely delivering knowledge but rather facilitating inquiry and co-learning with the students. With AI in the classroom, educators need to adopt the mindset of shared inquiry alongside learners, one in which they guide students throughout the process of learning rather than possess knowledge. Scholars argue that educators must adopt the mindset of shared inquiry alongside learners, guiding students throughout the process of learning rather than positioning themselves solely as knowledge holders (King et al., 2022; Fischer et al., 2023; Tan et al., 2024). This shift challenges traditional hierarchies of authority and pedagogy in higher education classrooms.

Another shift in the dynamics of teaching and learning is related to guarding ethical AI use. Fischer et al. (2023) explains that issues of bias, privacy, and access require educators to play the role of ethical guardians to enforce appropriate AI use. In other words, educators need to take responsibility for how AI is used by students to ensure fairness and promote integrity. These new dimensions were not traditionally part of a faculty member's roles and responsibilities. They emerged with AI, and they require critical reflection and dialogue to reconstruct one's understanding of how teaching and learning look post-AI. In the UAE context, this reflection is of paramount importance given the cultural bias and the limited linguistic variations in most AI models.

In conclusion, Mezirow's Transformative Learning Theory demonstrates how AI adoption among faculty members is more than just a technical issue. It is a human and moral process that makes teachers question who they are and how they teach. AI can be a great way to help teachers grow professionally, but only if they are encouraged to think critically and accept their evolving roles as facilitators, co-learners, and moral leaders. Since transformation happens through reflection and dialogue with others who share the same background and experience, it is important to create safe spaces for educators to openly discuss issues directly impacting their profession. It is also important that professional development opportunities focus on a wider range of issues other than technical integration, such as the ethical, moral, and cultural implications of integrating AI in teaching and learning.

Context of the Study

The United Arab Emirates has positioned itself as a global leader for artificial intelligence by placing AI as a top priority in its national agendas. This started back in 2017 when the UAE appointed its first Minister of Artificial Intelligence, the very first nation worldwide to take such a bold step signaling its global aspirations to be a center of innovation (UAE Government, 2017). Following that was the launch of the UAE National Artificial Intelligence Strategy 2031, which stresses the need for integrating AI into all sectors (UAE Ministry of Cabinet Affairs, 2018). The UAE Centennial 2071 Vision also places AI at its center, emphasizing the need for the UAE to be an example of successful AI use and utilization (UAE Centennial Vision 2071, 2017). Educational institutions, bearing these policies in mind, are expected to take steps towards integrating AI in effective ways to contribute to diversifying the economy and making it more knowledge-based rather than oil-based (Khaleej Times, 2021).

Despite the UAE's position in AI leadership, research on the use of AI in higher education in the country remains limited (Al-Kendi & Al-Mehairi, 2022). The goal of this study is to capture the intersection of global intersections with local practices. In a diverse and multicultural setting like the UAE, where faculty members come from a wide range of educational and cultural backgrounds, it is crucial for researchers to explore the shifting dynamics of teaching and learning in the AI era. The voices of the educators in this study offer important insights into the reality of using AI in higher education, which can inform practices in other contexts globally. This can help shape national and institutional frameworks at a time of uncertainty and change (UNESCO, 2023). AI adoption in UAE higher education is also impacted by national quality assurance and governance frameworks, including standards related to academic integrity, assessment, data privacy and responsible AI use. Entities like the Commission for Academic Accreditation (CAA) and institutional quality assurance units set metrics for how assessment tasks are designed, how AI use should be acknowledged, and how program quality is monitored, which in turn influences how faculty experiment with AI in their teaching.

Review of Current Research

Artificial intelligence has taken education by storm. From large language models to a wide range of tutoring platforms, translation apps, and assessment tools, AI has a lot of potential for customizing teaching and learning and differentiating instruction for students. In recent years, researchers have explored how higher education institutions utilize artificial intelligence for teaching, research, and assessment as well as how they address the ethical issues associated with AI utilization (Ifenthaler, 2024; Zawacki-Richter et al., 2019). Researchers note that AI use in higher education presents a shift in how teaching and learning will look in the future (King et al., 2022; Fischer et al., 2023).

To clearly understand the role that AI currently plays in higher education, especially in connection to faculty roles and perspectives, we draw on literature on five major themes: teaching, research, administrative work, assessment, and ethics.

1. Artificial Intelligence and Teaching

Teaching is an area that has been widely impacted by AI adoption, especially in higher education. Many AI-driven tools that adapt content, differentiate instruction, and give suggestions for classroom activities promise to make teaching and learning more personalized (Chen, Chen, & Lin, 2020; Tan et al., 2024). With the rise of technologies that offer feedback, customize learning for the needs of diverse learners, and generate materials, faculty members can significantly cut down on the amount of time needed for planning and preparation. That, in return, provides many professors with the opportunity to focus on other impactful tasks such as mentoring, facilitating dialogue, and fostering critical thinking and professional growth among learners (King et al., 2022).

Recent studies highlight how AI has transformed the role of faculty members from transmitters of knowledge to facilitators and partners inquiry. King et al. (2022) and Fischer et al. (2023) describe this as adaptive expertise. Adaptive expertise refers to a faculty member's ability to seamlessly switch between efficiency-driven routines and innovative, inquiry-oriented pedagogy. With AI adoption, faculty members see themselves more as facilitators of inquiry-based learning instead of gatekeepers who possess knowledge and authority in the classroom. This mindset shift is linked to Mezirow's Transformative Learning Theory (TLT) that frames this study. By engaging in critical reflection and professional learning, professors can see alternative pathways to teaching and learning in higher education. This eventually leads to more nuanced professional identities that shape how they see themselves and their roles as experts in their subject matters (Mezirow, 1991).

Research also shows that there is a discrepancy in terms of how much professors are utilizing AI in their teaching and preparation. While some seem to be excited about the possibilities, others are skeptical and hesitant to adopt it (Dawson et al., 2023). In the UAE specifically, a country that is very diverse in terms of language and culture, many professors fear that AI systems may fail to represent the needs of their students (UNESCO, 2023). With AI systems often favoring dominant cultures and languages, professors fear that AI-generated content can be biased, which can impact their ability to create culturally responsive spaces for all learners (UNESCO, 2023).

Overall, research on the impact of AI on teaching and learning in higher education captures examples of excitement and promise as well as others of hesitancy and fear. While faculty members are eager to use tools and resources that allow them to work on impactful research projects, for instance, they are faced with the challenge of questioning their roles and responsibilities in a time where AI tools can automate much of their work, resulting in questions about the future and the value of their expertise.

2. Artificial Intelligence and Research Practices

AI has also impacted research across areas of discipline. It is now commonly used for data analysis, generation of literature, analysis of research articles, and predictive modeling. Many faculty members have recently reported that AI has helped them process large data sets. identify gaps, and form hypotheses with speed (Jordan & Mitchell, 2020; van Dis et al., 2023). These new nuances in the way that research is conducted do not only come with benefits but also with challenges. Conducting research using AI raises questions about academic originality and authorship.

Many researchers even argue that research conducted with the use of AI should be counted as co-authored literature (King et al., 2022). This adds a new dimension to what it means to be a professor in the age of AI. It is, ultimately, not only about utilizing AI for research but rather about one's ability to critically use it to accelerate the pace at which research is conducted while preserving originality, integrity, depth, and contextualization (Yusuf, Pervin, & Román-González, 2024). Higher education in the UAE is unique because of the diverse backgrounds of faculty members who teach in the country (Ridge, 2014). Faculty members also have different perceptions of research and innovation that are shaped by their former experiences in their home countries and/or previous institutions (Badrasawi et al., 2021). Institutions in the UAE, on the other hand, are striving to gain credibility and legitimacy and position themselves as lead organizations in the GCC and beyond (Wilkins, 2010; Kosmützky

& Krücken, 2014). Consequently, many faculty members are left questioning what counts as valid research in the age of AI (Yusuf, Pervin, & Román-González, 2024).

Again, the rapid change of how research is conducted now is yet another force that prompts professors to re-question their roles and professional identities. Understanding how professors in such a multicultural and aspirational context perceive the promise and the threat of AI use in research is important for creating future policies and practices that promote scholarly responsibility and rigor.

3. Artificial Intelligence and Administrative Work

Many universities all over the world have started using a wide range of AI-powered tools to automate processes in student admissions, scheduling, and workload allocations (Al-Abdullatif & Gameel, 2023). Many also use tools that allow them to predict student performance and flag issues that might impact student performance so that assistance is provided when needed (Zawacki-Richter et al., 2019).

Research has recently highlighted the merits of automating administrative tasks for educators, especially in higher education (Luckin et al., 2022). Many faculty members appreciate the reduction of administrative burdens so that they have more time for scholarly work and service-related assignments (Holmes et al., 2022). However, many are worried that automating tasks such as grading and assessment can impact feedback quality and differentiation of instruction (Chen et al., 2020). Research also shows that many faculty members feel uneasy about utilizing AI to make decisions about admissions and advising on the institutional level (Williamson & Eynon, 2020). The concern is that such practices might undermine accountability in higher educational settings.

Putting the context in mind, the UAE is a country where relationships and human connection are crucial for success in any setting and especially in higher education. It is important to hear the viewpoints of faculty members on how they balance efficiency by using AI while also maintaining human connections and building relationships with students. This is yet another aspect through which educators would need to reassess their priorities and create a balance that allows them to meet the institutional demands of efficiency and automation while also creating personalized learning experiences for diverse learners.

4. Artificial Intelligence and Assessment Practices

An area that has been greatly impacted by AI is assessment. There are many tools that can support faculty members in creating formative assessment practices to monitor student progress and track their learning. There are also tools that can automate grading, adjust test levels, and detect plagiarism (Smutny & Schreiberova,

2020). Despite all of that, AI has also brought brand-new issues and concerns to the surface. With AI tools such as ChatGPT, students can generate work, complete assignments, and solve problems using AI (Cotton et al., 2023). This requires institutions and educators to rethink the role of assessment in learning and how student learning gains can be evaluated in authentic ways that fully capture their growth and development.

Research shows that educators have different responses to the assessment dilemma in the age of AI. While some suggest completely banning AI in assessment, others recommend redesigning assessment tasks to avoid reliance on AI-generated content. Some recommendations include oral presentations, project-based assessment, reflective journals, and process-based assignments that focus on reasoning, application of key concepts, and creativity rather than a final product (Dawson et al., 2023). The assessment dilemma requires extensive pedagogical change on the side of faculty members, which in many cases can result in increased workloads for many (Zawacki-Richter et al., 2019). There is no question that AI use among students has highlighted the need to steer away from traditional assessment practices and move towards meaningful forms of evaluation (Holmes et al., 2022). However, without institutional clarity and professional development support, many faculty continue to be unsure about how to do the latter (Luckin et al., 2022).

Shifting attention to the context of the UAE, universities in the country follow the guidelines set forth by the Commission for Academic Accreditation (UAE Ministry of Education, 2019). It is important to capture faculty thoughts and reflections on issues concerning plagiarism and misuse of AI to understand how they intersect with national priorities around quality assurance (Al Karam, 2021). This context deepens the need for reflective dialogue with faculty members to learn about how they maintain standards while also embracing innovation.

5. Ethical Issues in Adopting Artificial Intelligence

AI integration in education comes with a wide range of ethical dilemmas. Some of these include data privacy, algorithmic bias, accessibility, and equity (Fischer et al., 2023; Dieterle et al., 2024). A UNESCO report in 2023 emphasizes that AI must be built and created with transparency and inclusivity to avoid widening the gaps of inequality among learners worldwide.

In the context of higher education, faculty members are increasingly called to be ethical custodians so that they can guide students to critically use AI (Fischer et al., 2023). That presents a new dimension to the professional identity of faculty members: one in which they do not only have to teach with AI but also about AI (King et al., 2022). These new responsibilities do not only impact the pedagogies used in higher education classrooms but also add to the workload of many professors worldwide (Selwyn, 2024). Such nuances are often overlooked and insufficiently researched (Williamson & Molnar, 2022).

In the UAE, where Arabic is the official language of the country, issues about linguistic and cultural bias present a bigger challenge. With most mainstream AI systems often underperforming in Arabic compared to English, there is a bigger chance the AI-generated content is culturally inappropriate (UNESCO, 2023). Even when English is utilized in AI search, bias about the context, the culture, and the needs of students in the UAE can still be an issue. Without sufficient training on AI prompting and critical literacy, faculty members would struggle to generate culturally relevant materials. Students would also be exposed to content that is not representative of their needs and backgrounds. These concerns shed light on the importance of culturally responsive AI use and integration (Gay, 2018). UAE universities, given the unique dynamics of the country, could play a revolutionary role in incorporating Arabic and cultural perspectives into AI design (Abdelghani, 2022).

Research shows that the ethical dimension of AI use impacts faculty well-being (Knox, 2023). Faculty need to not only adopt new technologies but also navigate how these technologies can be used fairly in their work and with their students (Zawacki-Richter et al., 2019). Faculty also need to navigate the worries of AI taking over their roles if they do not continuously participate in professional learning to upskill themselves (Selwyn, 2024). For AI to be ethically integrated in higher education, support should be provided to faculty members not only in terms of technical training but also through creating spaces for dialogue and reflection that address the human aspect of this transformation (Fischer et al., 2023).

Looking at the Bigger Picture

Current studies on AI and education illustrate that AI has potential promise in personalizing learning, expediting planning, and enhancing research endeavors. Despite all of that, there is also concern about bias, academic integrity, shifting roles, and professional identities. This presents new nuances for both faculty members and higher education institutions in terms of planning workloads, professional training, and institutional policies and recommendations. In the UAE, a multicultural nation with a strong Arab and Muslim identity, it is also crucial to carefully examine issues of equity, linguistic and cultural bias, and data privacy. The literature reviewed in this section shows both opportunities and challenges of AI use in higher education, emphasizing the need for culturally responsive, context-specific approaches to AI integration.

METHODOLOGY

Study Design

The study utilizes a qualitative research approach, which is a great fit for exploring perspectives and sharing reflections. Qualitative research allows for the collection of nuanced accounts and experiences, which help provide insight into how faculty members perceive AI, how they utilize it, and how it impacts their professional identities (Creswell & Poth, 2018). Within this approach, a case study design is used to contextualize the experiences of higher education faculty members in the UAE. Case study design offers in-depth analysis of phenomena while highlighting different perspectives among participants (Yin, 2018). We viewed this work as a multi-site qualitative case study of nine faculty members working in higher education institutions across the UAE. Each faculty member served as the primary unit of analysis, viewed within the broader UAE higher education system.

Participants

We interviewed nine university professors across disciplines and emirates in the UAE. Purposive sampling was used to ensure that professors were selected based on their professional roles and direct experiences with AI (Palinkas et al., 2015). For this reason, we asked professors to recommend colleagues that they knew were interested in reflecting on their experiences with AI. This approach provided access to relevant and informed perspectives while maintaining a good sample size for in-depth qualitative analysis. All faculty members in this study had a minimum of five years of experience, with some crossing the ten-year mark. Table 1 below introduces the participants of the study. Pseudonyms are used to identify all participants. Participants were selected purposively based on their current use and integration of AI in teaching, research, assessment, or administrative work. Invitations were sent via institutional email and professional networks. When participants suggested potential colleagues, we applied the same inclusion criteria to reduce bias.

Table 1. Participants' Demographics and Academic Backgrounds

Name	Age Group	Gender	Discipline	Emirate/Region
Walid	35-45	M	Educational Leadership	Sharjah
James	45-55	M	Interdisciplinary Studies	Abu Dhabi
Maya	35-45	F	Special Education	Abu Dhabi
Kareema	45-55	F	Linguistics/TESOL	Sharjah
Wilson	45-55	M	Philosophy	Ajman
Murat	35-45	M	Early Childhood	Sharjah
Dalia	45-55	F	AI	Dubai
Fatima	35-45	F	Pharmacy	Al Ain/Abu Dhabi
Sybil	25-35	F	Computer Science	Sharjah

Instruments

Semi-structured interviews were used as the main data collection tool. This allowed us to focus on the main domains that we wanted to explore, namely teaching, research, assessment, ethical concerns, and future directions. This also allowed flexibility to sidetrack and explore discipline-specific issues or nuances that each participant brought up (Kallio et al., 2016).

Interviews lasted around 30-60 minutes each and were conducted virtually via Zoom. We ended each interview by asking participants about a motto or a tagline that reflected their relationship with AI. This question always inspired further reflection and summarized the mixed emotions that faculty members experience while integrating AI into their daily work.

The core interview protocol included sections on participants' AI use in teaching, research, assessment, and administration as well as benefits and risks; institutional policies and supports; and shifts in professional identity. The closing "motto" prompt was analyzed inductively as metaphorical representation of how participants made sense of AI in their professional lives.

Procedure

Data Collection

Before the study commenced, we obtained ethical approval from our institution to conduct this research. Professors were contacted using their institutional emails or professional platforms such as LinkedIn and the UAE Research Map. Each participant received an invitation that summarized the purpose and goals of the study. Upon agreeing to participate, they completed a consent form. With participants' permission, all interviews were audio-recorded and transcribed using a research-specific transcription application. In addition, various notes were taken during the interview to capture specific details about the context or the depth of the conversation. The combination of interview transcripts and interview notes was used to identify patterns and establish connections with our theoretical framework and literature review.

Data Analysis

Thematic analysis was used to analyze the interview data in a systematic approach (Braun & Clarke, 2006). We started by reading the transcripts multiple times to familiarize ourselves with the data and gain a better understanding of the common issues discussed by the participants. This was followed by coding several text sections based on key ideas and experiences. Coding took place in iterative processes: an initial open-coding phase to capture prominent ideas, a second cycle to cluster related codes, and a final thematic phase to refine broader patterns across participants. Codes were organized into bigger themes that reflected the repeated patterns in the participants' reflections. These themes were then aligned with our research questions and study focus to generate a comprehensive understanding of the opportunities and challenges of utilizing AI in higher education in the context of the UAE. Both researchers engaged in separate and independent data analysis and then came together to discuss the findings. This practice was important to ensure data validity and inter-rater reliability.

RESULTS

Attitude and Mindset toward AI

The first theme that emerged from the analyses was attitude and mindset. This theme referred to how professors feel about AI and the beliefs and perceptions they have, which shape and impact their engagement with AI. Across the interviews, participants' attitudes varied from curiosity and positivity to hesitation, with one participant presenting a contrasting attitude of resistance. Most of the participants' responses indicated a positive attitude towards AI, where the professors were open to exploring and using AI tools.

One professor captured this by saying,

I found it a new opportunity, as another steppingstone that we could use to enhance our teaching as well as our students' learning experiences.

Another participant said:

I think it helps me to reduce the time needed for preparation.

A third participant reinforced this point:

Though at the beginning, we were a little bit resistant and reluctant, exploring it, I found out that it is very essential and very important for teachers because it kind of saved a lot of time.

Some professors expressed uncertainty as they navigate AI and its benefits and downsides.

This was described by one participant:

I would say AI is good but dangerous.

Another participant reported:

I've run into so many people who say, 'You're not using this! It will help you do things. It's so easy. I'm afraid of something that's easy, so I probably don't use it as much as I should.

Some reported that they are not very familiar with AI, and many professors expressed caution about it because of its limitations. As noted in one of the interviews:

I'm not there yet. So I don't feel comfortable yet using AI for teaching.

This was supported by a similar comment:

I'm a little bit behind using AI. I'm not learning; I'm not doing much self-learning on new AI tools.

Another professor reported:

I think as time goes on, I'm probably getting more into, like, how I could really use it... I'm still learning what other research practices can be supported by AI. So learning is on the go.

In contrast to the general positive perspective, one professor showed a strong resistance to AI, viewing it as a threat to the teaching profession. They argued:

I still prefer to use my PowerPoint and just give examples from my experience. I don't know if you can call it old school, but interactive tools such as Mentimeter and ClassPoint. Yes, I'm there, but I'm not using AI in my classes yet.

Taking a different angle, a professor said:

I hate it because of the fear of replacement.

And then elaborated:

AI is scary to me, scary to the future of pharmacy, and maybe to the future of many jobs, not only pharmacy... I don't know how it will help me in the future or be against me in the future.

Some professors adopted a pragmatic view of AI. One participant put it plainly:

There is no escape from this.

Another said:

It's here to stay. It's like the calculator; you might not like it, but it's here to stay. I don't think that we're going to get rid of it by not liking it.

One professor voiced this subtheme clearly:

Today or tomorrow, all of us will start using AI!

This theme shows that professors are still figuring out their attitude and position toward AI. While their values and experiences differ, they are taking a practical approach, aiming to develop a responsible response to AI. These attitudes suggest that professors are in an early stage of developing their understanding and mastery of AI as they gain more experience with it every day. These patterns go hand in hand with the tenets of Transformative Learning Theory, where emerging dilemmas, critical questioning, and negotiated meaning-making shape how adults redefine their frames of reference to new technologies.

AI as a Thinking and Pedagogical Partner

This theme referred to how professors use AI to think, plan, design, and evaluate learning. Professors described AI as their thinking and idea-generation partner.

It's more like a thinking partner than a substitute ... Because now with the help of AI, I can really simplify the more complex topics.

Another professor reported:

I would use it to prepare my assignments. I use ChatGPT or Gemini.

They described AI as a helpful assistant for teaching tasks and preparation. They talked about using AI to simplify complex ideas for students, generate case studies, summarize content, and handle many administrative tasks.

As one professor stated:

It is a supportive tool, not replacing me but supporting me during my teaching and my preparation ... I used to struggle finding case studies and scenarios, and I used to sit down on my own, but instantly you can get them. Now on AI, it's like it's like a huge difference.

Another one stated:

For education, we do a lot of reading, so it simplifies the reading, and it summarizes the readings.

They explained that they had to feed AI the input, explain the context, and go back and forth with their thinking partner to get the optimal output.

So, for example, deciding on the title that I used, or for example, before submitting my manuscript to a journal.

They also discussed how they used AI to critique and enhance their work.

I remember I said, 'Check if my paper is okay, pretend you are the reviewer, and be so harsh, and please criticize me on this paper.

When professors were asked to describe AI and the role it plays for them, they answered as follows:

AI is my best assistant.

It's my friend, but I don't use it blindly.

AI is my friend. I mean, really, my friend. I love it.

Considering AI as their teaching assistant, professors approached AI with a critical and realistic mindset. They recognized both its capabilities and limitations. They reported that they questioned the accuracy and quality of AI, leading them to use their professional judgment to evaluate any AI-generated output.

As one professor remarked:

I had to edit a lot before I shared a couple of prompts with the students. So yeah, it's amazing if we really know this, the steps, and to what extent it can help us. I think I see an AI tool as a baby that you train on how they think with you so they can serve you better. I actually call it a personal assistant. It is a personal virtual assistant.

This aligns with another professor's view:

You still have to do your own research to make sure that whatever information you're getting is actually valid and credible and comes from a good source.

This theme shows that professors use AI in a purposeful way that supports thinking and planning, but always under their guidance and driven by their expertise. They view AI as a helpful and supportive tool, but not as one that changes the core of their teaching. This suggests that professors are intentionally integrating AI to make their work more efficient while steering the learning process. In Transformative Learning Theory terms, for many participants AI functioned as encouraged them to reconsider assumptions about expertise, and what counts as effective pedagogy and meaningful teaching in higher education.

Changes in Students' Engagement, Confidence, and Classroom Dynamics

This theme explores how professors perceived AI as a tool affecting students' learning and classroom dynamics. Professors observed that AI is reshaping students' engagement, confidence, and learning behaviors in many different ways. Many reported that integrating AI can boost students' confidence by providing a virtual partner that can help with articulating ideas, simplifying concepts, and checking understanding, and therefore, making students feel more confident.

Students felt they were achieving something using AI. This was very, very helpful in that part.

A second professor shared a similar view:

I have noticed an increase in self-confidence because they feel more confident now. They have an assistant with them, so you see more participation, whereas if they're starting from scratch, without using any AI, then you see some students disappear in the background, like they're trying not to participate.

Another said:

Of course, students are much more engaged because they can really understand, and they can relate to real-world cases and scenarios.

And this theme was further confirmed by the remark:

AI has promoted student engagement more than before because, again, of the kinds of questions and the kinds of activities I'm able to provide in a short period of time, compared to me, again, sitting and writing up a case study.

Contrary to that, some professors described a decline in critical thinking and collaboration because some students rely on AI rather than engage in deep cognitive work or group discussion.

Students used to work together. But now, they have another peer, an additional virtual peer.

Another professor confirmed the same point:

I think it's very common now because students have access to information so much easier now than before. And they believe that they can do it on their own. But again, they're always missing out on the point that they need others, because learning is a communal practice; we learn by being with other people.

Very close to this point, one participant explained:

I saw many students who are now just interested in doing the task by themselves. So I'm telling them, "Look, group work is actually a part of this, so it's how you learn how to interact." So it's hard to get them into groups.

Another reported:

They're not as active in the classroom ... Looking around, you can tell they go to AI because all the answers are perfect. You know, the answers are perfectly written and well crafted, with no typos, no spelling errors, nothing.

Another participant reflected:

Their words sound more digital; they're talking in kind of like a more digital type of way. I'm serious. Like just to listen to their voices, it sounds kind of animated. It sounds really fast, like a fast pitch.

Some professors discussed engagement as a reflection of their teaching regardless of AI:

When I'm designing my lesson, my focus is on engagement. How am I going to make sure that the students are with me? I also try to focus on the engagement beyond the classroom. So, it's not easy for me to answer the question because it's really linked to the way I teach and the way I plan my teaching and my students' learning experiences. So for me, my values haven't changed with AI. I've always focused on engagement.

These mixed perspectives highlight the negative and positive effects of AI as both a motivator for learning and, at the same time, a barrier to critical thinking and students' collaborative engagement. Because of that, professors resorted to teaching students how to use AI in a responsible, ethical, and critical way.

I encourage my students to use AI and integrate AI into their assignments wisely and ethically.

You still need to double-check. This brings us back to years ago when we used to teach students about fact-checking. So, nothing has changed. They still need to go and check the information.

A professor also added:

We should educate our students and educate people in terms of getting information. Then they can use AI tools as an assistant... I told my students it is a supportive tool. But it's not like the only decision-maker.

Another participant reflected:

I tell them, "You can use AI, but I need you to just disclose that. Just say you use AI.

This theme shows that AI is changing how students participate and learn, but not always in a consistent way. While some students become more confident and engaged because of the use of AI, others rely on it and do not engage in collaborative work. Several professors emphasized that true engagement depends on how they teach, not on the presence of AI. These observations suggest that professors need to create a learning environment where critical thinking and collaboration are embedded.

Transformative Reconfiguration of Professional Identity and Pedagogical Role

This theme explores how professors in the era of AI started to renegotiate their identity, authority, and roles. Participants emphasized how confident they are of their roles as pedagogical experts despite the rapid evolution of AI and digital tools. They discussed how the fundamental principles of good teaching, such as fostering students' critical thinking and building relationships with students, will remain grounded in human practice.

One professor captured this by saying,

Teaching is a work of art, but it's also a work of the heart.

Another one noted in the interview:

The whole idea of prompting is really using your own expertise because you know exactly what you're looking for. So, to get something that is really high-quality and contextual, you have to prompt in the right way.

A second professor shared his perspective:

The type of teaching or writing that I follow is not threatened by AI ... You always have to customize AI because you know about the topic more than anybody else.

This aligns with another professor's view:

Engagement doesn't come from AI. It comes from my thinking and my design of the assignment. As I told you, I mean, AI wouldn't have given me this assignment if I hadn't given it what I want ... I am the one who is revising, I am the one who is inputting the information, and I am the one who is deciding.

This belief and commitment to human-centered teaching shaped how professors perceive AI's role in their work. They highlighted their own expertise and professional judgment, positioning themselves as the primary authority and decision-makers who interpret AI-generated output. At the same time, professors described experiencing identity shifts and reflective growth, explaining that exploring AI and working in the AI era has forced them to rethink aspects of their roles because knowledge and information are now widely accessible. Alongside these reflections, one participant expressed professional uncertainty, voicing concerns about being replaced by AI. They said:

AI came just as a reminder to tell us to stop and look at your teaching practices and methodology. You're not doing it right." And this is why AI can take your place So, it's just a reminder. But it is not threatening to me.

Another professor reported:

New technologies are emerging, and it's growing... Every day, it grows very fast. If you are not able to, you know, keep the pace of adopting and incorporating these technologies into our curriculum. We will be left behind ... We should rethink our assessment styles."

This theme shows that AI is prompting professors to think deeply about who they are as educators and experts. While they hold onto the core values of good teaching, they are also adapting, learning, and rethinking parts of their roles and who they are as professionals. These identity shifts and reflections align closely with Transformative Learning Theory, in which educators engage in critical reflection, explore alternative role dimensions, and integrate new nuances of understanding who they are as experts, facilitators, and ethical leaders in AI-rich environments.

Institutional Policy, Support, and Training Gaps

Professors pointed to the limited institutional support and training they received on how to use AI confidently and appropriately. Some said they don't know how to use AI, especially given the lack of professional development and unclear expectations for its use.

A participant said:

They want everyone to use it because they want to be up-to-date ...But they're not teaching teachers how to use it ... As we also have to keep pace, even these policies will have to be revisited every now and then because there are new developments.

Another participant stated:

I would embrace it, but we need to understand how it's used, and there's no source to give me information on how to actually use it properly in my work. If I have a workshop or anything like this.

Another professor stated:

I think it needs many rules in the future to regulate how it can be used in a good way.

Some of the participants emphasized that effective AI integration requires research-informed guidance. They described investing time and energy into using AI tools but not achieving their desired outcomes because of lack of training.

One professor said:

Maybe I don't know how to use AI. By the way, I need some professional development, I think, on how to use it more efficiently, because I end up—okay, here's the paper—writing an abstract for me to submit to a conference, and I include good details in the front, conference here, and these are the themes for the conference, and I give so many details, and then I get the abstract, and the abstract sounds like it's AI generated.

Another professor articulated this strongly by saying,

We need more research. We need more research on AI and its usage in higher education and in schools so we can make more informed decisions about how our programs and our courses, how our teacher education curricula and higher education program curricula can be redesigned, and how they can be rethought to integrate the maximum possible AI concepts, ideas, and ways of usage into these programs to really prepare the future generation, future graduates, for this AI-driven world.

This data shows that even though professors are eager to use AI and integrate it into their teaching and research, they do not feel fully confident in their skills in using it the right way. This suggests that there is a need to focus on AI literacy and professional development opportunities for college professors in order to enhance AI adoption and efficiency.

Perceptions on Cultural Responsiveness and Bias

This theme captures professors' concerns about the extent to which AI-generated content is culturally responsive. Professors reflected on their own experiences, describing how AI sometimes generates content that does not align with their students' culture and context or educational setting.

I know that these tools are supportive, and sometimes they create good content, but maybe not appropriate content, and so on. So first, I have to check in terms of cultural appropriateness.

Participants noted that AI reflects a Western perspective and favors certain languages. It sometimes generates responses that are biased or misaligned with their students' cultural backgrounds.

Is it culturally sound? Is it culturally relevant? Are they looking at everybody, or are they just looking at one particular background?

Professors also highlighted issues related to linguistic bias and explained how these limitations are problematic for them and their work and research.

So, biased for cultures, yes, but it's biased for English, that I can definitely tell you, given the project we're working on for Arabic. Even though we found that it's improving, teaching Arabic, like teaching reading comprehension in Arabic, is improving, especially the paid versions, which are usually much better. And I'm not sure why, but the paid versions are more culturally sensitive. This is very interesting.

These concerns show that professors do not see AI as culturally responsive as it should be. They recognize the need to critically review and contextualize AI-generated content to ensure it is culturally relevant to their context. This prompts a need for ethical and inclusive AI design, one that honors different languages and represents traditionally marginalized groups.

DISCUSSION

The purpose of this study is to explore how faculty members in higher education institutions across the United Arab Emirates view the integration of AI in their teaching, research, assessment, and administrative work. Guided by Mezirow's (1991) Transformative Learning Theory, the study's goal was to understand not only the practical aspects of AI integration in higher education but also its impact on the mindset and professional identity of faculty members. The results of this study show both alignment with global research findings as well as context-specific insights given the unique nature of the higher education industry in the UAE.

Faculty Attitudes and Mindset

Regarding faculty attitudes and mindsets, the results reveal that most participants approach AI with curiosity, openness, and cautious optimism, while some have reservations about AI use. The view of AI as a personal assistant that facilitates tasks such as literature searching, drafting materials, and differentiating ideas for diverse learners is aligned with prior scholarly findings that highlight AI's potential to enhance productivity and pedagogical design (Chen et al., 2020; King et al., 2022). Similarly, concern about overreliance on AI and loss of academic originality is a theme that emerges in global discussions regarding the risk associated with AI use in higher education (Yusuf et al., 2024; Selwyn, 2024).

These mixed attitudes can easily be traced back to Mezirow's (1991) theory of transformation in which adults grapple with dilemmas, engage in critical reflection, and start questioning their previous experiences, roles, and assumptions. Faculty in this study demonstrated that AI use and integration go beyond technical adoption. It, instead, involves a process of ongoing reconstruction and re-examination of their professional identities.

Teaching and Learning

Findings related to teaching and learning show that faculty are utilizing AI to plan lessons, create examples and case studies, and tailor materials to student needs. These findings are consistent with global trends in which AI is described as a tool that allows educators to move towards student-centered learning (Fischer et al., 2023; King et al., 2022). Participants stressed that while AI can generate ideas and create content, their pedagogical expertise and cultural responsiveness remain central to effective teaching. This focus on human judgment and intelligence supports the argument that AI can enhance but not replace the relational and interpretive dimensions of academic work, especially in a multicultural setting such as the UAE. At the student level, faculty members noted that AI-supported tools can foster confidence by helping them express ideas, develop a deeper understanding of issues, and reduce anxiety. These findings are consistent with research that describes AI as a tool for personalized learning and scaffolding (Cotton et al., 2023).

On the other hand, many faculty members also expressed concern that overreliance on AI use can impact students' critical thinking and cognitive engagement. This tension amplifies the need for explicit instruction on ethical and critical AI use among students (Fischer et al., 2023; Holmes et al., 2022).

Professional Role and Identity

The findings also indicate that faculty members are undergoing significant shifts in professional identity as they navigate AI integration. Many faculty members affirmed their roles as pedagogical experts and ethical custodians, even though they also acknowledged that AI has made it easier for students to generate content. This dynamic reflects broader debates about how expertise is defined in the age of AI. It also sheds light on the importance of adaptive expertise, where faculty move fluidly between efficient routines and innovative, inquiry-driven approaches (King et al., 2022).

While some faculty interpreted AI as an opportunity for growth and continuous learning, others expressed fear and anxiety about the perceived devaluation of their work. Again, this is consistent with global trends on the affective dimensions of AI integration in higher education (Jordan & Mitchell, 2020; Selwyn, 2024).

Institutional Policy and Cultural Relevance

Institutional conditions emerged as a major factor shaping how faculty engage with AI. Participants shared concerns about the limited professional development, inconsistent policies related to assessment and academic integrity, and significant variability in access to AI tools. This is consistent with global findings that indicate that institutions are not yet fully prepared to support responsible AI use and integration (Luckin et al., 2022; Zawacki-Richter et al., 2019). Faculty members also spoke about the importance of cultural and linguistic responsiveness in AI use. They expressed concern about how AI-generated content reflects dominant or generalized perspectives that do not align with the UAE's cultural, linguistic, and educational realities. Recent research trends highlight the underperformance of AI systems in Arabic and the risks of misrepresentation. In the UAE, a context where Arabic is the official language and where national visions focus on cultural identity and innovation, the need for context-sensitive AI tools is particularly crucial.

To sum up, the findings reinforce the idea that AI integration in higher education is not solely a technical issue. Instead, it is a deep human, ethical, and pedagogical process that requires faculty to reflect on their roles, values, and responsibilities. With a context like the UAE, these insights are particularly relevant, as they provide guidelines for institution policies, recommendations, and future directions in exploring the role of AI in higher education.

CONCLUSION

This study examined how artificial intelligence is impacting faculty roles and professional identities in higher education institutions in the UAE. Drawing on semi-structured interviews with nine professors from diverse backgrounds and emirates, the study confirms that AI is seen as a valuable teaching and learning tool. At the same time, faculty members shared major concerns pertaining to academic integrity, overreliance on AI tools, equity, and cultural relevance.

Reflecting on faculty's responses, they all engaged in a transformative learning process as they questioned the promise and challenge of AI use and integration.

Drawing on Mezirow's (1991) framework, AI is prompting faculty members to rethink their authenticity, expertise, and what counts as solid teaching and learning.

LIMITATIONS

The limitations of this study can be attributed to the limited number of faculty members who participated in it. While the sample size is good for in-depth qualitative analysis, it does not capture the full spectrum of perspectives among educators in the UAE. The data in this study is also based on self-reported experiences, which can be heavily influenced by the participants' familiarity with AI tools and institutional cultures. The study also focused on faculty perspectives solely and did not include the voices of other stakeholders such as students, administrators, and policymakers. Finally, the study was conducted at a time of rapid change in technology, innovation, and AI adoption. With time, faculty attitudes may change and evolve, especially as institutions start introducing AI-related frameworks. These limitations highlight the need for future research that is broader and longitudinal.

RECOMMENDATIONS

The implications for practice, policy, and future research emerging from this study can be summarized as follows. First, there is a need to invest in AI literacy professional development initiatives in the UAE. These initiatives should go beyond technical training to include ethical, critical, and cultural issues related to AI use and integration. These initiatives will help faculty understand how AI can complement rather than replace their pedagogical knowledge and content-area expertise.

Another recommendation is to develop clear and coherent policies to guide and govern how AI can be used in teaching, assessment, and research. These policies should focus on the principles of transparency, academic integrity, and responsible practice. This will not only streamline ethical use of AI but also eliminate uncertainty among educators and students alike. A third recommendation is to address equity and access issues related to AI use and integration to ensure fair use and minimize disparity among users. This is particularly relevant in such a diverse context as the UAE, in which there is a discrepancy in socioeconomic backgrounds. The goal is to ensure access to all. There is also a need to support and develop culturally responsive AI platforms that address the needs of not only the UAE but the whole region. Universities in the UAE can play a vital role in contributing to Arabic language datasets and initiating cultural perspectives in AI design and evaluation.

Finally, institutions should prioritize faculty well-being by creating spaces for dialogue and reflection. Communities of practice are urgently needed to provide faculty with opportunities to share their experiences and navigate changes, challenges, and opportunities collectively. This is especially important as technology continues to evolve and shape the way institutions operate and faculty members approach teaching, learning, and research endeavors.

Future research could include longitudinal studies that follow faculty over time as institutional AI policies keep evolving to trace how differing governance arrangements shape AI integration in higher education. There is also a need to incorporate the perspectives of students, academic leaders, and policymakers to develop more holistic and multi-level understandings of how AI continues to reshape teaching, learning, and academic work in the region.

REFERENCES

Abdelghani, N. (2022). Artificial intelligence and Arabic language processing: Opportunities and challenges. *Journal of Arabic Linguistics*, *56*(2), 145–162.

Al-Abdullatif, A., & Gameel, B. (2023). Artificial intelligence–driven decision-making in higher education: Emerging practices and ethical concerns. *Education and Information Technologies*, *28*(4), 5231–5252.

Al Karam, A. (2021). Quality assurance and academic integrity in UAE higher education. *Journal of Higher Education Policy and Leadership Studies*, *2*(1), 49–62.

Al-Kendi, R., & Al-Mehairi, S. (2022). The adoption of artificial intelligence in universities across the United Arab Emirates. *International Journal of Educational Technology in Higher Education*, *19*, 38.

Badrasawi, K., Zaki, W., & Mustafa, F. (2021). Understanding research identities among faculty in Gulf universities. *International Journal of Research in Education and Science*, *7*(4), 1043–1062.

Braun, V., & Clarke, V. (2006). Using thematic analysis in psychology. *Qualitative Research in Psychology*, *3*(2), 77–101. DOI: 10.1191/1478088706qp063oa

Centennial Vision, U. A. E. 2071. (2017). *Centennial 2071 strategic document.* UAE Government.

Chen, W., Chen, R., & Lin, Y. (2020). Artificial intelligence in higher education: A systematic review. *Journal of Educational Technology & Society*, *23*(2), 103–118.

Commission for Academic Accreditation (UAE Ministry of Education). (2019). *Standards for institutional licensure and program accreditation*. Ministry of Education.

Cotton, D. R. E., Cotton, P. A., & Shipway, J. (2023). ChatGPT, assessment, and academic integrity: Student and staff perspectives. *Innovations in Education and Teaching International*, *60*(4), 1–12.

Creswell, J. W., & Poth, C. (2018). *Qualitative inquiry and research design: Choosing among five approaches* (4th ed.). SAGE.

Dawson, P., ChatGPT Detection Working Group, & Sutherland, K. (2023). Rethinking assessment in the age of generative AI. *Assessment & Evaluation in Higher Education*, *48*(7), 1–15.

Dieterle, E., Becker, S., & Williams, C. (2024). Ethical AI in education: Balancing innovation and equity. *Computers & Education*, *192*, 104629.

Fischer, C., Davis, L., & Dougherty, S. (2023). Educators as ethical leaders in AI-rich classrooms. *Computers & Education. Artificial Intelligence*, *4*, 100143.

Gay, G. (2018). *Culturally responsive teaching: Theory, research, and practice* (3rd ed.). Teachers College Press.

Holmes, W., Anastopoulou, S., Schafer, B., Payne, A., Smith, M., & Gray, E. (2022). AI in higher education: Risks, opportunities, and future directions. *British Journal of Educational Technology*, *53*(6), 1355–1373.

Holmes, W., Bialik, M., & Fadel, C. (2019). *Artificial intelligence in education: Promises and implications for teaching and learning*. Center for Curriculum Redesign.

Ifenthaler, D. (2024). Digital transformation and AI adoption in universities: A global overview. *Technology. Knowledge and Learning*, *29*(3), 677–694.

Jordan, M. I., & Mitchell, T. (2020). Artificial intelligence: Evolution, opportunities, and challenges. *Science*, *349*(6245), 255–260. DOI: 10.1126/science.aaa8415 PMID: 26185243

Kallio, H., Pietilä, A., Johnson, M., & Kangasniemi, M. (2016). Systematic methodological review: Developing semi-structured interviews. *Journal of Advanced Nursing*, *72*(12), 2954–2965. DOI: 10.1111/jan.13031 PMID: 27221824

Khaleej Times. (2021). The UAE pushes forward as a global leader in artificial intelligence. https://www.khaleejtimes.com

King, A., Fischer, C., & Johnson, W. (2022). Toward adaptive expertise: Rethinking faculty roles in AI-mediated learning environments. *Computers & Education*, *185*, 104529.

Knox, J. (2023). AI, automation, and the academic self: Reframing digital labor. *Postdigital Science and Education*, *5*(1), 14–29.

Kosmützky, A., & Krücken, G. (2014). Transnational university rankings and the quest for legitimacy. *Higher Education*, *68*(3), 411–424.

Luckin, R., Holmes, W., Griffiths, M., & Forcier, L. B. (2016). *Intelligence unleashed: An argument for AI in education*. Pearson Education.

Luckin, R., Smith, M., Baines, L., & Dolan, R. (2022). AI readiness in universities: Frameworks for strategic decision-making. *International Journal of Artificial Intelligence in Education*, *32*(3), 771–792.

Mezirow, J. (1991). *Transformative dimensions of adult learning*. Jossey-Bass.

Palinkas, L. A., Horwitz, S., Green, C. A., Wisdom, J., Duan, N., & Hoagwood, K. (2015). Purposeful sampling for qualitative data collection and analysis in mixed-method implementation research. *Administration and Policy in Mental Health, 42*(5), 533–544. DOI: 10.1007/s10488-013-0528-y PMID: 24193818

Ridge, N. (2014). *Education in the UAE: Drivers and challenges*. Dubai School of Government.

Selwyn, N. (2024). *The future of AI in higher education: Critical questions and emerging tensions*. Polity Press.

Smutny, P., & Schreiberova, P. (2020). Chatbots for learning: A comprehensive review. *Computers & Education, 151*, 103862. DOI: 10.1016/j.compedu.2020.103862

Tan, S., Wong, L., & Ng, M. (2024). AI-enabled personalization in higher education. *Journal of Computer Assisted Learning, 40*(1), 233–248.

UAE Government Media Office. (2017). The UAE appoints the world's first minister of artificial intelligence. https://www.mediaoffice.ae

UAE Ministry of Cabinet Affairs. (2018). *UAE National Artificial Intelligence Strategy 2031*. UAE Government.

UNESCO. (2023). *Guidance for generative AI in education and research*. UNESCO Publishing.

van Dis, E. A. M., Bollen, J., Zuidema, W., van Rooij, R., & Littman, M. (2023). Large language models and the future of academic research. *Nature, 620*, 115–118.

Wilkins, S. (2010). Higher education in the GCC: Accessibility, quality, and the role of private providers. *Journal of Higher Education Policy and Management, 32*(4), 401–414.

Williamson, B., & Eynon, R. (2020). Algorithmic decision-making in higher education. *Learning, Media and Technology, 45*(1), 87–106.

Williamson, B., & Molnar, A. (2022). The political economy of educational AI: Platforms, power, and policy. *Educational Theory, 72*(3), 323–342.

Yin, R. K. (2018). *Case study research and applications: Design and methods* (6th ed.). SAGE.

Yusuf, Z., Pervin, N., & Román-González, M. (2024). Scholarly responsibility in the age of AI: Rethinking authorship, rigor, and expertise. *Computers & Education. Artificial Intelligence, 4*, 100152.

Zawacki-Richter, O., Marín, V. I., Bond, M., & Gouverneur, F. (2019). Systematic review of research on artificial intelligence applications in higher education. *International Journal of Educational Technology in Higher Education*, *16*(1), 39. DOI: 10.1186/s41239-019-0171-0

Chapter 2
Human Collaboration in the Age of AI:
Building Responsible Digital Competencies in Education

Areej ElSayary
http://orcid.org/0000-0002-5554-0069
Zayed University, UAE

Karim Ragab
http://orcid.org/0000-0003-1337-3562
Al Ittihad Private School - Mamzar, UAE

ABSTRACT

Integrating Artificial Intelligence (AI) into education transforms how teaching and learning are conducted. AI technologies, such as adaptive learning platforms and intelligent tutoring systems, offer the potential to personalize instruction, provide real-time feedback, and optimize administrative tasks. However, alongside these benefits come challenges related to bias, fairness, transparency, and the need for human oversight. This chapter explores the role of AI in education, emphasizing the critical digital competencies that educators and students must develop to collaborate effectively with AI. It also addresses the ethical considerations associated with AI, including bias mitigation and the promotion of equity. Furthermore, the chapter discusses the challenges and opportunities of incorporating AI into curricula and lifelong learning, highlighting the need for investment in teacher training, equitable access to technology, and robust ethical frameworks to guide AI's responsible use in education. The future of AI in education hinges on fostering both technical and ethical literacy, ensuring that students are proficient in AI technologies and capable of shaping a more just and sustainable digital future.

DOI: 10.4018/979-8-2600-0328-2.ch002

INTRODUCTION

The advent of Artificial Intelligence (AI) has introduced profound changes across various fields, with education being a key area of transformation. While scholars broadly agree that AI is reshaping how schools manage operations, teachers deliver instruction, and students engage with learning materials (Huang, 2023; Wang & Lester, 2023), there is significant variation in how researchers characterize this transformation. Some emphasize AI's potential to enhance school management, optimize instructional strategies, and foster student self-development, pointing to evidence from educational settings where such benefits are already evident (Huang, 2023). Others adopt a more cautious stance, arguing that these benefits are contingent upon careful implementation and that claims about AI's transformative power often outpace empirical evidence (Gillani et al., 2023). This tension between optimism and caution reflects a deeper disagreement in the literature about whether AI represents a fundamental shift in educational practice or a more incremental evolution of existing technologies.

Before proceeding, it is important to clarify the key terms used throughout this chapter. Artificial Intelligence (AI) refers to computer systems designed to perform tasks that typically require human intelligence. In educational contexts, this includes systems that learn from data, recognize patterns, and make predictions or recommendations, such as adaptive learning platforms that adjust content difficulty based on student performance, or grading systems that evaluate student work. This chapter focuses primarily on machine learning-based AI systems, where algorithms improve through exposure to data rather than following pre-programmed rules. While the chapter occasionally references generative AI, systems like large language models that generate new text, images, or code based on patterns in training data, the primary focus is on AI systems designed to support, personalize, or automate specific educational functions.

Human-AI collaboration refers to the deliberate partnership between educators, students, and AI systems, where each contributes distinct capabilities. Humans bring judgment, contextual understanding, ethical reasoning, and the ability to recognize when AI outputs are inappropriate or harmful. AI systems bring speed, pattern recognition across large datasets, and the ability to personalize at scale. Responsible human-AI collaboration requires that humans maintain meaningful oversight and decision-making authority, particularly for high-stakes decisions affecting student learning and records.

This gap between promise and practice is central to this chapter. While vendors celebrate efficiency gains and personalization, empirical evidence reveals uneven benefits and emerging equity concerns (Bulut et al., 2024; Chan & Tsi, 2023). Understanding why this gap exists and how to bridge it requires examining not just what

AI can do, but also the competencies educators need, the ethical risks that emerge, and the governance structures that ensure responsible deployment.

The literature on AI in education reveals a critical insight: fairness, transparency, and accountability are not separate concerns to be balanced independently. Rather, they are deeply interconnected. The 'black box' nature of many AI systems directly undermines efforts to promote fairness and accountability (Gillani et al., 2023). This interconnection means that addressing one challenge without addressing the others may create new problems; for instance, automation designed to improve efficiency may inadvertently reduce transparency, making bias harder to detect.

To illustrate this interconnection, consider three common AI applications in education: adaptive learning platforms that personalize content, intelligent tutoring systems that provide one-on-one support, and data analytics tools that identify struggling students. Each offers genuine benefits, personalized instruction, continuous support, targeted interventions. Yet each also introduces specific risks: adaptive systems can perpetuate achievement gaps if training data reflects historical inequities; tutoring systems can create over-reliance if students don't engage critically; analytics tools can enable surveillance if not carefully governed (Ojha et al., 2023; Mello et al., 2023; Zhai et al., 2021).

Responsible AI integration requires simultaneous attention to four interconnected dimensions: (1) understanding specific AI use cases and their embedded assumptions about learning, (2) developing educator and student competencies to work effectively with these systems, (3) identifying and mitigating ethical risks, and (4) establishing governance mechanisms to ensure accountability. This chapter explores each dimension and their interdependence (Gillani et al., 2023; Tan & Subramonyam, 2023).

As AI becomes more ingrained in education, there is a growing need to prepare students for an AI-integrated future. This preparation involves developing digital competencies that enable students to work collaboratively with AI systems. These competencies include technical skills, critical thinking, ethical reasoning, and an understanding of AI's societal implications (Michaeli et al., 2023). Teachers are crucial in guiding students through this evolving landscape, helping them understand AI's fundamental principles, limitations, and potential impact on society (Kamalov & Gurrib, 2023). By fostering AI literacy, students can learn to use these technologies responsibly and ethically while also critically assessing the decisions made by AI systems (Gillani et al., 2023). Moreover, students should be encouraged to explore AI's applications in various fields, such as education, healthcare, and social services, thereby developing a sense of agency in shaping the future of AI technologies (Kamalov & Gurrib, 2023).

Integrating AI into education brings immense potential to personalize learning, streamline administrative processes, and enhance educational outcomes. However, it also introduces challenges that require thoughtful consideration, particularly around fairness, transparency, and ethical accountability. In order to fully harness AI's benefits while mitigating its risks, educators and students must develop the necessary digital competencies. These include technical skills for operating AI systems, a deep understanding of ethical issues, critical analysis of AI's outputs, and the ability to responsibly navigate its societal implications.

This chapter addresses AI in both K-12 and higher education settings, recognizing that while the contexts differ, the core challenges of responsible AI integration are similar across educational levels. Examples throughout the chapter draw from both contexts: secondary mathematics classrooms, elementary science instruction, and university biology courses. However, readers should note that implementation realities vary significantly across different contexts. K-12 schools often face greater resource constraints and stricter regulatory requirements regarding student data protection, while higher education institutions may have more autonomy in technology adoption but face distinct challenges related to scale and institutional change. Where context-specific considerations are important, they are noted explicitly. The chapter's central argument, that responsible AI integration requires simultaneous attention to use cases, competencies, ethics, and governance, applies across educational levels, though the specific strategies for implementation will vary. This chapter will explore the fundamental questions: *How can AI be integrated responsibly into education? What competencies do educators and students need to collaborate effectively with AI? How can ethical considerations be embedded into the use of AI-driven educational tools?*

A FRAMEWORK FOR RESPONSIBLE HUMAN-AI COLLABORATION IN EDUCATION

The integration of AI into education cannot be approached as a purely technical or pedagogical challenge; it requires a holistic framework (See Figure 1) that simultaneously addresses four interconnected dimensions: (1) AI use cases and applications, (2) required digital competencies, (3) ethical risks and mitigation strategies, and (4) governance and institutional oversight (Chan, 2023; Chan & Colloton, 2024; Unesco, 2023; Prazeres & Pina, 2024). These dimensions are not sequential or independent; rather, they form a dynamic system in which decisions made in one area directly influence outcomes in the others.

Figure 1. A holistic framework that addresses four interconnected dimensions.

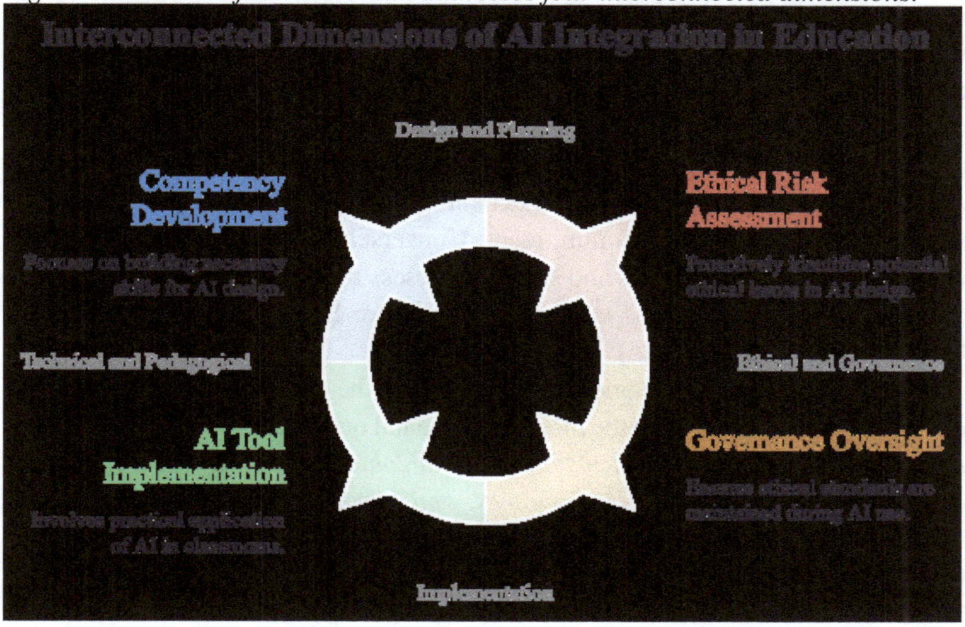

Throughout this chapter, we use the term "AI systems" to refer to the specific technologies discussed, including adaptive learning platforms, intelligent tutoring systems, grading systems, and data analytics tools. We distinguish between these application-specific systems and the broader concept of "AI" as a field. Our focus is on how specific AI applications function in educational settings, the competencies they require, the ethical risks they introduce, and how institutions can govern them responsibly. We do not attempt to address all AI applications or all possible educational uses of AI; rather, we focus on the most commonly deployed systems and the most pressing challenges they present.

To illustrate this interdependence, consider an institution implementing an AI-driven grading system. The choice of use case (automated assessment) directly shapes the competencies educators must develop (understanding algorithmic decision-making, recognizing bias in training data). Simultaneously, this use case introduces specific ethical risks (algorithmic bias, lack of transparency, reduced human judgment) that demand corresponding governance mechanisms (bias audits, human review protocols, stakeholder accountability). Without attention to all four dimensions, institutions risk deploying AI systems that may be technically sophisticated but ethically problematic, or conversely, systems that are well-intentioned but lack the institutional capacity to implement them responsibly (Akbarighatar, 2024; Ibitoye et al., 2025; Sitnicka et al., 2025).

This framework, which connects use cases, competencies, ethics, and governance, serves as the organizing principle for this chapter. Rather than treating AI in education as a collection of isolated technologies or competencies, we position human-AI collaboration as a deliberate, multi-stakeholder endeavor that requires intentional design at every level. The framework recognizes that educators and students cannot develop meaningful competencies without understanding the ethical implications of AI systems, nor can ethical frameworks be implemented without clear governance structures and institutional commitment. Conversely, governance structures are only effective when educators and students possess the competencies to recognize and address ethical concerns in practice (Barnes & Hutson, 2024; Daher, 2025; García-López & Liñán, 2025).

By adopting this framework, we move beyond the question of *"What AI tools can we use in education?"* to the more fundamental question: *"How can we design, implement, and govern AI systems in ways that enhance learning while upholding our commitments to equity, transparency, and human agency?"* This reframing acknowledges that responsible human-AI collaboration is not a technical problem to be solved but an ongoing institutional and pedagogical practice that must be continuously refined through collaboration among educators, technologists, researchers, policymakers, and students themselves (Du et al., 2024; Ifenthaler et al., 2024; Unesco, 2023). Central to this approach is the understanding that the effectiveness and ethical soundness of AI integration are intrinsically linked to the situated nature of its implementation within diverse educational contexts (Han et al., 2025). Consequently, this framework emphasizes the necessity of developing comprehensive policies and educational standards that seamlessly integrate AI ethics and application into both curriculum and professional development, ensuring all stakeholders are equipped for responsible engagement (Mouta et al., 2023; Ren & Wu, 2025).

AI IN EDUCATIONAL SETTINGS

This section examines the first dimension of our framework: the diverse applications and use cases of AI in educational settings. Understanding these applications is essential not only for recognizing AI's pedagogical potential but also for identifying the competencies that educators and students must develop, as well as the ethical risks that require mitigation. As we examine specific AI applications, from learning management systems to intelligent tutoring and data-driven analytics, we will consider how each use case shapes the competencies required and the governance mechanisms necessary to ensure responsible deployment. Artificial Intelligence (AI) has become an integral component of modern education, transforming how instruction is delivered and how students interact with learning materials. The literature on AI applications in education reveals a consistent pattern: researchers and practitioners celebrate specific technological capabilities, adaptive content delivery, real-time feedback, pattern recognition in student data, while simultaneously raising concerns about the pedagogical and ethical implications of these same capabilities. From AI-powered learning management systems to intelligent tutoring and data-driven analytics, AI is reshaping educational settings in K-12 and higher education environments. Yet this reshaping is neither uniform nor uncontested. While some scholars argue that AI enables more responsive, student-centered instruction (Ojha et al., 2023), others contend that the rush to implement these technologies often bypasses critical questions about whether they actually improve learning outcomes or merely create the appearance of innovation (Zhai et al., 2021).

This section explores this productive tension in the literature, between the promise of AI-enhanced personalization and the reality of implementation challenges, between technological capability and pedagogical wisdom, and between efficiency gains and equity concerns. While AI offers many advantages in personalizing learning and improving instructional outcomes, it also raises ethical concerns related to fairness, bias, and the role of human oversight. Understanding these applications requires moving beyond a simple catalog of tools to examine how different AI systems embody different assumptions about learning, teaching, and the role of human judgment in education.

AI in Classrooms: Transforming Learning Platforms

One of the most impactful uses of AI in education is through AI-powered learning management systems (LMS). These systems can personalize the learning experience by adapting content and pacing to meet individual student needs, offering real-time feedback for students and teachers (Akgün & Greenhow, 2021). For example, an AI-powered LMS might adjust the difficulty of lessons based on a student's progress, ensuring that the material remains appropriately challenging. This personalization level can increase student engagement and learning outcomes as students receive more tailored instruction.

Beyond learning management, intelligent tutoring systems are another prominent application of AI in education. These systems offer one-on-one support, providing customized guidance and feedback that can be adjusted based on a student's performance (Mello et al., 2023). Unlike traditional tutoring methods, intelligent tutors can be available around the clock, providing continuous support without time or location constraints. This capability makes learning more accessible and allows teachers to focus on more complex tasks such as mentoring, curriculum design, or addressing individual students' emotional and social needs (Bulut et al., 2024).

CASE STUDY 1: Adaptive Learning in Secondary Mathematics (K-12)

The Scenario: Lincoln High School implemented an AI-powered adaptive learning platform in algebra classes to personalize instruction. The system adjusted problem difficulty based on student performance and provided real-time feedback. Initially, teachers celebrated efficiency gains—they could identify struggling students quickly. However, after one semester, data revealed a troubling pattern: students from lower-income backgrounds were consistently assigned to lower difficulty levels and remained there, while affluent students progressed rapidly.

Framework Analysis:

Use Case: The school chose automated personalization to scale instruction.

Competencies: Teachers lacked training to recognize that the AI's "personalization" was actually reproducing existing achievement gaps.

Ethics: The algorithm's training data reflected historical inequities; the system perpetuated rather than mitigated bias.

Governance: No audit process existed to catch this problem; decisions were delegated entirely to the system. The school's experience illustrates a critical lesson: without competent educators who understand algorithmic bias, and without governance mechanisms to review AI outputs, even well-intentioned personalization can amplify inequity. The school subsequently implemented teacher training on bias recognition and established quarterly audits of student assignment patterns.

AI-Driven Data Analytics and Personalized Learning

Data analytics is another transformative aspect of AI in education. AI-powered data analytics tools can help teachers identify learning patterns, knowledge gaps, and areas where students might be struggling. These insights allow for more targeted interventions, ensuring instruction better aligns with each student's needs (Zhai et al., 2021). AI can enhance student engagement and improve learning outcomes, as instructional strategies can be continuously adjusted based on real-time data.

However, reliance on AI for personalized learning and assessment raises questions about AI-generated output's validity, reliability, and fairness. AI-driven grading systems, for example, are often used to assess student performance, offering rapid feedback and reducing the grading burden on teachers (Akgün & Greenhow, 2021). While such systems can streamline the grading process, they also introduce concerns regarding bias and consistency. Some AI algorithms may unintentionally favor certain groups of students based on variables such as language use, socioeconomic background, or geographic location (Bulut et al., 2024). This highlights the need for robust ethical frameworks to guide the implementation of AI in grading and assessment, ensuring that all students are treated equitably.

CASE STUDY 2: AI-Driven Grading in Higher Education

The Scenario: A large university deployed an AI grading system in an introductory biology course with 400 students. The system evaluated short-answer exam responses and provided immediate feedback. Instructors appreciated reduced grading time. Yet when faculty reviewed a sample of AI-graded responses, they discovered the system consistently scored lower when students used non-standard terminology or English as a second language, despite correct scientific understanding. Students from underrepresented groups had systematically lower grades.

Framework Analysis:

Use Case: Automation was chosen for efficiency.

Competencies: Faculty had not been trained to audit AI outputs or understand how language variation affects machine learning models.

Ethics: The system encoded linguistic bias from its training data, creating an equity problem invisible without critical examination.

Governance: No human review process existed for high-stakes decisions. The case demonstrates that efficiency gains (reduced grading burden) came at an ethical cost (biased assessment). The university responded by implementing a hybrid model: AI assists with initial scoring, but faculty conduct a human review of all grades, particularly for borderline cases. This restored human judgment to high-stakes decisions.

AI as a Learning Partner: Enhancing Collaboration and Feedback

In addition to serving as a tool for instruction and assessment, AI can function as a collaborative learning partner for both students and teachers. AI systems that offer real-time feedback and adaptive learning strategies allow for a more interactive and engaging learning environment (Mollick & Mollick, 2023). For instance, AI can assist students in problem-solving tasks by suggesting approaches or highlighting areas where the student might need additional help. This collaboration enhances the learning experience, promoting active learning and self-directed inquiry.

However, for AI to be a beneficial learning partner, students must understand its capabilities and limitations. AI literacy, the ability to understand how AI systems work and their potential biases, is a crucial competency for students to develop. Without this understanding, students may over-rely on AI outputs or accept them without critical evaluation (Kamalov & Gurrib, 2023). Educators must ensure that students engage with AI in a way that fosters critical thinking and ethical reasoning, recognizing the importance of human oversight in using these technologies (Gillani et al., 2023).

CASE STUDY 3: AI as Collaborative Learning Partner (K-12, Elementary)

The Scenario: A fourth-grade science teacher used an AI chatbot to help students design experiments. Students posed questions ("Will plants grow faster with more sunlight?"), and the AI suggested experimental designs. Initially, students engaged enthusiastically. However, the teacher noticed that some students accepted the AI's first suggestion without thinking critically, while others questioned and refined the suggestions. Students who questioned the AI learned more; those who deferred to it learned less.

Framework Analysis:

Use Case: AI was positioned as a collaborative partner to enhance inquiry.

Competencies: Students are required to train to engage critically with AI, recognizing that AI suggestions could be incomplete or biased.

Ethics: Without critical engagement, students risked outsourcing their thinking to an algorithm.

Governance: The teacher established norms, requiring students to justify their acceptance or rejection of AI suggestions and to undergo peer review of AI-assisted work. The case shows that AI collaboration requires competence (critical thinking) and governance (accountability structures). When the teacher explicitly taught students to question AI outputs and created accountability mechanisms, the technology became a genuine learning partner rather than a shortcut.

Implications for Teaching and Learning: Redefining Educational Roles

As AI technologies take on more routine tasks in the classroom, the roles of both teachers and students are shifting. With AI handling administrative and instructional tasks such as grading, attendance tracking, or content delivery, teachers can focus on higher-order educational functions (Resnick, 2024). These include mentoring students, fostering critical thinking, and guiding ethical reasoning, all of which are skills that cannot be easily replicated by machines. AI thus allows educators to spend more time on activities that require human insight, creativity, and emotional intelligence.

Nevertheless, the increasing use of AI in education also raises concerns about the potential displacement of teachers. Some fear that as AI systems become more advanced, they could replace certain teaching functions altogether (Ng et al., 2023). While this fear is not unfounded, viewing AI as a complementary tool rather than a replacement for human educators is essential. Professional development is crucial in this context. Teachers must be trained to use AI technologies effectively and collaborate with AI in ways that enhance, rather than diminish, the learning experience.

Additionally, the integration of AI into education has the potential to amplify existing biases and inequities. AI systems are only as objective as the data they are trained on, and without careful attention to issues of bias, these technologies could exacerbate disparities among students (Chan & Tsi, 2023). To address this, it is essential to establish governance frameworks that ensure ethical AI deployment in schools. Ongoing collaboration between educators, AI developers, researchers, and policymakers will be necessary to create systems prioritizing fairness, equity, and inclusivity (Bulut et al., 2024).

AI fundamentally transforms educational settings, offering tools to personalize learning, provide real-time feedback, and enhance student engagement. However, integrating AI into classrooms must be carefully managed to ensure that it supports, rather than undermines, the role of human educators. Ethical considerations, including the need for transparency, fairness, and bias mitigation, are paramount to the responsible use of AI in education. Teachers and students alike must develop the skills to engage critically with AI technologies, ensuring that they can collaborate with these tools to enhance learning while upholding ethical standards.

DIGITAL COMPETENCIES FOR AI COLLABORATION IN EDUCATION

Building on our examination of AI use cases, this section addresses the second dimension of our framework: the digital competencies that educators and students must develop to collaborate effectively with AI. These competencies are not generic 'AI skills' but are specifically shaped by the use cases examined in the previous section and the ethical considerations that follow. As we explore computational thinking, data literacy, critical thinking, and ethical reasoning, we will emphasize how these competencies enable educators and students to recognize ethical risks and contribute to governance processes that ensure the responsible use of AI. As AI continues to shape the future of education, it is crucial to develop a comprehensive set of digital competencies that enable students to collaborate effectively and responsibly with

AI technologies. These competencies encompass not only technical skills such as computational thinking, data literacy, and an understanding of machine learning but also soft skills like creativity, adaptability, collaboration, and critical thinking. Together, these abilities empower students to use AI as a tool and as a partner in solving complex problems and shaping ethical, innovative solutions.

Foundational Digital Competencies and Soft Skills for AI Collaboration

For students to engage meaningfully with AI, they need a robust foundation in both technical competencies and soft skills, yet the literature reveals an important gap between this principle and its implementation. While technical skills provide the ability to understand and interact with AI systems (Michaeli et al., 2023), soft skills enable students to navigate the ethical and creative dimensions of AI collaboration (Rožman et al., 2023). However, most educational institutions and curricula prioritize technical skills, often treating ethical reasoning, critical thinking, and creativity as secondary or supplementary (Ng et al., 2023). This prioritization reflects a broader assumption in the field: that understanding how AI works is more important than understanding when and whether AI should be used. Combining these two areas is essential for developing well-rounded, AI-literate individuals capable of making informed, ethical decisions in an increasingly AI-driven world (Borenstein & Howard, 2020; Michaeli et al., 2023), yet achieving this integration requires reconceptualizing what counts as "competence" in AI education, moving beyond technical proficiency to include ethical judgment and critical awareness.

1. Computational Thinking and Problem-Solving

The literature on digital competencies for AI collaboration reveals an important but often unexamined tension: the relationship between technical skills and creative or ethical reasoning. While computational thinking, the ability to break down complex problems, recognize patterns, and develop algorithmic solutions, is widely recognized as fundamental to working with AI (Michaeli et al., 2023), scholars increasingly argue that technical competence alone is insufficient. Students must learn to approach problems systematically, applying logical thinking to create solutions that AI can enhance or automate. However, a growing body of research suggests that this systematic, algorithmic thinking must be complemented, and sometimes counterbalanced, by creative and critical capacities (Rožman et al., 2023; Hubert et al., 2024). Creativity plays a critical role beyond logical problem-solving, not merely in finding new applications for AI technologies but in questioning whether particular applications should be pursued at all. This raises a pedagogical question that the literature has only begun to address: *How do educators cultivate the kind of creative and ethical thinking that can push back against AI's capabilities, not just extend them?*

Encouraging students to think creatively enables them to push the boundaries of what AI can accomplish, but it also requires developing the judgment to recognize when those boundaries should not be pushed. This distinction, between expanding AI's capabilities and exercising restraint in their application, is crucial for responsible human-AI collaboration but remains underexplored in most competency frameworks.

Worked Example: Consider a student analyzing college application data using AI. Rather than simply asking the AI "Which colleges should I apply to?", a computationally thinking student breaks the problem down: "What factors matter? (academics, location, cost, culture) How might AI bias the recommendations? (toward wealthy schools? toward certain demographics?) What data is the AI using?" By decomposing the problem and questioning the AI's logic, the student moves from passive consumption to active problem-solving, using AI as a tool rather than an oracle.

2. Data Literacy and Critical Thinking

In AI-driven environments, data literacy is indispensable. Students must know how to collect, interpret, and critically analyze data, as AI systems depend heavily on large datasets (Gascon et al., 2023). Understanding the potential biases and limitations of data-driven decision-making ensures that AI outputs are valid and reliable. Alongside technical data skills, students must also develop critical thinking abilities, allowing them to critically evaluate AI-generated information, question its reliability, and assess its broader societal implications (Hubert et al., 2024).

Worked Example: A high school student receives an AI-generated report showing that students in her school who use AI tutoring systems score higher on standardized tests. Before accepting this conclusion, she asks critical questions: "Who uses AI tutoring? (likely students whose families can afford it) What else might explain the score difference? (prior achievement, family resources, test preparation?) Is correlation being confused with causation?" By applying critical thinking to data, she recognizes that the AI's findings may reflect selection bias rather than the AI's effectiveness. This is data literacy in action.

3. Understanding Machine Learning and Ethical Reasoning

Understanding machine learning principles is crucial for students to engage with AI technologies meaningfully. This includes knowing how AI systems learn from data, the inherent biases in these systems, and how those biases can impact outcomes (Ferrara, 2023). Students need to be aware of the ethical issues surrounding AI, such as algorithmic bias, privacy concerns, and unequal access. Ethical reasoning plays a central role in AI collaboration, helping students navigate complex moral questions and ensuring that AI systems are used in ways that promote fairness, equity, and transparency (Özer et al., 2024).

Worked Example: A teacher learns that an AI system predicts which students will drop out of college. She asks: "What data trained this model? (past student records) Does that data reflect current students? (demographics have changed) What happens if the system flags a student as 'at-risk'? (might trigger interventions that help, or stigmatization that harms) Who benefits from this prediction? (the institution, which can improve retention rates, or the student, who gets support?) Ethical reasoning means asking not just "Can we predict this?" but "Should we, and for whom?"

4. Adaptability and Collaboration

In the rapidly changing AI landscape, students must develop adaptability, the ability to quickly learn and adjust to new tools and technologies. As AI evolves, so will the skills required to work alongside it. Students must be prepared to continually update their knowledge and skills in response to new developments. Additionally, collaboration is critical when working with AI. Many AI projects require interdisciplinary teamwork, where students must work with peers to design, implement, and evaluate AI systems (Rožman et al., 2023). Collaborative problem-solving teaches students to integrate multiple perspectives, ensuring that AI systems are functional and ethical.

Worked Example: A team of students designs an AI chatbot to help younger students with homework. They discover the chatbot sometimes gives incorrect explanations. Rather than accepting this limitation, they adapt by adding a feature that allows younger students to flag confusing answers, creating feedback loops that improve the system. They also establish norms: the chatbot is a starting point, not a final answer. Students must verify their suggestions. Through this collaborative process, adapting the tool, establishing norms, and incorporating feedback, they develop both technical and ethical competence.

Integrating AI into Curricula

Educational institutions must adopt a forward-thinking approach to integrating AI into their curricula to effectively build these digital competencies and soft skills. This requires teaching the technical aspects of AI and addressing its ethical and societal impacts. Schools should provide students with theoretical knowledge and practical experiences, ensuring they are well-equipped to navigate the challenges and opportunities presented by AI technologies.

1. Introducing AI Concepts Early

Schools can introduce AI-related topics at earlier educational stages to build a foundational understanding of AI among younger students. Topics such as basic coding, algorithmic thinking, and AI ethics can be introduced in elementary and middle schools, gradually progressing to more complex concepts like machine learning and data analysis in higher grades (Michaeli et al., 2023). Early exposure to AI can demystify the technology and foster interest in STEM-related fields.

2. Practical AI Experiences

Practical, hands-on experiences are essential for helping students understand how AI works in real-world contexts. Students can engage in activities such as designing simple AI-powered applications, developing chatbots, or working with machine learning models to classify data (Cassidy et al., 2023). Additionally, participating in AI-themed projects, such as developing AI tools for social good or creating AI solutions for environmental challenges, can help students apply their knowledge in meaningful ways. These activities encourage creativity, critical thinking, and the ethical application of AI while also providing students with tangible skills for future careers.

3. Interdisciplinary Learning and Societal Impacts

AI should not be confined to technology or computer science classes. Interdisciplinary approaches that integrate AI into subjects such as social studies, economics, and even literature can help students explore the societal impacts of AI across various domains (Wang & Lester, 2023). For example, students might analyze the role of AI in healthcare or law enforcement, exploring the ethical dilemmas associated with AI decision-making in these fields. By integrating AI into a broader range of subjects, schools can help students see the connections between technology and society, fostering a more holistic understanding of AI's implications.

4. Collaborative and Project-Based Learning

Collaborative learning environments incorporating AI can enhance student engagement and deepen their understanding of the technology. For instance, students can work together on project-based learning activities, designing and implementing AI systems to solve real-world problems (Mollick & Mollick, 2023). This approach builds technical and collaborative skills and encourages students to think critically about the ethical challenges of AI development and deployment.

5. Simulations and Real-world Applications

Schools can integrate AI simulations into the curriculum, allowing students to explore how AI is used in climate science, economics, or healthcare fields. For example, students might use AI tools to simulate climate change scenarios, helping them understand the role of AI in addressing global challenges. These real-world applications provide practical experience and teach students how to work with AI responsibly, keeping societal benefits and ethical concerns in mind (Huang, 2023).

In today's AI-driven world, students must develop technical and soft skills to collaborate effectively with AI technologies. Foundational digital competencies such as computational thinking, data literacy, and an understanding of machine learning principles are crucial for engaging with AI on a technical level. However, these must be complemented by soft skills like creativity, adaptability, collaboration, and ethical reasoning to ensure that students can apply AI responsibly and thoughtfully in their future endeavors.

To build these competencies, educational institutions must integrate AI into their curricula in practical and interdisciplinary ways. Early exposure to AI concepts, hands-on experiences, and project-based learning can all contribute to a deeper understanding of how AI works and how it can be used to address societal challenges. By fostering AI literacy and promoting ethical awareness, schools can empower students to navigate the complexities of AI-enhanced education and become responsible, informed participants in an AI-driven world (Cassidy et al., 2023; Khan & Bose, 2021; Michaeli et al., 2023; Rožman et al., 2023).

ETHICAL CONSIDERATIONS IN HUMAN-AI COLLABORATION

As AI continues to influence various aspects of education, it is critical to address the ethical considerations arising from using AI technologies in schools and classrooms. While AI offers opportunities to enhance learning outcomes and personalize instruction, it also presents bias, fairness, and accountability risks. Educators must not only teach students how to use AI but also how to engage with it ethically, ensuring that AI technologies are deployed responsibly in educational settings. This section delves into the ethical challenges of AI, the importance of fostering ethical digital citizens, and the practical strategies for integrating ethics into AI education.

Bias in AI Systems

One of the most pressing ethical concerns in AI-driven education is the issue of bias in AI systems, yet the literature reveals important disagreements about the nature, scope, and solutions to this problem. AI algorithms are trained on vast datasets, and if these datasets are not carefully curated, they can reflect and perpetuate existing societal biases. Teaching students about the risks of bias in AI is crucial for developing a critical understanding of how these technologies operate and their potential limitations (Ferrara, 2023). Others argue that this technical framing obscures deeper structural issues: that bias in AI systems is not merely a flaw to be fixed but a reflection of biases embedded in educational institutions, assessment practices, and society itself (Chan & Tsi, 2023). From this perspective, attempting to "debias" an AI system without addressing institutional biases is at best incomplete and, at worst, misleading, as it creates a false sense of fairness while perpetuating systemic inequities.

A common example of bias in education is seen in AI-driven grading systems. While these systems can streamline the grading process, they may inadvertently favor certain groups of students over others due to biases in the training data (Bulut et al., 2024). For instance, students from different linguistic or cultural backgrounds may be disadvantaged if the AI system is primarily trained on data that reflects a specific demographic.

The literature on this issue reveals a critical tension between two competing imperatives: the desire to automate and scale assessment (which motivates the adoption of AI-driven grading) and the commitment to equitable, contextually sensitive evaluation of student learning. These two imperatives are not easily reconciled. Automation often requires standardization, which can erase the contextual details that make assessment fair and meaningful for diverse learners. Moreover, the lack of transparency in many AI systems, known as the "black box" problem, makes it difficult for educators to understand how grading decisions are made, which raises concerns about fairness and accountability (Gillani et al., 2023). Yet even when transparency is improved, educators and students may lack the expertise to interpret AI decision-making processes, raising questions about whether transparency alone is sufficient to ensure ethical use.

Students and educators must be trained to recognize and question potential biases in AI systems to mitigate these risks. This includes understanding how biases are introduced, how they can be identified, and what measures can be taken to reduce their impact. However, the literature suggests that such training is often framed as a technical competency, learning to use bias detection tools or interpret model outputs, rather than as a critical practice of questioning the legitimacy of using AI for high-stakes decisions in education. Transparent AI models and human oversight ensure that AI-driven tools promote fairness rather than perpetuate inequalities (Ferrara, 2023), yet the literature reveals that human oversight itself can be compromised by automation bias, the tendency of people to favor automated decisions over human judgment, even when the automated decision is questionable (Gillani et al., 2023).

This suggests that addressing bias in AI-driven education requires not just technical solutions or individual competencies but systemic changes in how institutions approach assessment and decision-making.

Worked Example: An educator reviews an AI system that recommends which students should be placed in advanced mathematics courses. She notices the system recommends fewer girls than boys, despite similar performance. She investigates: the training data came from historical enrollments, which reflected gender bias in course placement. The AI learned and reproduced this bias. By recognizing this pattern, the educator can intervene, either by retraining the system with more balanced data or by implementing human review of recommendations. Without this critical examination, the system would have perpetuated historical inequity.

Automation Bias: When Human Oversight Fails

A critical governance risk that deserves explicit attention is automation bias, the tendency of people to favor automated decisions over human judgment, even when the automated decision is questionable (Chen et al., 2023; Laux, 2023). In educational contexts, this manifests when educators or administrators accept AI recommendations without scrutiny because they trust the system or lack confidence in their own judgment. For example, a teacher might accept an AI-generated grade without reviewing the underlying work, assuming the system is more objective than human grading. Or an administrator might accept an AI recommendation for course placement without considering contextual factors that the system cannot capture (Deepshikha, 2025; Swiecki et al., 2022).

Automation bias undermines the human oversight that is supposed to mitigate AI risks. To address this, institutions must: (1) Establish mandatory review protocols: Require human review of all high-stakes AI decisions, with documented justification for accepting or overriding the AI recommendation. (2) Train educators to question AI: Help educators develop confidence in their professional judgment and understand that questioning AI is a sign of rigor, not distrust. (3) Rotate responsibility: Avoid assigning the same person to review AI outputs repeatedly, which can lead to complacency. (4) Monitor for automation bias: Track whether humans consistently accept AI recommendations without meaningful review, which signals that human oversight has become performative rather than substantive (Bonthu & Goel, 2025).

Developing Ethical Digital Citizens

As AI technologies become more embedded in everyday life, schools must take an active role in developing ethical digital citizens who possess technical skills and understand the societal impact of AI, and use it responsibly (Chaudhry et al.,

2022). The development of ethical digital competencies should be framed as a core component of digital citizenship education. In this context, students learn how to interact with AI systems and ensure that their use of AI promotes equity, fairness, and social good.

Ethical reasoning is an essential skill in an AI-driven world. Students must be taught to identify potential harms that AI technologies might cause and take steps to mitigate those risks (Borenstein & Howard, 2020). This includes understanding the ethical dilemmas that arise from using AI, such as privacy concerns, data misuse, and algorithmic bias. By fostering ethical reasoning, educators help students develop the ability to think critically about AI's role in society and make informed decisions about how it should be used.

A key goal of ethical digital citizenship is ensuring that AI technologies are used to promote equity and fairness. This means developing AI systems that are inclusive and accessible to all students, regardless of their background, and that actively work to reduce rather than exacerbate educational inequalities. Students should learn how to assess whether AI systems are designed and implemented in ways that respect the rights and dignity of all individuals.

Ethical digital citizenship also involves engaging with collaborative governance models that bring together multiple stakeholders, educators, AI developers, policymakers, and community members, to shape the responsible development and deployment of AI in education (Nguyen et al., 2022). These frameworks are essential for addressing complex issues like data privacy, algorithmic accountability, and transparency in AI systems. Collaborative governance ensures that diverse perspectives are considered when deciding how AI should be integrated into educational settings.

By embedding these ethical considerations into AI education, schools can equip students to become informed, responsible, and engaged digital citizens, ready to navigate the complexities of human-AI collaboration in the 21st century (Holmes et al., 2021).

Worked Example: Students in a civics class analyze how AI is used in criminal justice systems. They learn that some systems predict recidivism with higher error rates for certain racial groups. They debate: Should these systems be used? If so, how can bias be addressed? Should humans have final say over AI recommendations? Through this analysis, students develop ethical digital citizenship, not just technical skills but the ability to ask critical questions about AI's societal impact and to advocate for responsible deployment.

Governance and Institutional Oversight in AI Implementation

Effective governance of AI in education requires establishing clear institutional structures, policies, and accountability mechanisms that ensure responsible deployment across all dimensions of the framework. While competence and ethics are essential, they are insufficient without governance structures that translate principles into practice. Institutions must establish three key governance elements: (1) decision-making authority and transparency, (2) audit and accountability mechanisms, and (3) stakeholder engagement and oversight (Nguyen et al., 2022; Radanliev et al., 2024; Solanki et al., 2022).

Decision-Making Authority and Transparency. Institutions should establish clear policies specifying who decides whether to adopt an AI system, on what criteria, and through what process. This requires moving beyond vendor recommendations or individual educator preferences to a deliberate, transparent process involving educators, administrators, parents, and students (Fitas, 2025; Kasztelnik, 2024). Key questions include: Has the system been tested for bias? What data does it use? Who has access to student data? What are the alternatives? Transparent decision-making ensures that AI adoption reflects institutional values rather than efficiency pressures alone.

Audit and Accountability Mechanisms. Institutions must implement regular audits of AI systems in use, examining whether they produce equitable outcomes across student populations. This includes bias audits (comparing outcomes by race, gender, socioeconomic status, and language background), assessment validity checks (verifying that AI-driven grades correlate with other measures of learning), and transparency reviews (ensuring educators understand how systems make decisions). Audits should occur at least annually and whenever significant changes are made to systems or student populations. When audits reveal problems, institutions must establish clear protocols for remediation or discontinuation (Fraidan, 2024; Simbeck, 2023).

Stakeholder Engagement and Oversight. Governance requires ongoing collaboration among educators, administrators, technology staff, parents, and students. Rather than delegating AI decisions to technical experts alone, institutions should establish AI oversight committees that include diverse perspectives and can identify concerns that technical staff might miss (Fitas, 2025; Ifenthaler et al., 2024). Students and parents should have meaningful input into decisions about data use and AI systems affecting their learning and records. This collaborative approach ensures that governance reflects the values and concerns of those most affected by AI systems.

Incorporating Ethics into AI Education

Embedding ethical thinking into AI education is critical for ensuring that students are proficient in using AI technologies and capable of thinking critically about their broader implications. There are several practical ways to integrate ethics into

AI-related coursework, helping students navigate the ethical dilemmas associated with AI use in various fields.

One effective method for teaching ethics is through the use of *case studies*. In classroom discussions, students can analyze real-world examples of ethical dilemmas related to AI use in healthcare, law enforcement, and education (Engelmann et al., 2024). For instance, students might examine how AI is used to make decisions in predictive policing, where algorithmic bias could lead to disproportionate targeting of certain groups. Students learn to apply ethical principles to real-world problems by engaging with these case studies, developing a deeper understanding of AI's societal impact.

Another approach is incorporating ethics into *project-based learning*. When students work on AI-related projects, they should be encouraged to think about the ethical dimensions of their work. For example, if a project involves designing an AI application for education, students should consider how the system could affect different populations and what steps could be taken to ensure it operates fairly. This approach helps students connect ethical theory with practical application, reinforcing ethics' importance in designing and deploying AI systems.

Schools can also introduce *ethical guidelines* for the use of AI technologies. These guidelines can provide students a framework for making moral decisions when working with AI, covering data privacy, consent, transparency, and bias mitigation. By following these guidelines, students learn to engage with AI technologies in ways that respect individual rights and promote social good.

Ethical considerations are central to the responsible use of AI in education. As AI continues to influence how students learn and how teachers assess performance, it is essential to address bias, fairness, and accountability issues. Educators must teach students how to identify and mitigate bias in AI systems while also fostering a broader understanding of ethical digital citizenship. This involves developing technical skills and cultivating the ability to think critically about the societal impact of AI technologies.

By incorporating ethics into AI education through case studies, project-based learning, and ethical guidelines, schools can ensure that students are prepared to navigate the ethical challenges of AI collaboration. Ultimately, the goal is to develop informed, responsible digital citizens who are equipped to use AI in ways that promote fairness, equity, and transparency in an increasingly AI-driven world (Borenstein & Howard, 2020; Chaudhry et al., 2022; Engelmann et al., 2024; Holmes et al., 2021; Nguyen et al., 2022).

Addressing Key Risks: Data Privacy, Consent, and Vendor Accountability

Beyond bias and fairness, AI deployment in education introduces specific risks that require targeted governance responses. Three critical areas demand institutional attention: data privacy and consent, assessment validity, and vendor accountability.

Data Privacy and Consent. AI systems require vast amounts of student data, academic records, behavioral patterns, and demographic information to function. Institutions must establish clear policies governing data collection, use, and retention (Nagaraj et al., 2023). Specifically: (1) Minimize data collection: Collect only data necessary for the stated educational purpose; avoid collecting sensitive information (race, religion, family income) unless directly relevant. (2) Obtain informed consent: Parents and students should understand what data is collected, how it is used, and who has access. Consent should be specific to each system, not blanket approval. (3) Establish data retention limits: Specify how long student data is retained and ensure it is securely deleted when no longer needed (Huang, 2023). Without these protections, institutions risk violating student privacy and enabling misuse of sensitive information.

Assessment Validity. When AI systems make high-stakes decisions (course placement, grading, graduation eligibility), institutions must verify that these systems are valid measures of student learning. This requires: (1) Validation studies: Compare AI-generated grades or recommendations with human expert judgments and other measures of student performance. (2) Bias testing: Examine whether AI systems produce equitable outcomes across demographic groups. (3) Transparency about limitations: Educators and students should understand the system's error rates and when human judgment should override AI recommendations (Ansari & Qamari, 2025; Mishra, 2024). Deploying unvalidated assessment systems risks making consequential decisions based on flawed measures.

Vendor Accountability and Transparency. Many AI systems are proprietary tools developed by external vendors, creating information asymmetries where institutions don't fully understand how systems work. Institutions should: (1) Require vendor transparency: Demand documentation of training data, model architecture, and known limitations. (2) Establish service level agreements: Specify performance standards, audit rights, and remediation procedures if systems fail or produce biased outcomes. (3) Retain institutional control: Avoid vendor lock-in by ensuring data portability and the ability to discontinue systems without losing access to student records (Boscardin et al., 2023; Karimi & Khawaja, 2023). Without accountability mechanisms, institutions become dependent on vendors who have limited incentive to prioritize equity or transparency.

Teaching Students to Collaborate with AI

As AI continues to transform educational practices, it is essential that students not only learn how to use AI tools but also how to collaborate with them effectively and responsibly. AI's role in education extends beyond automation and convenience; it offers new avenues for enhancing critical thinking, problem-solving, and collaborative learning. However, to fully realize these benefits, students must develop the skills to work alongside AI systems, understanding their limitations while utilizing their capabilities. This section explores the use of AI as a collaborative tool in the classroom, the role of project-based learning with AI, and the development of a symbiotic relationship between human intelligence and AI technologies.

In today's classrooms, AI can be a powerful *collaborative tool*, enhancing student learning experiences by assisting with research, project management, and personalized feedback. AI-powered tools, such as research assistants or project management applications, enable students to streamline certain aspects of group work, focusing on higher-order thinking tasks such as critical analysis, creative problem-solving, and ethical decision-making (Cassidy et al., 2023). For example, students might use AI to quickly gather and organize research data, giving them more time to analyze their findings and develop insights.

AI-driven tools can significantly improve the *efficiency and productivity* of collaborative work. For instance, AI-powered project management software can automate task delegation and track group progress, helping students organize their job more effectively. AI tools can also assist in brainstorming sessions by generating suggestions, offering insights, or even predicting possible outcomes based on existing data. However, it is essential to ensure that these technologies support, rather than dominate, the learning process (Mollick & Mollick, 2023).

While AI can enhance learning, students must be encouraged to maintain a *critical engagement* toward AI outputs. Blindly deferring to AI-generated conclusions risks undermining the development of critical thinking skills. Educators should implement strategies that require students to justify their use of AI and actively evaluate AI outputs (Chang et al., 2023). For example, peer review of AI-assisted work or classroom discussions about AI's recommendations can foster a more reflective and engaged approach. This ensures that students understand that AI is a tool that must be questioned, interpreted, and validated by human reasoning.

Various AI models, such as *AI-tutors, AI-coaches, and AI-mentors*, can offer personalized feedback and adaptive instruction, supporting students in real-time (Mollick & Mollick, 2023). AI-tutors can help students master specific subjects by adjusting the difficulty of content based on performance, while AI-coaches can offer advice on skills development. These models provide personalized learning experiences, allowing students to learn independently. However, students should also be taught to interpret the AI's recommendations critically, understanding that AI systems are not infallible and require human oversight.

AI should be viewed as a collaborative partner in education rather than a replacement for human educators. By teaching students to engage critically with AI technologies, educators help them develop the skills needed to use AI tools to augment their own learning and problem-solving processes rather than as substitutes for human thinking.

Project-Based Learning with AI

Project-based learning (PBL) incorporating AI can further enhance students' understanding of AI technologies and how they can be applied in real-world contexts. This approach allows students to work hands-on with AI tools, deepening their technical knowledge while fostering essential skills such as collaboration, problem-solving, and ethical reasoning (Ojha et al., 2023). Through AI-infused PBL, students are exposed to the full scope of AI's potential and limitations, allowing them to grapple with the challenges of developing and deploying AI responsibly.

Practical AI Experiences

Engaging in hands-on AI projects allows students to interact directly with AI technologies, helping them develop practical skills. For example, students might design and deploy an AI-powered application to address a real-world issue, such as using AI to predict environmental changes or streamline healthcare processes (Mollick & Mollick, 2023). These experiences not only enhance students' technical abilities but also help them understand the ethical challenges that arise from using AI, such as privacy concerns and bias in decision-making.

Project-based learning enables students to see AI's practical applications and encourages them to solve *real-world challenges* using AI technologies. In doing so, students develop a deeper understanding of both the power and limitations of AI. For instance, they might explore how AI can optimize resource allocation in humanitarian aid or how it can support decision-making in urban planning. However, through these projects, students also learn to identify and mitigate the potential harms that AI can cause, such as biases in data or unintended social consequences (Ojha et al., 2023).

Incorporating *ethical dilemmas* into project-based learning ensures that students not only focus on the technical aspects of AI but also consider the broader societal implications of their projects. Educators can prompt students to think about questions like: How might this AI system affect different populations? What safeguards can be implemented to ensure fairness? What are the long-term consequences of deploying this AI technology? Addressing these questions during AI projects helps students integrate ethical reasoning into their technical work, preparing them to become responsible innovators.

Developing Human-AI Symbiosis in Education

A key goal of teaching students to collaborate with AI is helping them understand and embrace the symbiotic relationship between humans and AI. Rather than viewing AI as a tool that replaces human judgment, students should be taught that AI complements human capabilities, each playing distinct but interdependent roles in solving complex problems.

AI excels at processing vast amounts of data, identifying patterns, and making predictions based on statistical models. For example, AI can simulate climate models, forecast economic trends, or analyze large datasets in biomedical research (Huang, 2023). Students should learn to utilize these *strengths of AI* in tasks that require computational power or data analysis, freeing up human capacity for higher-level critical thinking, creativity, and ethical decision-making.

Despite AI's advanced capabilities, *human oversight* remains essential in ensuring that AI is used responsibly and ethically. Educators must teach students the importance of ethical decision-making and how human intelligence is needed to interpret AI's outputs. For instance, while AI can provide predictive insights, human judgment must assess the broader ethical and social implications of acting on those predictions (Holstein & Aleven, 2021). Students must understand that AI is a tool to assist human reasoning, not to replace it.

Ultimately, the goal is to empower students to become active partners in shaping the future of *human-AI collaboration*. By developing the ability to work symbiotically with AI, students can utilize both human strengths (creativity, ethical reasoning, and critical thinking) and AI's computational capabilities to address complex societal challenges (Mollick & Mollick, 2023). This collaborative approach ensures that students can contribute meaningfully to developing and applying AI technologies in ways that promote positive social change.

Teaching students to collaborate with AI is essential to preparing them for an AI-driven future. AI can be a powerful tool for enhancing collaboration, problem-solving, and critical thinking, but students must learn to engage with these technologies critically and responsibly. Educators can equip students with the skills and mindset needed to work alongside AI effectively through AI-supported project-based learning and developing a human-AI symbiosis.

By fostering a balance between human creativity, ethical decision-making, and AI's computational capabilities, educators can empower students to become active participants in shaping the future of human-AI collaboration. Through practical experiences, critical evaluation, and a commitment to ethical responsibility, students will be prepared to navigate the opportunities and challenges that AI presents in both educational and professional contexts (Holstein & Aleven, 2021; Huang, 2023; Mollick & Mollick, 2023; Ojha et al., 2023).

CHALLENGES AND OPPORTUNITIES IN EDUCATING FOR AI COLLABORATION

As AI continues to evolve and become integral across various industries, education faces numerous challenges in incorporating AI technologies, but these also present significant opportunities. The responsible integration of AI into educational settings can enhance student engagement. Still, barriers such as limited teacher training, unequal access to technology, and the ever-evolving nature of AI require attention. This section discusses these challenges, highlights the potential for student empowerment, and explores the role of AI in lifelong learning and career development.

Challenges in AI Education

One of the primary challenges in teaching AI and its ethical implications is the *limited availability of teacher training*. Many educators do not possess the necessary background in AI to confidently incorporate it into their teaching. The rapid pace of technological change exacerbates this issue, as educators must continually update their knowledge and skills to keep up with new advancements (Ojha et al., 2023). Current professional development programs often fail to provide teachers with the comprehensive training required to teach AI's technical and ethical aspects. This lack of preparedness can hinder the successful integration of AI into the curriculum. However, the challenge extends beyond availability to the practical realities of implementation. Professional development requires significant time and resources. Effective teacher training in AI competencies typically requires 40-80 hours of initial instruction, plus ongoing professional learning throughout the year (Tan & Subramonyam, 2023). This represents a substantial commitment for schools already stretched thin with existing professional development requirements. Teachers must learn not only how to use AI tools but also how to recognize bias, conduct audits, evaluate AI outputs critically, and teach these competencies to students. Additionally, professional development must be sustained; one-time workshops are insufficient for developing the depth of understanding needed for responsible AI integration. Schools must budget for ongoing coaching, collaborative planning time, and access to expert resources, costs that many institutions struggle to afford. Beyond training, teacher workload presents a significant implementation barrier. Integrating AI responsibly requires educators to take on additional responsibilities: reviewing AI outputs for bias, conducting audits of student outcomes, participating in governance committees, and redesigning curricula to incorporate AI literacy. These tasks occur on top of existing teaching responsibilities, often without corresponding reductions in other duties. Teachers report that AI integration, when implemented hastily without addressing workload, contributes to burnout rather than efficiency gains. Responsible implementation requires institutions to acknowledge these additional demands and either reduce other responsibilities or provide time during the school day for AI-related work. Without addressing workload, even well-trained teachers may resist AI adoption or implement it superficially.

Another significant challenge is the *inequitable access to AI technologies*. Many schools, particularly in less privileged regions, lack the technological infrastructure to support AI education. This can include insufficient access to high-quality computers and internet connectivity and a lack of AI-specific software and learning tools (Ojha et al., 2023). Beyond hardware, implementing AI systems involves substantial ongoing costs: licensing fees for AI platforms (ranging from thousands to hundreds of thousands of dollars annually), data storage and security infrastructure, technical support staff, and regular system updates. The resulting digital divide places students in under-resourced schools at a disadvantage, making it more challenging to gain the digital competencies necessary to succeed in an AI-driven future. For schools operating on limited budgets, the decision to invest in AI often means reducing spending in other areas, such as smaller class sizes, special education services, or arts programs. This creates difficult trade-offs that institutions must navigate carefully, ensuring that AI adoption does not come at the expense of other educational priorities (Tan & Subramonyam, 2023).

Additionally, the *rapid evolution of AI technologies* presents a unique challenge for educational systems. AI is advancing so quickly that teaching materials and curricula can become outdated quickly. Keeping up with these changes is difficult for schools and educators, who must continuously revise and update their instructional methods to stay relevant (Wang & Lester, 2023). This creates an implementation challenge: institutions must decide whether to adopt cutting-edge AI tools (which may be unstable or unproven in educational settings) or wait for more mature, well-tested systems (which may lag behind current capabilities). Additionally, institutions must plan for system transitions; when AI platforms are discontinued or replaced, institutions must migrate data, retrain staff, and redesign curricula, a costly and disruptive process.

Perhaps most critically, institutions face an evaluation challenge: How do they know whether AI implementation is actually improving learning? Many schools adopt AI systems based on vendor claims or efficiency gains (e.g., reduced grading time) without systematically evaluating whether these systems improve student learning outcomes. Rigorous evaluation requires comparing student outcomes with and without AI, controlling for other variables, and examining outcomes across different student populations to ensure equity. This requires expertise in research design and data analysis that many schools lack. Without rigorous evaluation, institutions may continue using systems that are ineffective or harmful, or may abandon systems that could be beneficial if implemented differently. The absence of clear evidence about AI's actual impact on learning creates uncertainty about whether the significant investments required are justified. To overcome these challenges, schools and educational policymakers must take a realistic, phased approach to AI integration. This includes: (1) Realistic budgeting: Calculate true costs (hardware, software, training, staff time, evaluation) and secure sustainable funding rather than relying on one-time grants. (2) Workload management: Explicitly reduce other responsibilities when adding AI-related work, or provide dedicated time during the school day. (3) Sustained professional development: Invest in multi-year training programs with ongoing coaching and support, not one-time workshops. (4) Careful vendor selection: Prioritize systems that are transparent, have evidence of effectiveness, and align with institutional values. (5) Rigorous evaluation: Build in systematic evaluation from the start, examining whether AI actually improves learning and whether benefits are equitably distributed. (6) Incremental implementation: Start with pilot programs in limited contexts, learn from implementation, and scale gradually rather than system-wide adoption. This deliberate, evidence-based approach requires patience and resources but increases the likelihood that AI integration will be sustainable and beneficial (Akgun & Greenhow, 2021).

Opportunities for Student Empowerment

Despite these challenges, integrating AI in education offers significant opportunities for *empowering students.* By developing digital competencies, students are better positioned to shape the future workforce actively. AI is rapidly becoming a critical component in industries such as healthcare, finance, and technology, and students who are proficient in AI will have a competitive edge in these fields (Rožman et al., 2023). AI education equips students with the technical skills to innovate and lead in their chosen professions. Still, it also instills a deeper understanding of how AI can solve complex problems and address global challenges (Farrow, 2023).

In addition to developing technical skills, AI education provides an opportunity to nurture students as *ethical digital citizens.* By teaching students to evaluate the societal impact of AI, educators can help them become active agents of change, capable of shaping the responsible development and deployment of AI technologies (Wang & Lester, 2023). For instance, students can be taught to recognize bias in AI systems and to advocate for fairness and equity in AI applications. This focus on ethical reasoning ensures that students do not merely use AI technologies but also consider their decisions' moral and societal implications. Schools can cultivate a generation of students who are not passive consumers of AI but somewhat proactive collaborators in shaping a more responsible and equitable digital future (Ibrahim et al., 2022).

AI in Lifelong Learning and Career Development

As AI becomes increasingly integrated into various sectors, educational systems must prepare students not only for their initial careers but also for the *long-term evolution of work*. The dynamic nature of the modern job market means that many professions will undergo significant changes due to AI, and workers will need to continually update their skills to stay relevant. Schools can address this challenge by integrating *AI competencies into career and technical education (CTE)* programs, helping students develop the skills needed to work alongside AI systems in a wide range of fields (Wang & Lester, 2023). Understanding how AI is applied in different contexts is crucial for future success in engineering, healthcare, marketing, or the creative industries.

Moreover, *lifelong learning* will become increasingly important as AI reshapes the workforce. AI-powered personalized learning platforms offer a promising solution, enabling individuals to continually upskill and reskill throughout their careers (ElSayary, 2023). These platforms can tailor educational experiences to meet the specific needs of each learner, providing targeted recommendations for new skills based on their career path and industry trends. Schools can play a critical role in fostering a lifelong learning mindset among students, emphasizing the importance of adaptability and continuous self-improvement. By teaching students to view education as a constant process, schools can prepare them for the ever-changing demands of the AI-driven economy.

The integration of AI into education presents both significant challenges and exciting opportunities. On the one hand, barriers such as limited teacher training, resource disparities, and the rapid evolution of AI technologies must be addressed to ensure equitable and effective AI education. Schools, policymakers, and technology companies must collaborate to develop solutions that empower educators and students to thrive in this new environment. On the other hand, AI education provides a unique opportunity to empower students with the skills and ethical understanding necessary to lead in an AI-driven world.

AI education can help shape a generation of responsible, informed digital citizens by equipping students with both technical competencies and a strong ethical framework. Furthermore, the focus on lifelong learning and career development ensures that students will be prepared to adapt to the evolving demands of the workforce.

Ultimately, by addressing the challenges and capitalizing on the opportunities presented by AI in education, we can cultivate a future where human-AI collaboration is responsible, equitable, and empowering for all (ElSayary, 2023; Ibrahim et al., 2022; Rožman et al., 2023; Wang & Lester, 2023).

CONCLUSION

In the rapidly evolving landscape of education, integrating Artificial Intelligence (AI) offers immense opportunities and significant challenges. AI can potentially enhance educational outcomes by personalizing learning, improving instructional efficiency, and providing real-time feedback to students and educators. However, as this technology becomes more ingrained in schools, it raises critical concerns about bias, transparency, accountability, and equity (Huang, 2023; Gillani et al., 2023).

To navigate these complexities, it is essential that educators and students alike develop the necessary digital competencies that will allow them to collaborate effectively with AI systems. These competencies include technical skills such as computational thinking, data literacy, and an understanding of machine learning, alongside essential soft skills like creativity, critical thinking, and ethical reasoning (Ferrara, 2023; Michaeli et al., 2023). Together, these skills will enable individuals to engage responsibly with AI technologies, ensuring they are used to promote fairness, equity, and social good (Borenstein & Howard, 2020).

Moreover, as AI reshapes the future workforce, education must adapt by preparing students not just for the jobs of today but for a lifelong journey of learning and professional development (Wang & Lester, 2023). AI-powered learning platforms offer flexible, personalized education pathways that allow individuals to continuously upskill and reskill throughout their careers (ElSayary, 2023). However, achieving the full potential of AI in education will require a concerted effort to address systemic barriers, such as inadequate teacher training and unequal access to AI technologies (Tan & Subramonyam, 2023).

Ultimately, by fostering both digital and ethical literacy, schools can empower students to succeed in an AI-driven world and shape it in ways that reflect human values and ethics. As AI increasingly integrates into education and society, responsible human-AI collaboration will be crucial to creating a more equitable, innovative, and sustainable future (Mollick & Mollick, 2023; Kamalov & Gurrib, 2023).

Future Directions

Looking ahead, several key areas should be the focus of educational institutions, policymakers, and researchers to ensure that AI is integrated into education responsibly and effectively.

First, there is a pressing need to invest in *teacher training and professional development programs.* Teachers must have the technical knowledge and ethical understanding to guide students through AI-enhanced learning environments. As AI continues to evolve rapidly, ongoing professional development opportunities will be essential in helping educators stay updated on the latest advancements and teaching strategies related to AI (Tan & Subramonyam, 2023).

Second, addressing *access and equity issues* is critical for successfully integrating AI into education. Many schools, particularly in underserved communities, lack the necessary resources and infrastructure to support AI technologies (Ojha et al., 2023). Efforts must be made to bridge this digital divide, ensuring that all students, regardless of their socioeconomic background, have equal access to the tools and technologies that are shaping the future of education (Chan & Tsi, 2023).

Another important consideration is the development of *ethical frameworks for AI use in education.* These frameworks must address key concerns such as data privacy, bias mitigation, and algorithmic transparency. Collaborative efforts between educators, policymakers, AI developers, and researchers will be necessary to create guidelines that ensure AI is used to align with ethical standards and promote fairness (Nguyen et al., 2022; Borenstein & Howard, 2020).

Additionally, integrating AI into *interdisciplinary and real-world learning* opportunities will be essential for preparing students to engage with AI technologies in meaningful ways. AI should not be confined to STEM fields alone but should be introduced across various subjects, helping students explore how AI impacts different domains, such as healthcare, law enforcement, and the environment (Wang & Lester, 2023). This interdisciplinary approach will give students a broader understanding of AI's societal implications (Michaeli et al., 2023).

Finally, fostering a lifelong learning culture will ensure that students remain adaptable and resilient in an ever-changing job market. AI will continue to reshape industries and career paths, and students must be prepared for ongoing professional development (Wang & Lester, 2023). AI-powered personalized learning platforms can play a significant role in helping individuals continuously update their skills and knowledge throughout their careers, allowing them to remain competitive in a dynamic workforce (ElSayary, 2023).

By focusing on teacher training, equitable access, ethical AI frameworks, interdisciplinary learning, and lifelong education, educators and policymakers can ensure that AI is integrated into education in a responsible and transformative way. Through collaborative efforts, we can create an educational landscape where AI enhances human potential, promotes equity, and fosters a more ethical and sustainable future (Mollick & Mollick, 2023; Rožman et al., 2023).

REFERENCES

Akbarighatar, P. (2024). Operationalizing responsible AI principles through responsible AI capabilities. *AI and Ethics*, *5*(2), 1787–1801. DOI: 10.1007/s43681-024-00524-4

Akgun, S., & Greenhow, C. (2021). Artificial intelligence in education: Addressing ethical challenges in K-12 settings. *AI and Ethics*, *2*(3), 431–440. DOI: 10.1007/s43681-021-00096-7 PMID: 34790956

Ansari, S. R., & Qamari, I. N. (2025). Artificial intelligence and students' cognitive learning outcomes with bibliometric and content analysis for future research agenda. *Discover Education*, *4*(1), 441. Advance online publication. DOI: 10.1007/s44217-025-00865-0

Barnes, E., & Hutson, J. (2024). Navigating the ethical terrain of AI in higher education: Strategies for mitigating bias and promoting fairness. *Forum for Education Studies.*, *2*(2), 1229. DOI: 10.59400/fes.v2i2.1229

Bonthu, C., & Goel, G. (2025). Autonomous Supplier Evaluation and Data Stewardship with AI: Building Transparent and Resilient Supply Chains. *International Journal of Computational and Experimental Science and Engineering*, *11*(3). Advance online publication. DOI: 10.22399/ijcesen.3854

Borenstein, J., & Howard, A. (2020). Emerging challenges in AI and the need for AI ethics education. *AI and Ethics*, *1*(1), 61–65. DOI: 10.1007/s43681-020-00002-7 PMID: 38624388

Boscardin, C. K., Gin, B., Golde, P. B., & Hauer, K. E. (2023). ChatGPT and Generative Artificial Intelligence for Medical Education: Potential Impact and Opportunity. *Academic Medicine*, *99*(1), 22–27. DOI: 10.1097/ACM.0000000000005439 PMID: 37651677

Bulut, O., Beiting-Parrish, M., Casabianca, J. M., Slater, S. C., Jiao, H., Song, D., Ormerod, C. M., Fabiyi, D. G., Ivan, R., Walsh, C., Rios, O., Wilson, J., Yildirim-Erbasli, S. N., Wongvorachan, T., Liu, J. X., Tan, B., & Morilova, P. (2024). The rise of artificial intelligence in educational measurement: opportunities and ethical challenges. *arXiv (Cornell University).* https://doi.org//arxiv.2406.18900DOI: 10.48550

Cassidy, D., Borgne, Y. L., Bellas, F., Vuorikari, R., Rondin, E., Sharma, M., Niewint-Gori, J., Gröpler, J., Gilleran, A., & Kralj, L. (2023). Use Scenarios & Practical Examples of AI Use in Education. *arXiv (Cornell University).* https://doi.org//arxiv.2309.12320DOI: 10.48550

Chan, C. K. Y. (2023). A comprehensive AI policy education framework for university teaching and learning. *International Journal of Educational Technology in Higher Education*, *20*(1), 38. Advance online publication. DOI: 10.1186/s41239-023-00408-3

Chan, C. K. Y., & Colloton, T. (2024). *Generative AI in higher education.* https://doi.org/DOI: 10.4324/9781003459026

Chan, C. K. Y., & Tsi, L. H. Y. (2023). The AI revolution in Education: Will AI replace or assist teachers in higher education? *arXiv (Cornell University).* https://doi.org//arxiv.2305.01185DOI: 10.48550

Chang, D. H., Lin, M. P., Hajian, S., & Wang, Q. Q. (2023). Educational design principles of using AI chatbot that supports Self-Regulated learning in education: Goal setting, feedback, and personalization. *Sustainability (Basel)*, *15*(17), 12921. DOI: 10.3390/su151712921

Chaudhry, M. A., Cukurova, M., & Luckin, R. (2022). A Transparency Index Framework for AI in education. *arXiv (Cornell University).* https://doi.org//arxiv.2206.03220DOI: 10.1007/978-3-031-11647-6_33

Chen, Y., Ahn, M. J., & Wang, Y. (2023). Artificial intelligence and Public Values: Value impacts and governance in the public sector. *Sustainability (Basel)*, *15*(6), 4796. DOI: 10.3390/su15064796

Daher, R. (2025). Integrating AI literacy into teacher education: A critical perspective paper. *Discover Artificial Intelligence*, *5*(1), 217. Advance online publication. DOI: 10.1007/s44163-025-00475-7

Deepshikha, D. (2025). A comprehensive review of AI-powered grading and tailored feedback in universities. *Discover Artificial Intelligence*, *5*(1), 251. Advance online publication. DOI: 10.1007/s44163-025-00517-0

Du, K., Geiger, J., Killen, T., Porta, A. E., & O'Brien, T. (2024). The Paradigm Shift in education in Big Data Era: Exploring the intersection of historical assessment frameworks and AI-Powered assessment methods in education. *Journal of Education and Training Studies*, *12*(2), 22. DOI: 10.11114/jets.v12i2.6582

ElSayary, A. (2023). An Investigation of Teachers' Perceptions of Using ChatGPT as a Supporting Tool for Teaching and Learning in the Digital Era. *Journal of Computer Assisted Learning*, •••, 1–15. DOI: 10.1111/jcal.12926

Engelmann, S., Choksi, M. Z., Wang, A., & Fiesler, C. (2024). *Visions of a Discipline: Analyzing Introductory AI Courses on YouTube. FAccT '24: Proceedings of the 2024 ACM Conference on Fairness, Accountability, and Transparency.* https://doi.org/DOI: 10.1145/3630106.3659045

Farrow, R. (2023). The possibilities and limits of XAI in education: A socio-technical perspective. *Learning, Media and Technology*, *48*(2), 266–279. DOI: 10.1080/17439884.2023.2185630

Ferrara, E. (2023). Fairness and Bias in Artificial intelligence: A brief survey of sources, impacts, and mitigation strategies. *Sci*, *6*(1), 3. DOI: 10.3390/sci6010003

Fitas, R. (2025). Inclusive education with AI: Supporting special needs and tackling language barriers. *AI and Ethics*, *5*(6), 5729–5757. DOI: 10.1007/s43681-025-00824-3

Fraidan, A. A. (2024). Anticipatory Thinking and AI-Driven Assessments: A Balanced Approach to AI Integration in Education Aligned with Saudi Vision 2030. *African Journal of Biomedical Research*, •••, 619–628. DOI: 10.53555/AJBR.v27i3.2560

García-López, I. M., & Trujillo-Liñán, L. (2025). Ethical and regulatory challenges of Generative AI in education: A systematic review. *Frontiers in Education*, *10*, 1565938. Advance online publication. DOI: 10.3389/feduc.2025.1565938

Gascon, G. M., Wallman, K. K., Ravula, S., Cappelleri, J., Lee, J., Lum, K., Nagaraja, C. H., Paul, S., Roy, D., & Wu, E. (2023). DSLA 2023: Facing the dangers of data illiteracy. *Significance*, *20*(5), 26–29. DOI: 10.1093/jrssig/qmad077

Gillani, N., Eynon, R., Chiabaut, C., & Finkel, K. (2023). Unpacking the "Black box" of AI in education. *arXiv (Cornell University)*. https://doi.org//arxiv.2301.01602DOI: 10.48550

Han, B., Coghlan, S., Buchanan, G., & McKay, D. (2025). Who is Helping Whom? Student Concerns about AI-Teacher Collaboration in Higher Education Classrooms. *Proceedings of the ACM on Human-Computer Interaction*, *9*(2), 1–32. DOI: 10.1145/3711104

Holmes, W., Porayska-Pomsta, K., Holstein, K., Sutherland, E., Baker, T., Shum, S. B., Santos, O. C., Rodrigo, M. T., Cukurova, M., Bittencourt, I. I., & Koedinger, K. R. (2021). Ethics of AI in Education: Towards a Community-Wide framework. *International Journal of Artificial Intelligence in Education*, *32*(3), 504–526. DOI: 10.1007/s40593-021-00239-1

Holstein, K., & Aleven, V. (2021). Designing for human-AI complementarity in K-12 education. *arXiv (Cornell University)*. https://doi.org//arxiv.2104.01266DOI: 10.48550

Huang, L. (2023). Ethics of Artificial intelligence in Education: Student privacy and data protection. *Science Insights Education Frontiers*, *16*(2), 2577–2587. DOI: 10.15354/sief.23.re202

Huang, L. (2023). Ethics of Artificial intelligence in Education: Student privacy and data protection. *Science Insights Education Frontiers*, *16*(2), 2577–2587. DOI: 10.15354/sief.23.re202

Hubert, K. F., Awa, K. N., & Zabelina, D. L. (2024). The current state of artificial intelligence generative language models is more creative than humans on divergent thinking tasks. *Scientific Reports*, *14*(1), 3440. Advance online publication. DOI: 10.1038/s41598-024-53303-w PMID: 38341459

Ibitoye, A. O., Nkwo, M. S., & Orji, R. (2025). Rethinking responsible AI from ethical pillars to sociotechnical practice. *AI and Ethics*, *5*(6), 6207–6223. DOI: 10.1007/s43681-025-00809-2

Ibrahim, M. B., Dadeh, T., & Rola, F. (2022). Student Activities in Organizing, Learning Motivation and Self-Adjustment (Case Study In Ptkin Students). *Edukasi Islami Jurnal Pendidikan Islam*, *11*(4), 417. DOI: 10.30868/ei.v11i4.3271

Ifenthaler, D., Majumdar, R., Gorissen, P., Judge, M., Mishra, S., Raffaghelli, J., & Shimada, A. (2024). Artificial intelligence in Education: Implications for policymakers, researchers, and practitioners. *Technology Knowledge and Learning*, *29*(4), 1693–1710. DOI: 10.1007/s10758-024-09747-0

Kamalov, F., & Gurrib, I. (2023). New era of Artificial intelligence in Education: Towards a sustainable Multifaceted Revolution. arXiv (Cornell University). https://doi.org//arxiv.2305.18303DOI: 10.48550

Karimi, H., & Khawaja, S. (2023). The impact of artificial intelligence on higher education in England. *Creative Education*, *14*(12), 2405–2415. DOI: 10.4236/ce.2023.1412154

Kasztelnik, K. (2024). Artificial Intelligence-Assisted Curriculum Development: Innovations in designing educational content for the 21st century learner. *Journal of Higher Education Theory and Practice*, *24*(11). Advance online publication. DOI: 10.33423/jhetp.v24i11.7367

Khan, F., & Bose, D. (2021). Artificial Intelligence enabled Smart Learning. *arXiv (Cornell University)*. https://doi.org//arxiv.2101.02991DOI: 10.48550

Laux, J. (2023). Institutionalised distrust and human oversight of artificial intelligence: Towards a democratic design of AI governance under the European Union AI Act. *AI & Society*, *39*(6), 2853–2866. DOI: 10.1007/s00146-023-01777-z PMID: 39640298

Mello, R. F., Freitas, E., Pereira, F. D., Cabral, L., Tedesco, P., & Ramalho, G. (2023). Education in the age of Generative AI: Context and Recent Developments. *arXiv preprint arXiv:2309.12332*.

Michaeli, T., Seegerer, S., & Romeike, R. (2023). What Students Can Learn About Artificial intelligence — Recommendations for K-12 Computing Education. *arXiv (Cornell University)*. https://doi.org//arxiv.2305.06450DOI: 10.1007/978-3-031-43393-1_19

Mishra, S. (2024). Revolutionizing Education: The impact of AI-Enhanced Teaching Strategies. *International Journal for Research in Applied Science and Engineering Technology*, *12*(9), 9–32. DOI: 10.22214/ijraset.2024.64127

Mollick, E. R., & Mollick, L. (2023). Assigning AI: Seven Approaches for Students, with Prompts. SSRN *Electronic Journal*. https://doi.org/DOI: 10.2139/ssrn.4475995

Mouta, A., Pinto-Llorente, A. M., & Torrecilla-Sánchez, E. M. (2023). Uncovering Blind Spots in Education Ethics: Insights from a Systematic Literature Review on Artificial Intelligence in Education. *International Journal of Artificial Intelligence in Education*, *34*(3), 1166–1205. DOI: 10.1007/s40593-023-00384-9

Nagaraj, B. K., A, K., R, S. B., S, A., Sachdev, H. K., & N, S. K. (2023). The Emerging Role of Artificial intelligence in STEM Higher Education: A Critical review. *International Research Journal of Multidisciplinary Technovation*, 1–19. https://doi.org/DOI: 10.54392/irjmt2351

Ng, D. T. K., Leung, J. K. L., Su, J., Ng, R. C. W., & Chu, S. K. W. (2023). Teachers' AI digital competencies and twenty-first century skills in the post-pandemic world. *Educational Technology Research and Development*, *71*(1), 137–161. DOI: 10.1007/s11423-023-10203-6 PMID: 36844361

Nguyen, A., Ngo, H. N., Hong, Y., Dang, B., & Nguyen, B. T. (2022). Ethical principles for artificial intelligence in education. *Education and Information Technologies*, *28*(4), 4221–4241. DOI: 10.1007/s10639-022-11316-w PMID: 36254344

Ojha, S., Narendra, A., Mohapatra, S., & Misra, I. (2023). From Robots to Books: An Introduction to Smart Applications of AI in Education (AIED). *arXiv (Cornell University)*. https://doi.org//arxiv.2301.10026DOI: 10.48550

Özer, M., Perc, M., & Suna, H. (2024). Participatory management can help AI ethics adhere to the social consensus. *İstanbul Üniversitesi Sosyoloji Dergisi / İstanbul University Journal of Sociology, 0*(0), 0. https://doi.org/DOI: 10.26650/SJ.2024.44.1.0001

Prazeres, F. G., & Silva-Pina, A. (2024, October 30). *AI Integrated Learning for Higher Education Social Science Educators*. https://dergipark.org.tr/tr/pub/usdad/issue/86150/1529088

Radanliev, P., Santos, O., Brandon-Jones, A., & Joinson, A. (2024). Ethics and responsible AI deployment. *Frontiers in Artificial Intelligence*, *7*, 1377011. DOI: 10.3389/frai.2024.1377011 PMID: 38601110

Ren, X., & Wu, M. L. (2025). Examining teaching competencies and challenges while integrating artificial intelligence in higher education. *TechTrends*, *69*(3), 519–538. DOI: 10.1007/s11528-025-01055-3

Resnick, M. (2024, March 27). *Generative AI and Creative Learning: Concerns, Opportunities, and Choices [Online forum post]*. An MIT Exploration of Generative AI. https://doi.org/DOI: 10.21428/e4baedd9.cf3e35e5

Rožman, M., Tominc, P., & Vrečko, I. (2023). Building skills for the future of work: Students' perspectives on emerging jobs in the Data and AI Cluster through artificial intelligence in education. *Environment and Social Psychology*, *8*(2). Advance online publication. DOI: 10.54517/esp.v8i2.1670

Simbeck, K. (2023). They shall be fair, transparent, and robust: Auditing learning analytics systems. *AI and Ethics*, *4*(2), 555–571. DOI: 10.1007/s43681-023-00292-7

Sitnicka, S., Mursalov, M., Mammadov, H., Babaiev, D., & Zhou, Y. (2025). Ethics, Institutions, Infrastructure, and Governance in AI National-Level Readiness: A Hidden driver of Banking transformation. *Business Ethics and Leadership*, *9*(3), 290–304. DOI: 10.61093/bel.9(3).290-304.2025

Solanki, P., Grundy, J., & Hussain, W. (2022). Operationalising ethics in artificial intelligence for healthcare: A framework for AI developers. *AI and Ethics*, *3*(1), 223–240. DOI: 10.1007/s43681-022-00195-z

Swiecki, Z., Khosravi, H., Chen, G., Martinez-Maldonado, R., Lodge, J. M., Milligan, S., Selwyn, N., & Gašević, D. (2022). Assessment in the age of artificial intelligence. *Computers and Education Artificial Intelligence*, *3*, 100075. DOI: 10.1016/j.caeai.2022.100075

Tan, M., & Subramonyam, H. (2023). More than Model Documentation: Uncovering Teachers' Bespoke Information Needs for Informed Classroom Integration of ChatGPT. *arXiv (Cornell University).* https://doi.org//arxiv.2309.14458DOI: 10.48550

Unesco. (2023). Guidance for generative AI in education and research. In *UNESCO eBooks*. https://doi.org/DOI: 10.54675/EWZM9535

Wang, N., & Lester, J. (2023). K-12 Education in the Age of AI: A Call to Action for K-12 AI Literacy. *International Journal of Artificial Intelligence in Education, 33*(2), 228–232. DOI: 10.1007/s40593-023-00358-x

Zhai, X., Chu, X., Chai, C. S., Jong, M. S. Y., Istenic, A., Spector, M., Liu, J., Yuan, J., & Li, Y. (2021). A Review of Artificial Intelligence (AI) in Education from 2010 to 2020. *Complexity, 2021*(1), 1–18. DOI: 10.1155/2021/8812542

Chapter 3
AI-Enhanced Educational Motivation in Collaborative Learning Environments

Ibrahem Mohammad Alamoush
http://orcid.org/0009-0007-8728-4227
Sharjah Education Academy, UAE

ABSTRACT

Education is undergoing a profound transformation thanks to artificial intelligence. AI has reshaped collaborative learning. In Arabic language education, AI stands out as a solution to morphological, semantic, and dialectal challenges. Initiatives such as the Sird Scale, the Zay Scale, and the Tal'a and Mubkar tests are pioneering Arabic models that use artificial intelligence for personalization and motivation. Despite these developments, issues of privacy, algorithmic bias, and cultural sensitivity remain central, with the teacher continuing to play a key role as the designer of learning. The future trend confirms that successful smart education is based on a balance between technology and human vision.

1. INTRODUCTION

Recent years have seen remarkable developments in the use of artificial intelligence and a qualitative shift in collaborative learning, due to rapid advances in AI technologies and educational applications. Reviews such as the Kovari study (2025), the integration of AI tools, particularly machine learning, natural language process-

DOI: 10.4018/979-8-2600-0328-2.ch003

ing (NLP), and recommender systems, has reshaped the techniques of collaboration among learners and made the educational environment more adaptive and smarter.

It has contributed to increased motivation and engagement through real-time feedback systems and predictive analytics that can identify learners at risk of falling behind and provide immediate support. Thus, collaborative learning is no longer just human interaction between peers but has become an smart system that integrates algorithms and human interaction to build more effective and inclusive learning environments.

Educational motivation is a dynamic process that is built through interaction between the learner, the content, the activities, and the educational context, and is not limited to external incentives or final results. Collaborative learning refers to an educational model based on organized interaction between learners to achieve common goals, with distributed roles and responsibilities, rather than simply traditional group work. Here, artificial intelligence contributes to enhancing both individual and social motivation by analyzing interaction patterns in groups, providing intelligent feedback, and supporting more interactive and responsive collaborative learning environments that meet the needs of learners.

Considering these rapid changes, recent research trends have emerged linking artificial intelligence and motivation and interaction strategies in education, especially in the context of gamification as an educational approach based on the principles of play. Torres-Toukoumidis, et al. (2024) note that the integration of gamification techniques with artificial intelligence has become one of the most influential trends in modern education, as it enables the creation of more stimulating and personalized learning experiences. With proper handling of challenges related to technical readiness, accessibility, and privacy protection, an immense potential to reshape the educational process is something to look for.

From this perspective, this chapter seeks to analyze the potentials of using artificial intelligence in building stimulating collaborative learning environments and explore how these approaches can contribute to the development of Arabic language education within a evolving digital context. Despite the growing research momentum in the use of artificial intelligence and gamification in education, studies focus on Western educational environments with advanced technical infrastructure, along with limited representation of educational contexts in the Arab or developing worlds. (Almelhes, 2024).

Often, the integration of AI and language learning is approached from a general technical or motivational perspective, without an in-depth analysis of the collaborative dimensions or group dynamics that arise in AI-supported learning environments (Gini, 2025; Kovari, 2025). However, pioneering Arab initiatives have recently begun to emerge, contributing to bridging this gap, such as Zay Center, SARD Scale, Al Dhad Scale and TAL'A and Mubakkir. These efforts invest in artificial intelligence technologies for language analysis and personalized learning, language assessment, and the promotion of language motivation in a way that keeps up with global trends. This chapter seeks to analyze these practices considering the theoretical frameworks of collaborative learning and smart motivation, and to explore how they contribute to the development of an authentic Arab model for smart education that combines technology and cultural dimension.

The current chapter does not aim to provide a technical overview of artificial intelligence tools, but rather seeks to present an educational analysis focusing on the dimensions of motivation and collaborative interaction in smart educational environments, especially in the context of Arabic language education, highlighting the specificity of this field compared to general studies in AI-supported education.

The chapter also aims to analyze the integration of motivation, games, and artificial intelligence within the context of cooperative learning, focusing on employing these approaches in teaching and assessing Arabic as a field that combines linguistic complexity with cultural richness. It seeks to offer a critical and applied reading of Arab models that represent a growing trend toward smart education and language motivation; to reveal how artificial intelligence technologies can be leveraged to enhance interaction, collaboration, and motivation within educational environments. The goal is to build a more comprehensive educational vision that links theory and practice and enriches the discussion on localizing artificial intelligence technologies in Arab and global education. Furthermore, this I seek through this chapter to reframe the relationship between technology, motivation, and collaboration from a humanistic and cultural perspective, highlighting the integration of smart tools into a participatory learning environment that respects the linguistic and cultural specificities of learners.

The chapter consists of six interrelated sections. The first section about background of the topic and outlines the chapter's objectives. The second section presents the theoretical framework linking artificial intelligence, motivation, and cooperative learning. The third section discusses cooperative learning in the digital age as an AI-supported educational approach. The fourth section focuses on Arabic language education considering AI and smart motivational design. The fifth section offers an applied analysis of selected pioneering Arab initiatives. The chapter concludes with a sixth section addressing ethical considerations and future trends in smart education.

2. ARTIFICIAL INTELLIGENCE AND MOTIVATIONAL DESIGN IN EDUCATION: A THEORETICAL FRAMEWORK

This section establishes the theoretical framework that guides the analysis in this chapter, explaining the conceptual foundations that link artificial intelligence and motivational design to education, and how they interact to support the design of learning environments based on motivation, interaction, and personalization. In contrast, motivational design and gamification principles have provided an educational framework that rethinks the concept of motivation by employing challenges, rewards, and feedback to increase engagement and persistence in the educational process (Subhash & Cudney, 2018). This section reviews the theories and models that explain this integration, showing how AI can function as a tool that supports motivational design, capable of enhancing interaction and collaboration within educational environments, particularly in Arabic language education, which combines linguistic complexity with cultural richness.

2.1 The Evolution of AI in Education

The use of AI has shifted from expert educational systems in the 1980s, which relied on specific rules to simulate teacher decisions, to smart educational systems, which have emerged in the last two decades and are capable of analyzing learner data and providing feedback tailored to their individual needs. Létourneau, et al., (2025) showed that the development of these systems has contributed to the creation of learning environments capable of learning from learners' behavior and responses, and automatically modifying their content to achieve greater effectiveness, paving the way for a new generation of smart learning environments that combine machine learning algorithms and predictive analytics, shifting from the traditional teacher-centered model to an adaptive model that places the learner at the center of the educational process.

With the development of deep learning and predictive analytics technologies in the last decade, AI applications in education have moved to a more mature stage characterized by the ability to dynamically personalize and guide learning experiences. Létourneau et al. (2025) also emphasized that integrating artificial intelligence into the design of educational environments depends on combining real-time monitoring of learner performance with continuous feedback, which increases levels of motivation and engagement in the educational process. These results indicate that artificial intelligence is no longer just an analytical tool but has become a smart educational mechanism that contributes to the development of more equitable and effective educational models, capable of continuously and renewably adapting to learners.

This transformation has extended to the structure of the educational environment itself, establishing what are known as smart learning environments. These environments represent a new phase in the digital transformation of education, employing data analysis algorithms and deep learning technologies to provide personalized and adaptive learning experiences (Tabuenca, et al., 2024). Smart classrooms redefine educational interaction by combining instant communication and real-time monitoring of learners' performance and reshaping educational activities based on their responses. Schools and universities thus become dynamic learning systems capable of continuously adapting to different learner styles and contexts, while enhancing the role of data in educational decision-making. (Zhang, et al. 2024)

This development indicates that artificial intelligence has become an essential design element in building motivational learning experiences capable of prediction and intelligent human interaction. The findings of Létourneau et al. (2025) confirm that the effectiveness of smart teaching systems is linked to the degree to which they integrate motivational elements into instructional design, such as immediate feedback, personalized learning paths, the use of challenges, and content progression tailored to the learner's readiness.

The shift in educational AI research includes the emergence of the concept of "educational emotional intelligence," an approach that aims to understand the emotional dimension of learners and adapt the learning process according to their psychological and motivational state (Klimova & Pikhart, 2025). Some smart educational systems have become capable of analyzing facial expressions, voice tone, and digital behavior patterns to assess the emotional state of learners, whether they feel bored, confused, or excited, and then adjust the level of difficulty or type of activity accordingly, making motivation an integral part of the smart structure of the educational system itself.

In light of this shift in the nature of smart systems, the role of teachers in educational environments has also changed. Instead of being the sole source of knowledge, teachers are now seen as designers of the educational experience and facilitators of motivation, directing artificial intelligence toward learning objectives and balancing the relationship between machine analysis and human motivation. Létourneau et al (2025) and Zhai et al (2021) have shown that the effectiveness of smart educational systems depends largely on the presence of teachers to interpret the data produced by the system and translate it into motivating educational strategies, thereby enhancing the integration between artificial intelligence and the role of the teacher.

With the expansion of AI applications, new ethical challenges have emerged regarding the use of learner data and protecting learners from algorithmic bias. Some systems still lack clear standards of transparency and accountability in the collection and use of educational data, which can negatively affect learners' trust and motivation. Therefore, it has become necessary for technological transformations to be accompanied by ethical educational frameworks that ensure fairness and equity in smart educational experiences and guarantee that AI systems are tools that support human motivation rather than restrict it. (Marín, et al., 2025)

New generations of smart systems are no longer content with improving academic achievement, but seek to build learning environments that interact with the emotional and cognitive state of learners and support their independence and collaboration.

Finally, the relevant educational literature in this section indicates that AI in education has moved from being primarily a technical support tool to becoming a fundamental design component for reshaping learning environments through data-driven personalization, adaptive feedback, and instructional models that place the learner at the center of the educational process.

2.2 Motivational Design Principles in AI-Supported Educational Transformations

Taking into consideration the conceptual development of artificial intelligence in education, the need emerged to redefine the principles of motivational design in smart educational environments, moving beyond traditional concepts of motivation toward an educational approach based on data, interaction, and adaptive intelligence. Létourneau et al. (2025) explain that motivation in smart environments is no longer a purely psychological concept, rather it has become a design element integrated into educational systems themselves, where algorithms analyze learners' responses and provide personalized feedback that contributes to enhancing engagement and sustained interest.

While in linguistic contexts, Xiao et al. (2025) showed that emotion-based smart education systems contribute to increasing motivation by enhancing learners' self-confidence and regulating emotions during online learning, which is reflected in higher levels of joy and achievement. These findings support what Pikhart & Klimova (2025) has pointed out about the importance of the ethical and emotional dimension in building stimulating learning environments, where motivation becomes more effective when learners feel that the system treats their emotional state with fairness and human empathy, rather than merely as a source of data.

Predictive analytics has become one of the main pillars in the development of adaptive motivation within smart education systems. The prediction algorithms based on educational data analysis enable the system to detect early signs of decreased motivation, such as a decline in interaction frequency or an increase in error rates, allowing the system to intervene immediately by providing motivational feedback or adjusting the level of challenge to match the learner's abilities. This type of proactive analysis promotes what is known as "preventive motivation," i.e., motivation that seeks to prevent loss of motivation before it occurs, making the learning process more continuous and effective. (Zhang & Dong, 2024)

While in smart collaborative learning environments, multi-agent systems re-define motivation as a participatory social process, as they can monitor patterns of cooperation within educational groups, analyze member interactions, and then suggest smart interventions to improve the balance between individual and group participation. The use of collective motivation mechanisms, such as cooperative points and shared rewards, increases the level of positive interaction and enhances mutual trust among learners, leading to sustainable motivation based on team spirit and shared achievement. (Outay, et al, 2024)

These trends show that motivational design principles in AI-supported environments are based on integrating three interrelated dimensions: First, personalization: which ensures that content is tailored to the learner's abilities and interests; second: interaction, which produces continuous dialogic learning experiences; and third: emotional responsiveness, which takes into account the learner's emotional state and uses it pedagogically. According to this vision, motivation is not seen as an external process, but rather as a mechanism inherent in the design of the smart system, which seeks to achieve a continuous balance between challenge and support, performance and satisfaction, giving the learner a comprehensive human learning experience that combines technical competence and educational vision.

The previous literature shows that motivational design in AI-supported educational environments functions as an integrated tool in learning and teaching design, working to support personalization by increasing interaction and providing immediate feedback on maintaining learner engagement, and maintaining consideration of the learner's contextual, cultural, and educational differences.

2.3 How AI Integrates Personalization, Interaction, and Motivation.

An analysis of recent literature in the field of artificial intelligence in education indicates that new trends are no longer limited to the development of automated educational systems but aim to build smart learning systems that integrate personalization, interaction, and motivation into a single integrated framework. Studies in recent years have shown that the effectiveness of artificial intelligence in education depends primarily on its ability to understand learners, interpret their behavior, and adapt the learning environment to suit their cognitive and emotional styles (Létourneau et al., 2025; Zhai et al., 2021).

The personalization is the cornerstone of AI-supported education, as modern systems rely on deep learning algorithms and educational data analysis to identify learners' strengths and weaknesses and build dynamic learning paths that change according to performance. The combining real-time data analysis with predictive intelligence enables the system to instantly adjust the level of difficulty and feedback, ensuring that the learning experience is consistent with the learner's needs and pace of progress. This form of personalization seeks not only differentiation, but also adaptive equity in education, where each learner receives precisely tailored support (Merino-Campos, 2025).

Interaction in smart learning environments is linked to motivation, as it is a key channel for feedback and collaborative learning. The multi-agent systems represent an advanced stage of interaction, as they can analyze group conversations among learners and provide smart interventions to enhance collaboration or redirect dialogue when participation declines (Edwards, 2024). Xiao et al. (2025) also showed that conversation-based interaction between learners and smart systems contributes to improving linguistic confidence and reducing academic anxiety, as the system provides immediate support without human judgment, thereby enhancing self-motivation and sustained engagement. Repeated interaction with the system also enabled learners to receive immediate and linguistically correct feedback, which increased their motivation to continue self-practice. (Zhu &Wang, 2014)

The emotion detection systems using facial expression and voice analysis and interaction patterns help determine the level of attention, fatigue, or frustration in learners, allowing proper adaptation of educational activities. The immediate emotional response of smart systems enhances interactive motivation, as learners feel that the system interacts with them in a personal and genuine way, which increases cognitive and emotional integration simultaneously. This integration of emotional analysis and performance-based motivation is one of the most prominent manifestations of human-like artificial intelligence in contemporary education. (Fernández-Herrero, 2024)

The role of AI in motivation is not restricted to the individual level, but extends to the value and ethical level in the design of learning environments. That systems that consider fairness and transparency in processing learner data create more motivating and trusting environments, because learners realize that their assessment is the result of fair and unbiased analysis. The fairness in feedback is part of the motivational structure in smart education, as algorithmic bias or prejudice leads to a decline in the motivation of underrepresented groups. (Yin, et al., 2025)

The transformation in the use of artificial intelligence in education is no longer limited to improving technical efficiency, but has become an educational path that redefines the concepts of motivation, interaction, and personalization within human and smart learning environments. Motivational design is no longer just a tool, but a structural part of educational smart systems that are capable of predicting and responding to educational behavior emotionally in real time. With this knowledge, teaching practices are moving toward building collaborative learning environments supported by artificial intelligence, where motivation, interaction, and collaboration become a single integrated system redefines the roles of teachers and learners in our digital age.

In conclusion, the above indicates that integrating personalization, interaction, and motivation into AI-enhanced learning systems is a comprehensive educational change that encompasses cognitive, emotional, and ethical dimensions in an effort to create more equitable, responsive, and learner-centered educational environments.

3. COLLABORATIVE LEARNING IN THE DIGITAL AGE: AN EDUCATIONAL APPROACH SUPPORTED BY ARTIFICIAL INTELLIGENCE.

The integration of AI and collaborative learning is not limited to improving communication but also extends to building collective knowledge based on data and real-time performance analysis. The results of a study by Lu, et al. (2024) showed that multi-agent systems enable educational environments to efficiently manage educational dialogue by tracking learners' behavior and analyzing their contributions, then suggesting smart interventions to motivate low-participation learners and support balanced collaboration.

The importance of this human dimension in AI-supported collaboration stands out in the light of what Pikhart & Klimova (2025) have put forward, where they emphasized that ethical and emotional values have become an integral part of the design of smart educational environments. Effective collaboration is not simply achieved by exchanging knowledge, rather it requires building trust and belonging among individuals, which smart systems can promote through fairness in data processing and transparency in evaluation mechanisms. The ensuring equality in collective performance analysis contributes to promoting motivational justice within the team, as each learner feels that their efforts are fairly valued, which increases their commitment and participation.

Now, in this context, artificial intelligence become capable of supporting collective motivation through adaptive recommendations and data-driven collaborative activities, leading to deeper and more interactive learning (Susnjak, 2023) . Thus, collaboration in smart environments has become a blend of social interaction and computational intelligence, integrating cognitive, affective, and ethical aspects to create a collective learning experience based on mutual understanding and meaningful participation.

Based on these transformations, the researcher seeks to analyse the educational concepts that form the basis of collaborative learning and its socio-constructive pillars, then review the role of artificial intelligence in supporting teamwork and interaction, before discussing the relationship between motivation and collaboration in the design of smart learning environments, in an attempt to present an integrated vision of how to build balanced digital human collaboration in contemporary education.

We can understand learning in the digital age as an instructional approach that is constantly being redefined and constructed through AI, where intelligent analysis guides collective interaction and participation rather than just informal social interaction.

3.1 Key Concepts of Cooperative Learning and its Social Constructivist Underpinnings

Collaborative learning is one of the most advanced teaching concepts in the digital age, having evolved from a classroom interaction method to a comprehensive educational philosophy that redefines the relationship between learners and knowledge. Thanks to artificial intelligence technologies, the digital learning environment has become capable of embodying the core principles of collaborative learning by building open learning communities based on participation, discussion, and collective thinking. Becheru, et al. (2018) point out that analysing data from educational groups has provided a deeper understanding of student interaction patterns within smart classrooms, enabling systems to predict the level of collaboration and provide constructive interventions to improve collective performance.

Collaborative learning is fundamentally based on the principles of social constructivism, which views knowledge as being constructed through interaction between individuals within a shared cultural and social context, not in isolation. The artificial intelligence has become an effective tool in analyzing collective discourse and knowledge negotiation among learners, as modern systems can track collective thinking processes and infer patterns of shared understanding, representing a digital translation of social constructivist theory in its contemporary interactive form. Artificial intelligence tools have also helped reshape the concept of collective participation through real-time tracking systems capable of detecting hidden interactions, i.e., nonverbal contributions or implicit collaborative decisions that were not observable in traditional classrooms. This awareness of the level of participation has enabled educational institutions to develop learning models that encourage collective contributions and give learners a sense of belonging and shared responsibility. (Dinnar, et al., 2021)

The artificial intelligence has created collaborative learning environments capable of integrating human communication and smart media through collective recommendation algorithms allowing learners to choose participatory activities that best suit their needs and learning styles. This trend reinforces the idea of "collective empowerment," which makes every learner an active participant in knowledge construction and decision-making within the group, interacting with constructivist principles that view learning as an ongoing social negotiation process.

The cooperation cannot be achieved in isolation from the emotional state of the participants. Smart systems capable of recognising collective emotions, such as tension, integration or enthusiasm, can adjust the course of activities based on the general mood of students, leading to improved communication, reduced conflict and facilitated positive group learning (Salloum, et al., 2025). The understanding social and emotional contexts is a prerequisite for designing effective collaboration within smart environments, as collaborative processes require a delicate balance between computational intelligence and social intelligence. (Henriksen, 2025)

AI-supported educational environments have reinforced the concept of "collective intelligence, where knowledge has become the product of the interaction between human minds and algorithms. Educational systems are now able to collect and analyse individual contributions to generate shared knowledge, shifting from individual learning to collective learning based on participation and collaborative production. (Casebourne et al, 2025)

This make it clear that collaborative learning in the light of artificial intelligence is no longer just a complementary educational model, but has become a constructive approach linking the collective mind and technology. It is based on three pillars; cognitive (exchange of experiences and construction of shared meaning), affective (trust, respect, and collective motivation), and technical (recommendation algorithms and interactive analysis), which together form the basis for building smart social learning environments capable of developing human knowledge in a collaborative and renewable manner.

Translating these theoretical concepts into effective educational practice requires redesigning smart environments to be more capable of accommodating human and cognitive diversity within groups. The development of collaboration analysis tools should not be limited to performance tracking but should extend to enabling learners to understand their roles within the group through smart dashboards that display patterns of collective contributions in a transparent and interactive manner. This type of educational design based on "collaborative awareness" enables individuals to self-organise their learning within a collective context, transforming the smart environment into a space for both personal and social development.

Considering these shifts, predictive analytics emerge as a crucial element in understanding the dynamics of collaborative learning. Susnjak (2023) has shown that predictive algorithms based on social interaction data can detect signs of weakening cooperation or declining engagement before they occur, enabling smart systems to intervene proactively through motivational activities or group reconfiguration based on cognitive and emotional integration among individuals. This approach is a step towards 'preventive cooperation', which seeks to maintain continuity of interaction and achieve a balance between individual motivation and group harmony.

Thus, it can be said that collaborative learning in smart environments represents an integrated system that employs both machine learning and human interaction to build learning communities capable of continuous adaptation and development. It is not limited to improving academic performance, but also contributes to the development of communication skills, critical thinking, and collective creativity, and establishes a new educational culture based on participation, transparency, and shared responsibility. These foundations form the framework from which the modern roles of artificial intelligence in supporting teamwork and interaction emerge, which the researcher will discuss in the following section.

These reflections suggest that collaborative learning, when supported by AI, is consistent with and adds a developmental dimension to social constructivist theory, as shared knowledge is constructed through intelligent analysis of interaction, participation, and collective meaning-making.

3.2 The Role of Artificial Intelligence in Supporting Teamwork and Interaction.

Artificial intelligence is a key factor in redefining educational interaction and teamwork within digital environments, as its role has shifted from mechanical automation to cognitive and participatory support enabling groups to build knowledge in a more conscious and coordinated manner. Smart educational systems are no longer used solely to monitor student performance, but are now capable of analysing group interactions and providing immediate recommendations to improve communication and collaboration among them (Susnjak, 2023). These capabilities allow algorithms to function as cognitive partners that help set the pace of group dialogue, identify weaknesses in interaction, and suggest strategies that support inclusivity and fairness within the team.

One of the most notable developments in this field is multi agent systems, which enable artificial intelligence to interact with educational groups in a participatory manner. Lu, et al. (2024) showed that these systems monitor group conversations, analyse speech patterns, and generate smart interventions to encourage balanced student participation. They not only guide the dialogue but also monitor the quality and speed of the discussion and suggest mechanisms to the teacher or system to improve harmony and integration among members. These systems also provide quantitative and qualitative indicators of group collaboration that can be used to evaluate the effectiveness of educational communication in real time.

In the context of language education, a study by Xiao, et al. (2024) showed that AI-supported conversational learning systems contributed to improving the quality of linguistic interaction among learners, and acted as a mediator, providing immediate linguistic feedback, suggesting alternative vocabulary and structures, and motivating students to use language in real-life communication situations. This type of automated human interaction reduces communication anxiety and increases linguistic motivation, leaving a positive impact on collaborative performance within educational teams.

Shi (2025) points out that the integration of affective analysis into intelligent collaboration systems represented a qualitative shift in understanding group interaction. Systems equipped with emotion-recognition algorithms can interpret facial expressions, tone of voice, and typing speed to assess the emotional state of the group, then direct activities in line with the general mood. If the system detects signs of boredom or distraction, it can suggest stimulating interactive activities or redistribute roles among learners. This type of "educational emotional intelligence" is one of the most important areas of development in smart collaborative learning environments.

From a strategic perspective, the artificial intelligence has contributed to restructuring the role of teachers within collaborative environments, where their role is no longer limited to transferring knowledge, but has become one of designing the educational experience and facilitating interaction. Teachers use the data generated by the smart system to guide discussions, stimulate collective thinking, and tailor support to each group according to its immediate performance. This educational approach represents the "Analytical Teacher" model, which relies on artificial intelligence to make pedagogical decisions.

Xia et al. (2024) also reveal a new dimension of collaborative interaction, namely the ability of smart systems to support collaboration between learners from different cultures and linguistic backgrounds. These systems employ translation and semantic analysis algorithms to facilitate mutual understanding, thereby promoting the concept of "cultural justice" in educational interaction. This type of cross-cultural collaboration not only contributes to the development of language skills but also instils values of respect and global understanding in educational environments.

Considering these developments, it can be said that artificial intelligence is no longer just a tool to aid collaborative learning, but has become an active element in the dynamics of teamwork, managing dialogue, analysing emotions, and redistributing roles to ensure balanced participation. It combines machine analysis and social intelligence to build a learning environment capable of continuously responding to changes in individual and group behaviour. Through this integration, the features of "interactive educational intelligence" are revealed, which aims to achieve a balance between technology and humanity in designing more collaborative and equitable learning environments.

Considering the above, AI can be considered an influential factor that facilitates collaborative work and interaction by organizing communication mechanisms and forming comprehensive, emotionally aware, and data-informed collaborative practices within digital learning environments.

3.3 The Relationship between Motivation and Cooperation in the Design of Smart Learning Environments.

The relationship between motivation and collaboration in smart learning environments is crucial to understand modern learning mechanisms. Motivation is no longer viewed as an individual driver, but rather as a collective phenomenon built within an interactive and participatory context. Smart technologies based on artificial intelligence have redefined the concept of motivation from a social perspective, so that it no longer targets the learner as an independent individual, but as an active member of a dynamic knowledge network. Zhai, & Nezakatgoo (2025) have shown that smart systems that employ collective performance analysis and participatory feedback have a positive effect on increasing engagement, as learners feel that their achievements contribute to the success of the group, enhancing collective motivation and transforming it into a shared experience.

Combining gamification elements with group collaboration generates "social motivation," a state in which individuals interact with each other motivated by collective achievement rather than individual achievement alone. Activities that combine shared rewards and collective challenges increase the depth of interaction and prolong participation in online learning. It also emphasises that effective motivation is not achieved through competition, rather through cooperation that redefines success as a collective outcome, making smart environments more consistent with the principles of fairness and social belonging. (Riar, 2022)

Alamgir, et al. (2024) showed that intelligent feedback systems are one of the most important tools for combining motivation and cooperation, as they allow learners to receive immediate feedback on their performance within the group and highlight their contributions to achieving common goals. Motivation here is inseparable from collective awareness, as individuals feel that their personal progress is linked to the team's progress, and that their feedback is not merely an evaluation, but a motivational message that reinforces the spirit of collaboration. The design of collaborative feedback contributes to transforming the learning environment into a space of "mutual motivational feedback," based on positive support and collective appreciation.

Algorithmic justice in smart educational systems is a prerequisite for sustaining cooperative motivation (Yin, et al., 2025). When learners feel that their contributions are evaluated in fair and transparent manner, their trust in the system increases, reflecting directly on their motivation to participate. However, when there is bias in the distribution of rewards or recognition of effort, collective motivation declines and some individuals withdraw or become symbolically excluded. Therefore, collective assessment algorithms must be based on principles of predictive fairness that consider cultural, linguistic and social differences among learners.

We must consider a new dimension to understand the relationship between motivation and cooperation. Artificial intelligence can predict the level of group engagement through accurate indicators, such as the pace of interaction, tone of communication, and patterns of mutual support among members (Tan, et al, 2022). This allows the smart system to intervene early when motivation within the group declines, by activating collaborative tasks or additional incentives that maintain harmony and integration among learners. This approach is a step towards building what could be called "preventive motivation," which aims to avoid loss of motivation before it occurs through direct analysis of group data.

Thus, the relationship between motivation and collaboration in the design of smart learning environments is based on a complex integration of technical and human factors. Effective group interaction requires fair, continuous, and algorithmically managed motivation without losing its human touch. This vision shows that artificial intelligence is not merely a tool for managing educational teams, but rather a partner in building a comprehensive motivational environment that considers performance, emotions, and fairness simultaneously. From this perspective, the integration of motivation and collaboration can be considered one of the most important aspects of educational transformation in smart education, as it establishes a new learning culture based on participation and collective motivation and paves the way for the application of these principles in Arabic language teaching contexts, which will be discussed in the next section of this chapter.

Accordingly, the relationship between motivation and collaboration in smart learning environments is a dynamic interaction at the system level, with AI supporting collective participation while maintaining the central role of the learner, trust, and shared purpose.

4. TEACHING ARABIC LANGUAGE THROUGH AI-DRIVEN MOTIVATIONAL APPROACHES

Supporting Arabic language education with AI is a unique educational reality, rather than a development of existing AI-based language learning models for which AI models have been developed. The Arabic language is characterized by linguistic richness, represented by morphology, derivation, grammatical flexibility, rhetoric, and other linguistic features. There are educational challenges that require educational design that is particularly sensitive to context and linguistic origins. As a result, it is necessary to design AI-enhanced motivational Arabic language curricula with attention to linguistic diversity and the learner's context, rather than relying on learning models for other languages.

In recent years, Arabic language teaching has undergone qualitative transformations because of the rapid developments in artificial intelligence technologies, which have reshaped language learning environments by integrating machine language analysis, real-time interaction, and smart personalisation of learning. Arabic language teaching is no longer limited to traditional presentation methods or simple interactive media, but it now relies on knowledge systems capable of understanding, analysing and generating Arabic language, including morphological, syntactic and semantic processing, and utilising the results of this analysis to build language content tailored to learners. Artificial intelligence can facilitate Arabic language teaching through smart conversations, adaptive recommendations, and accurate automated assessments, making the learning process more effective and interactive. (Alabbas & Alomar (2024).

With this technological development, the need arise to redefine the pedagogical and linguistic challenges in teaching Arabic, especially given its lexical and syntactic peculiarities and its multiple dialects. Teaching Arabic faces fundamental difficulties related to the automatic representation of the language and the construction of accurate databases that reflect its linguistic and cultural characteristics. Therefore, it is necessary to develop artificial intelligence tools that take into account the differences in dialects and linguistic diversity among learners, which requires the construction of flexible educational models capable of adapting to this diversity (Al-Ghadhban & Al-Twairesh, 2020; Elsayed, et al, 2025). The development of smart Arabic education requires combining linguistic knowledge, educational design, and artificial intelligence into a single system that simultaneously promotes understanding, interaction, and motivation.

Therefore, there is a need to employ interactive motivation and educational gamification as modern approaches to enhance Arabic language learning. The integration of gamification and artificial intelligence contributes to increasing language motivation and learner engagement through challenge, reward, and instant feedback mechanisms (Alameddine, et al., 2025). This integration enables the creation of smart Arabic learning environments that take cultural specificity into account and reshape the relationship between the learner and the educational system. This section seeks to analyse linguistic and pedagogical challenges, highlight the importance of data-driven motivational approaches, and explore the implications of gamification and smart motivation principles on Arabic language learning, in order to outline an authentic Arabic model for language teaching in the digital age.

4.1 Linguistic and Pedagogical Challenges in Teaching Arabic

The following discussion does not seek to provide a comprehensive overview of all the challenges facing Arabic language education, but rather highlights selected linguistic, educational, and cultural dimensions that are particularly relevant to the design of stimulating learning environments based on AI.

Teaching Arabic in the digital age represents a field in which linguistic, technical, and pedagogical challenges intersect in an unprecedented way, as educational institutions seek to leverage the potential of artificial intelligence in analyzing the Arabic language and employing it educationally, while still facing profound problems related to the specificity of the language structure and the multiplicity of linguistic and cultural levels. Among the most prominent difficulties are the limited digital language resources and the scarcity of structured databases in Arabic compared to other languages, which hinders the development of smart educational systems capable of processing the Arabic language characterised with its flexibility and lexical accuracy. (Hanandeh, et al. 2024).

The linguistic challenge stems from the nature of the Arabic language itself, as it is a derivational language rich in morphological and semantic structures and multiple contexts. Elsayed, et al, (2025) pointed out that the automatic evaluation of Arabic texts faces problems in distinguishing between similar meanings and diverse structures that express the same meaning. They also emphasized that the absence of balanced standard data sets leads to variations in the accuracy of models in analyzing learners' styles, which negatively affects fairness in assessment and feedback within smart learning environments.

The challenge of dialects is one of the most prominent problems facing Arabic education systems, especially for non-native speakers. The multiplicity of Arabic dialects makes it very difficult to build unified education systems, as the syntax, vocabulary, and phonetic patterns differ between dialects, limiting learners' ability to switch smoothly between standard Arabic and dialects (Al-Ghadhban & Al-Twairesh, 2020). The use of artificial intelligence in dialect analysis requires in-depth training on real-world data that represents this diversity. Otherwise, linguistic models may contribute to widening the gap rather than bridging it.

Another challenge is designing conversational systems capable of comprehending the cultural and contextual nuances of Arabic conversation (Alhassan, et al. 2022), as Arabic learners interact linguistically and culturally alike. Artificial intelligence still has difficulty understanding the use of metaphors, similes, and idioms, which limits the effectiveness of smart dialogue systems in simulating natural communication and highlights the need to develop linguistic models capable of treating Arabic as an integrated cultural phenomenon.

From a pedagogical perspective, the lack of professional development for teachers in the field of artificial intelligence represents a major obstacle to the integration of these technologies into classrooms (Samin & Osman, 2024). The use of AI is often limited to the technical aspect without being accompanied by a shift in teaching philosophy. It is necessary to adopt a comprehensive vision that makes AI a tool for personalizing learning and enhancing self-motivation, rather than just a digital aid.

It should be noted that the gap between the design of smart systems in Arabic and their English counterparts is not only technical but also educational, as many Arabic systems lack language learning models that reflect real-life classroom practices and respond to the diversity of learner types (Alsheddi & Alhenaki, 2022). English-language systems often adopt a design based on analyzing user needs and adapting content according to performance, while most Arabic systems still rely on fixed models that do not allow for deep interaction or dynamic content customization.

On a cultural level, the use of generative language models in the Arabic domain encounters issues related to the sensitivity of values and language (Al-Khalifa, et al. 2023). Generative models sometimes reproduce cultural or linguistic stereotypes when dealing with the Arabic language, which requires increased human supervision in the design of educational content to ensure consistency with cultural and linguistic specificity. This challenge highlights the ethical dimension of teaching Arabic with artificial intelligence, which is inseparable from linguistic justice and identity representation.

On the other hand, the concept of Arabic language education is expanding to include diverse groups of learners, such as those with hearing impairments, adding a new human dimension to the educational challenge (Abbas, et al. 2021). Building smart education systems that take Arabic sign language into account requires integrating computer vision and physical signal processing technologies into a multimedia learning environment. This approach highlights the importance of smart Arabic education being inclusive, not limited to written or spoken fluency, but also considering alternative forms of communication.

One of the fundamental challenges in Arabic language education is the lack of integration between academic language content and the needs of the labor market or vocational education (Alabbas & Alomar, 2024). Intelligent language learning remains disconnected from real-world applications, whereas artificial intelligence can build bridges between linguistic and functional skills through guided conversations and professional scenarios in Arabic.

Based on the above, the future of smart Arabic language education will be influenced by the extent to which new technologies can represent language in multiple written, spoken, visual, or even kinetic forms, requiring the investment of advanced algorithms to process the multiple contexts of language (Qedear, et al. 2024) . With these linguistic, educational, and cultural challenges, smart Arabic educational frameworks should be developed to consider linguistic specificity and adopt motivational and interactive approaches.

4.2 The Need to Adopt Motivational and Interactive Approaches Based on Data

Arabic language education is undergoing a fundamental shift toward smart learning environments that use data analysis and automated interaction to enhance self- and group motivation among learners. The design of data-driven learning environments enables institutions to track learners' performance in real time and analyze their linguistic behavior to generate personalized learning paths that consider their strengths and weaknesses (Hanandeh, et al. 2024). Thus, the transition from standardized education to personalized learning represents the first step toward building genuine motivation among learners, as each learner feels that the system understands their linguistic needs and keeps pace with their progress.

Alabbas & Alomar (2024) present a model of smart linguistic interaction based on AI-guided dialogue, in which the smart assistant analyzes the learner's responses and adapts questions and learning situations to suit their level, providing immediate feedback that motivates the learner to continue communicating. The results showed that smart conversation-based interaction enhances language learning, builds self-confidence, and increases the desire for continuous self-learning, as it combines play and personal experience in a safe environment free from direct human evaluation.

Analyzing the educational discourse resulting from intelligent conversations enables educational systems to understand learners' linguistic thinking patterns and redirect them educationally (Alhassan, et al. 2022). It was therefore necessary to develop interactive, data-driven approaches to teaching Arabic. In this context, artificial intelligence does not merely generate content, but also interprets linguistic performance and converts it into quantitative indicators that can be used to measure progress, interaction, and emotional engagement simultaneously. This approach must be expanded by integrating semantic and emotional analysis of the Arabic language, so that motivation is based on a true understanding of the learner's situation and not just on repetition or automatic rewards.

One of the most prominent strengths of data-driven interactive approaches is their ability to integrate emotional dimensions into the learning experience (Alsheddi & Alhenaki, 2022). Modern systems are now able to monitor indicators of satisfaction, frustration, or hesitation by analyzing writing tone and response speed, and adjusting dialogue patterns to enhance motivation. A comparison between English and Arabic models also highlights that the future development of Arabic systems needs to shift the design focus from static content to adaptive content, which changes the dialogue based on the learner's psychological state and the context of the interaction, representing a qualitative shift towards intelligent humanistic education.

The importance of these models lies in building Arabic learning environments based on predictive analysis of motivation, in a system that relies on algorithms that learn from learners' preferences and behavior in the system to provide language materials appropriate to their level and interests (Meddeb, et al. 2021). These systems increase the effectiveness of learning and create a positive psychological connection between the learner and the content, because the selection process appears to learners to be the result of their own self-awareness rather than an external system. This sense of autonomy is one of the most important factors in internal motivation, which promotes perseverance and interest in the language.

Automatic text analysis develops academic motivation among Arabic language learners by providing assessments and feedback, and by analyzing the linguistic style, grammatical structure, and semantic content of topics written in Arabic. It provides learners with explanatory feedback that highlights strengths and areas for improvement. This type of smart assessment makes feedback motivational rather than merely evaluative, as it focuses on performance development rather than judgment, and contributes to building learners' linguistic confidence.

Here, teachers in smart learning environments should be viewed as facilitators of learning who use language performance data to guide students individually and collectively. Therefore, teachers must be trained to understand smart analysis tools and interpret their educational results, because the real motivation in smart education does not come from the system itself, but from the way it is used to support the human experience of learning. It is also important to pay attention to the sociocultural aspect, as these smart educational systems consider the cultural dimension of Arabic language, because the motivation of Arab learners is inseparable from their sense of identity and belonging. When we employ artificial intelligence in an Arabic educational environment, it should reflect the values of the language and its culture, and move away from imported models that measure motivation in Western cultures. In these data-driven interactive approaches, we must not limit ourselves to quantitative analysis; rather, they must be based on a qualitative understanding of the nature of Arab learners and their social and cultural context.

Adopting these interactive motivational approaches in Arabic language teaching can be considered a strategic step toward building language education that is both smart and humane. Artificial intelligence does not replace teachers, but rather reshapes their roles as facilitators and designers of interactive learning experiences that promote self-motivation and group collaboration. With the development of real-time performance analysis, Arabic learning environments are transforming into living learning systems that respond to learners' emotions and needs, contributing to the development of sustainable motivation towards the language. This paves the way for a discussion of the role of gamification and smart motivation in the design of Arabic language learning.

4.3 Reflection of the Principles of Gamification and Smart Motivation on Learning Arabic

Gamification is one of the most prominent recent trends in the development of Arabic language education in smart environments, as it combines elements of play and intelligent data analysis to build self-motivation and sustainability among learners. Artificial intelligence has not only changed the way language content is presented, but has also reshaped the learning experience itself to be based on challenges, rewards, and immediate feedback. The integration of gamification with performance analysis algorithms generates a noticeable increase in learner engagement, as behavioral data is used to generate progressive challenges that match the learner's level and reward them for their progress, enhancing their sense of achievement and enjoyment of learning. (Alameddine, et al., 2025).

Now, the question arises: how can artificial intelligence redesign gamification in the form of realistic professional conversations? It relies on conversational algorithms that transform the learning process into a gaming experience based on solving linguistic situations and problems. Each successful linguistic interaction earns the learner digital points or level progression, increasing self-motivation and making the learner an active participant in an interactive environment that simulates real-life situations (Alabbas & Alomar, 2024). Gamification in Arabic language teaching can go beyond entertainment to develop linguistic competence and professional communication at the same time.

Gamification in language education is not limited to individuals, but extends to building group interaction among learners through "shared dialogue tasks." It uses smart systems that manage collaborative conversation through play, with participants exchanging roles and being rewarded based on the quality of interaction and adherence to linguistic rules (Alhassan, et al. 2022). This enhances social motivation, as learning is achieved through collaboration and collective achievement rather than individual competition.

One form of gamification is treating dialect diversity as an interactive learning space. Al-Ghadhban & Al-Twairesh (2020) designed a smart assistant that allows learners to practice conversation in different Arabic dialects through fun language activities that encourage them to explore dialect differences. The system gives digital rewards for the correct use of local vocabulary or for successfully switching from dialect to standard Arabic, making dialect diversity a means of linguistic belonging and cultural motivation at the same time.

Despite these advantages, the effectiveness of gamification and AI-based motivation strategies in Arabic language learning remains closely linked to thoughtful instructional design, cultural sensitivity, and the avoidance of superficial reward structures that may limit intrinsic motivation.

To go beyond traditional methods, we use smart packaging by employing predictive analysis to adapt the level of difficulty and activity pattern to the learner's emotional and cognitive state. Modern systems can analyze interaction time, response speed, and body language (in virtual reality environments) to assess the level of effort or fatigue, then automatically adjusting the degree of challenge to ensure continued motivation without fatigue (Hanandeh, et al. 2024). This combination of emotional motivation and artificial intelligence restores the human language of education and makes the system more empathetic to the learner.

Gamification succeeds when it is based on a comprehensive educational approach. Rewards and visual elements alone are not enough to motivate learners unless activities are designed to serve specific language goals. Gamification must be part of a comprehensive motivational design that links linguistic performance with an intelligent analysis of the learner's needs, thereby achieving a reciprocal relationship between fun and academic mastery.

Despite the importance of gamification, Arab education systems still need to develop assessment models that include criteria for achievement and interactive behavior, not just correct answers. Effective gamified learning measures participation, time, and continuity, and rewards positive behavior within the platform (Alsheddi & Alhenaki, 2022). Comparing Western and Arab models, we find that Western smart systems often incorporate elements of "social challenge" and "digital identity," while Arab models continue to focus on results without a clear and developed learning path. This calls for the need to build authentic Arab gamification systems that consider the cultural and educational values specific to Arabic language.

Gamification principles can be used to motivate writing skills, as feedback from automated assessment can be turned into a motivating experience by awarding learners points or levels when they improve their sentence structure or avoid repeated grammatical errors. This approach redefines feedback as part of an endless educational game, making the learning process cumulative and continuous.

Gamification also plays an important role in helping people with hearing impairments, as it uses sign recognition systems to teach Arabic vocabulary and pronunciation to people with hearing impairments through activities based on movement, points, and rewards (Abbas, et al. 2021). This makes Arabic language teaching more inclusive and human, as motivation becomes part of a multisensory communication experience.

Open interaction between Arab users and generative language models has enabled a new form of "social gamification," whereby users learn through dialogue and discussion in a vast digital space without direct supervision. Learners who use Arabic text generation models develop language skills through trial and error, self-correction, and immediate feedback from the system, which are all elements resemble the dynamics of play in spontaneous learning. (Al-Khalifa, et al. 2023)

Based on the above, it is clear that gamification in Arabic language teaching is no longer just a means of entertainment, but has become an intelligent educational approach that combines technical analysis and human motivation. Artificial intelligence allows for the design of learning environments that adapt to the learner and respond to their momentary efforts, while the elements of play provide an emotional and cognitive framework that supports continuity and engagement. Thus, learning Arabic in the digital age is being reshaped into an enjoyable and effective experience that balances self-motivation, group interaction, and cultural connection to Arab identity, which form the foundations upon which the leading Arab initiatives in smart education presented in the following section will be built.

5. LEADING ARAB INITIATIVES AND SMART APPLICATIONS IN ARABIC LANGUAGE TEACHING

In recent years, several smart educational initiatives have emerged seeking to employ artificial intelligence technologies in content delivery or assessment to redesign language learning experiences, including motivation, interaction, and group personalization. This section focuses on the most prominent of these initiatives in the context of Arabic language teaching, analyzing how each has invested in AI to support learning or assessment and how it has integrated technical, pedagogical, and motivational dimensions. In this analysis, we seek to show how these Arab projects have become pioneers in building smart language environments and how they can create a sustainable motivational and collaborative climate for Arab learners, overcoming the traditional challenges associated with teaching Arabic and redefining the relationship between language and learning in the digital age.

This section will discuss three Arab initiatives that represent contemporary trends in smart Arabic language teaching: SARD scale as a model for early analysis and motivation; Al-Dhad scale as a standardized system based on smart linguistic analysis, with the aim of demonstrating how these models contribute to redefining the relationship between assessment, motivation, and learning in the smart Arabic environment, and TALA'A and Mubakkir (Arabic Language Assessments).

5.1 Zai Center and the SARD Scale: Intelligent Narrative and Reading Assessment

Zai Arabic Language Research Center at Zayed University is a pioneering research model in the development of smart language tools that combine linguistic cognitive analysis and artificial intelligence algorithms to identify learners' abilities in the Arabic language. One of its most notable projects is SARD (Smart Arabic Reading Diagnostic Tool), a comprehensive digital system designed specifically to assess the reading and comprehension skills of Arabic-speaking children in the early stages of learning. The project aims to move from traditional paper-based measurement to adaptive smart assessment based on the analysis of individual learner data, making assessment a structural part of the learning process itself (SARD Final English Report, 2024).

The SARD system consists of sixteen interactive activities that measure multiple dimensions of reading proficiency, such as phonological awareness, naming speed, letter recognition, auditory comprehension, vocabulary, and working memory (Arabisard, n.d.). The platform relies on machine learning algorithms that track the learner's performance momently, measuring their accuracy, speed, and emotional and cognitive responses. Based on this data, the system generates an instant diagnostic report showing the learner's level in each sub-skill and suggests teaching approaches appropriate to their individual situation. Thus, the assessment process becomes a continuous learning support tool, rather than just a final test to judge proficiency. (ZAI–Zayed Artificial Intelligence Center, n.d.)

One of the distinctive features of "SARD" is its adoption of an educational motivation approach through Affective Design. The platform offers an engaging virtual environment carefully designed to suit Arab children, where learners can choose a digital character to represent them during the assessment and interact with it through friendly voice dialogue (Arabisard, n.d.). This human-like digital interaction reduces test anxiety and boosts children's motivation to participate, as they feel they are embarking on a linguistic adventure rather than taking a rigid test. Field testing of the system has shown that this approach increases attention spans and improves the accuracy of responses, confirming the impact of psychological motivation on improving the quality of language assessment (SARD Final English Report, 2024).

Technically, SARD relies on temporal and cognitive analytics, monitoring click sequences, response speed, and number of attempts, and comparing them to developmental standards codified by age and grade level (ZAI–Zayed Artificial Intelligence Center, n.d.). This analysis enables the platform to detect early indicators of reading difficulties, such as slow processing or poor short-term verbal memory, and issue educational alerts that help teachers intervene at the right time. In this way, SARD combines predictive analysis with educational equity, providing each learner with an accurate description of their abilities and needs. (Arabisard, n.d.)

The use of artificial intelligence in “SARD” is also evident in its ability to identify and reduce this gap across school grades, enabling teachers to determine the level of student achievement and tailor a suitable curriculum for those students, helping them succeed in their classes. The school can also conduct a comprehensive survey to identify the strengths and weaknesses in Arabic phonics skills, including reading and writing Arabic texts, among all students from first to sixth grade. This will enable schools to develop their educational programs to cater to each student based on the previous assessment.

Instead of providing typical feedback, the platform provides diagnostic feedback that explains mistakes and their causes and suggests practical solutions. This type of “AI-driven” feedback motivates learners to develop their own strategies for independent self-learning. (ZAI–Zayed Artificial Intelligence Center, n.d.)

Although SARD represents an advanced model of AI-supported diagnostic assessment, its current application remains primarily focused on literacy and reading comprehension contexts. The effectiveness of the tool depends on the availability of trained specialists, appropriate technological infrastructure, and the alignment of its diagnostic results with classroom instruction. In addition, large-scale independent studies examining its long-term impact on reading development in diverse Arabic-speaking contexts remain limited, indicating the need for cautious interpretation when considering broader generalizations.

The importance of “SARD” is also evident in its ability to transform assessment into a motivating learning process, as each task is designed as a short linguistic challenge. This integration makes the measurement process both enjoyable and productive, redefining the relationship between motivation and assessment in Arabic education. The project is also a remarkable example of the integration of scientific research and field application, as it is based on the results of psychometric and psycholinguistic studies. The results of this tool not only serve practitioners, but its data can also be used to guide national education policies in the field of literacy and curriculum development, as it is an intelligent diagnostic system that goes beyond the classroom to become a tool for data-driven educational decision-making.

SARD provides an example of AI-driven assessment, which relies on emotional interaction and a sense of personal achievement. When learners receive a report detailing their progress in each skill and track their improvement over time, they feel that their efforts are valuable and become more motivated to continue. This is consistent with the view that a sense of competence, autonomy, and belonging are the keys to sustained motivation. (ZAI–Zayed Artificial Intelligence Center, n.d.)

“SARD” experience demonstrates how artificial intelligence can redefine the assessment process, transforming it into a motivating and personalized learning experience that combines linguistics, technology, and emotional motivation to build an authentic Arabic system for smart education. The project represents a pioneering step toward transforming assessment into a catalyst for learning and transforming artificial intelligence from a technical tool into an educational partner that enhances motivation and makes the Arabic language alive and renewed in the digital space. (Arabisard, n.d.)

Zay Center experience and the "SARD" scale represent an advanced Arab model in redefining language assessment as a motivational learning process based on artificial intelligence. It focuses not only on measuring performance, but also on analyzing linguistic knowledge and emotion in a single linguistic context, making it part of a new generation of smart learning tools that combine technology with human motivation. Although SARD primarily focuses on diagnosing reading and comprehension skills, it paves the way for a broader shift toward customized and adaptive Arabic learning systems that respond to learners' needs in real time.

5.2 Al-Dhad Scale (Miqyas AlDhad): Smart Analytics for Arabic Language Learning

Miqyas Al Dhad project represents a strategic shift in contemporary Arab education, as it seeks to integrate artificial intelligence with educational linguistic measurement to establish an integrated Arabic reading system that links the difficulty of texts to the level of readers' abilities from first to twelfth grade and beyond. (Zawya, 2025).

The philosophy behind the Al-Dhad Scale is based on the principle of data-driven smart assessment, whereby test results are converted into educational feedback that is used to personalize reading content for each learner. Al-Dhad Scale relies on Arabic text analysis deep learning algorithms that determine textual complexity from multiple infinite variables and match them to the reader's level as measured by standardized digital rapid assessments. Based on this match, the system suggests stimulating texts and readings that vary in difficulty according to the individual student's performance (Alef Education, 2024). This combination of computational linguistic analysis and educational motivation makes the scale an interactive learning tool rather than a rigid assessment method, as the system responds dynamically to the learner's behavior and adjusts the reading path according to actual performance data.

Al-Dhad scale also embodies a model of assessment and motivation integration in a single learning environment. The reports issued by the system are not mere Dhad scores, but they allow the monitoring of students progress and provide an explanatory description of what a Dhad score means, with appropriate reading suggestions that reinforce a sense of competence and progress. This approach translates the principles of self-motivation theory into a digital context, where autonomy, feedback, and a sense of accomplishment become key elements in motivating learners to continue reading and expanding their vocabulary. Press reports have indicated that the project is being implemented as part of "the largest field linguistic survey in the Arab world" and is expected to contribute to the reformulation of educational policies related to literacy (Zawya, 2025).

Technically, Al-Dhad scale is part of the smart architecture of Miqyas Al Dhad platform, which uses deep learning analytics to interpret linguistic performance patterns. The metric provides rich data that is used to train algorithms to predict reader behavior and suggest motivating content in the future. This transforms artificial intelligence from a descriptive role to a predictive one, enabling the system to continuously adapt to learners' needs (MetaMetrics & Alef Education, 2024). The Al-Dhad Scale can also be considered a fundamental step toward building an Arabic research infrastructure for natural language processing (NLP) and developing educational metrics that take into account the unique features of Arabic.

From a motivational perspective, Al-Dhad scale highlights the importance of transparency and linguistic fairness in increasing learner motivation. When students realize that assessment is based on fair scientific criteria rather than subjective judgments, their confidence in the educational process increases and they become more engaged in improving their performance. Here, artificial intelligence acts as a guarantor of objectivity in assessment, reinforcing "motivation based on linguistic fairness" (Zawya, 2025). The scale also provides a meeting point between scientific research and field application, as the collected data is used to guide decision-makers in designing adaptive reading curricula linked to students' actual levels.

Ultimately, Al-Dhad Scale embodies a new trend in Arabic education towards building linguistic artificial intelligence systems based on both graphical analysis and educational motivation. It does not aim to classify learners, but rather to empower them to control their learning journey based on objective data that translates into real motivation to progress. Al-Dhad Scale is therefore a fundamental building block in the development of an authentic Arab approach to smart education based on motivation and personalization, relying on artificial intelligence as an educational partner rather than merely a technological tool.

Despite the strong analytical basis of the Al-Dhad Scale, its effectiveness remains closely linked to consistent implementation across schools, teacher engagement with the data generated, and the availability of compatible Arabic reading materials, which may limit its impact in resource-poor educational contexts.

5.3 Diglossia: Tala'a and Mubakkir (Arabic Language Assessments)

Diglossia LLC is an organization specializing in the development of Arabic language assessment tools based on adaptive analysis and artificial intelligence. Its research and applied activities are focused on the Arab region, through strategic partnerships with Arab educational institutions. Since its inception, the company has contributed to building a knowledge bridge between educational assessment expertise in the Western world and the requirements of Arabic language education in the Arab cultural context, through the development of standardized tests supported by performance analysis algorithms and adaptive learning (Diglossia, n.d.).

The TALA (Test of Arabic Language Arts) is a digital assessment system for students in grades 3 through 11 that measures reading, comprehension, listening, and vocabulary skills in Modern Standard Arabic. The test was designed according to precise linguistic standards, with the aim of harmonizing international educational quality standards with the linguistic specificity of Arabic.

The Mubakkir test was developed in collaboration with the Arab Thought Foundation as part of the "Arabic21" initiative. It complements the Tala test but is geared toward early reading skills in children in the early years of basic education. It aims to diagnose reading abilities before they turn into learning difficulties, through a series of short activities that take only a few minutes and cover phonological awareness, visual word recognition, and auditory comprehension skills.

The two tests represent a practical application of the concept of assessment as learning, transforming measurement from a final evaluation process into a continuous learning process that provides learners with the information they need to improve their performance. The results are not presented as rigid grades, but are translated into explanatory feedback that shows the learner how to improve their performance and which areas need further development. The platform also allows teachers to track performance through interactive dashboards that enable them to monitor progress at the individual and group levels and make evidence-based educational decisions. This intersects with the principles of data-driven learning.

These two tests reinforce the concept of competence-based motivation, as learners feel a sense of accomplishment when they see their progress in real time through digital reports. The system relies on a delicate balance between challenge and ability; each task follows the next within a level close to the learner's zone of proximal development, creating a sense of positive challenge and keeping the learner in a state of "learning flow" that motivates them to continue progressing. Adaptive content personalization also promotes autonomy, as each learner has a unique experience within a path tailored to their individual needs, which is consistent with the principles of Self-Determination Theory in the context of language learning.

The two tests were designed to cover the broad spectrum of Arabic speakers in different countries, promoting the values of linguistic equity and educational equality in education. They also contributed to providing Arabic benchmark data that helps decision-makers understand the reality of Arabic language education and develop curricula and policies based on reliable quantitative indicators.

These two tests are among the most prominent serious Arab attempts to combine smart measurement, educational motivation, and linguistic analysis in a single educational environment, contributing to the transition of Arabic language education from traditional paper-based assessment to data-driven, motivational digital learning.

Considering the above, the three Arab initiatives, SARD Tool, Al-Dhad Scale (Miqyas al-Dhad), and TAL'A and Mubakkir represent a qualitative shift in the use of artificial intelligence in Arabic language education. The three initiatives essentially intersect in building customized smart systems that place the learner at the center of the educational process and leverage artificial intelligence to enhance efficiency and independence. Thus, it can be said that they are the nucleus for establishing an Arabic approach to smart education based on human motivation and interaction, paving the way for the transition from the technical use of artificial intelligence to its employment as an educational tool with an authentic cultural and human dimension.

While TAL'A and Mubakkir offer powerful adaptive assessment models grounded in psychological and linguistic theory, their effectiveness ultimately depends on contextual alignment with classroom practices, the teacher's ability to interpret adaptive observations, and ongoing institutional support to ensure meaningful integration beyond the assessment itself.

6. ETHICAL AND FUTURE CONSIDERATIONS IN AI-ENHANCED LANGUAGE EDUCATION

After reviewing Arab smart initiatives in Arabic language education and analyzing their motivational models, the need to reflect on the ethical, cultural, and future dimensions of smart education emerges. Here, ethical and future considerations emerge as an extension of the previous analysis of AI-enhanced motivations, collaborative learning, and practical Arab initiatives. In addition, it is an important framework for maintaining the smart and practical nature of Arabic language education. The expansion of artificial intelligence applications is not limited to improving performance or personalizing learning, but raises profound questions about fairness, transparency, privacy protection, and the role of humans in an algorithm-driven educational environment. Recent studies indicate that the success of smart education is not achieved by technology alone, but by adopting a humanistic educational approach that considers ethical and cultural values in the design of artificial intelligence systems (Belaid & Mâ ă, 2024; Al-Zahrani & Alasmari, 2024).

6.1 Ethical Dimensions of Smart Education

Recent educational literature has addressed several ethical challenges associated with the integration of artificial intelligence in education. Al-Zahrani & Alasmari (2024) pointed out that ethical risks can be divided into three levels: technical (algorithmic bias and lack of transparency in decision-making), educational (weak educational accountability in automated systems), and social (potential violation of privacy and undermining of trust in educational institutions). Smart education requires "algorithmic governance" that ensures accountability in system design, so that artificial intelligence is understood as a tool that supports human learning rather than replacing it. (Belaid & Mâ ă, 2024)

Algorithmic fairness is emerging as one of the most important contemporary challenges, since reliance on data that does not represent all groups can reinforce patterns of cultural or linguistic bias, which is something Henriksen et al. (2025) in their study on emotional and social learning in the context of generative intelligence have warned about. Zhang et al. (2024) also emphasized that "smart classroom" applications that rely on behavioral sensors may violate privacy if they are not built on the principles of transparency and informed consent. The study by Mohammadinejad & Mohammadhoseini (2020) highlighted the need to adopt clear policies for managing sensitive learner's data, whether it is linguistic texts or biometric indicators, emphasizing that "digital trust" has become an educational component rather than just a technical one.

Considering these challenges, the framework of "Responsible AI in Education" was proposed, based on three pillars: (1) Explainability to ensure transparency in the functioning of educational systems; (2) Accountability to define the ethical responsibility of programmers, teachers, and institutions; and (3) Human Oversight to maintain human sovereignty over educational decisions in smart classrooms. These principles are a fundamental step toward establishing ethical practices in smart Arab education. (Zhu, et al., 2025)

6.2 Cultural and Linguistic Sensitivity in Smart Education

In addition to technical fairness, the issue of cultural and linguistic sensitivity is prominent in the design of smart education systems, especially in the context of Arabic language with its diversity of dialects. Adapting literary texts using artificial intelligence requires "educational and cultural verification" to ensure that generated content does not conflict with the linguistic values or cultural contexts of learners. (Chatzichristofis et al., 2025)

Generative AI models designed for language teaching often show a structural bias toward Western patterns of discourse and cultural representation, making it necessary to train models on local Arabic data that takes into account semantic specificities (Zhang & Dong, 2024). Furthermore, linguistic and cultural diversity in training data is the decisive factor in achieving linguistic equity in smart education (Stade, et al., 2024).

From this perspective, building customized Arabic education systems takes on double importance, not only for developing technical performance, but also for preserving cultural and linguistic identity. Artificial intelligence in language education cannot be neutral; as its algorithms reflect implicit cultural perceptions of language and knowledge.

6.3 The Role of Humans in Smart Education

Despite the rapid advancement of artificial intelligence, literature confirms that teachers remain the central element in the smart ecosystem. The role of the teacher is evolving from "knowledge transmitter" to "learning experience designer," guiding artificial intelligence to deliver personalized learning without losing human interaction (Mzwri & Turcsányi-Szabo, 2025). The absence of full human supervision in automated systems may reduce learner motivation and limit the educational empathy necessary to build an effective learning relationship (Zhu et al., 2025).

Teachers express their concern that excessive automation will lead to the "dehumanization of education," calling for the promotion of the concept of "human-centered AI." Optimal integration is achieved when the smart system supports rather than replaces the teacher's decisions, and when learning data is used as a mean to understand learners rather than to monitor them. (Perez-Jorge, et al., 2025).

This approach is reinforced by the emphasis that the ethical framework for AI-supported education must be designed to preserve the emotional connection between teacher and learner as the core of motivation and collaboration in education. The teacher thus becomes a knowledge partner to the machine, employing its analytical capabilities to build an interactive learning environment based on mutual trust and respect. (Chatzichristofis et al., 2025)

6.4 Future Trends in Smart Education

Research findings indicate that education in the coming decade will shift toward generative personalized learning. Zhang & Dong (2024) explained that generative intelligence systems are now capable of creating language learning tasks that adapt in real time to learners' linguistic and emotional patterns. A study by Mzwri & Turcsányi-Szabo (2025) also showed that the use of prompt engineering enables designing of self-directed learning experiences based on deep interaction and internal motivation, to promotes independence and innovation.

To achieve future trends related to the context of Arabic language education, it is necessary to build incentive systems based primarily on authentic Arabic data and compatible with linguistic, cultural, and educational characteristics, rather than synthesizing models from other languages and translating them into Arabic.

In this context, gamified motivation emerges as one of the most important future trends. Gamified assessment systems will shape the future of educational evaluation, using game elements (levels, points, badges) to motivate learners to participate, while integrating smart analytics to personalize learning paths. (Alameddine, et al., 2025).

At the educational management level, AI optimization algorithms will contribute to supporting higher education decisions through predictive analysis of success and dropout rates, and directing educational resources according to individual needs. Considering these developments, future education must be based on the integration of generative intelligence and emotional intelligence, so that personalization is not limited to content, but extends to "personalizing the emotional experience" that takes into account the feelings and motivations of learners. (Xu, 2023)

6.5 Conclusion: Towards Humanistic Educational Intelligence

The expansion of smart Arabic education requires redefining the relationship between technology and humans. AI-based education should not be reduced to data analysis algorithms or content production but should be built on an ethical and cultural vision that makes AI a human partner that contributes to the development of motivation, the promotion of justice, and respect for linguistic and cultural diversity. Evidence from recent studies (Zhu et al., 2025; Chatzichristofis et al., 2025; Belaid & Mâ ă, 2024) that the future of successful smart education lies in balancing technical effectiveness with educational responsibility, and algorithmic personalization with human motivation.

Accordingly, this chapter argues that the ethical future of intelligent Arabic language education depends on integrating data governance, cultural sensitivity, and learner-centered design into AI-powered systems that support motivation, collaboration, and linguistic identity rather than pure technical proficiency.

REFERENCES

Abbas, S., Al-Barhamtoshy, H., & Alotaibi, F. (2021). Towards an Arabic Sign Language (ArSL) corpus for deaf drivers. *PeerJ. Computer Science*, *7*, e741. DOI: 10.7717/peerj-cs.741

Al-Ghadhban, D., & Al-Twairesh, N. (2020). Nabiha: An Arabic dialect chatbot. *International Journal of Advanced Computer Science and Applications*, *11*(3). Advance online publication. DOI: 10.14569/IJACSA.2020.0110357

Al-Khalifa, S., Alhumaidhi, F., Alotaibi, H., & Al-Khalifa, H. S. (2023). ChatGPT across Arabic Twitter: A study of topics, sentiments, and sarcasm. *Data 8(11),* 171, 1-19.

Al-Zahrani, A. M., & Alasmari, T. M. (2024). Exploring the impact of artificial intelligence on higher education: The dynamics of ethical, social, and educational implications. *Humanities & Social Sciences Communications*, *11*(1), 912. DOI: 10.1057/s41599-024-03432-4

Alabbas, A., & Alomar, K. (2024). Tayseer: A novel AI-powered Arabic chatbot framework for technical and vocational student helpdesk services and enhancing student interactions. *Applied Sciences (Basel, Switzerland)*, *14*(5), 2547. DOI: 10.3390/app14062547

Alameddine, M., Sabra, N., El Amaout, N., El Dakkoudi, A., El Jaouni, M. B., Hamadeh, R., Shanaa, A., & Saleh, S. (2025). Utilizing gamification, artificial intelligence, and mHealth for the professional development of maternal care providers: Exploratory pilot cross-sectional study assessing providers' satisfaction in primary health care centers in Lebanon. *JMIR Serious Games*, *13*, e53735. DOI: 10.2196/53735 PMID: 40929508

Alamgir, A., Roy, P., & Taverna, F. (2024). Levels of engagement of South Asian participants in health research: Effectiveness of community-based research (CBR) framework. *Journal of Scientific Research and Reports*, *30*(9), 880–897. DOI: 10.9734/jsrr/2024/v30i92415

Alhassan, N. A., Albarrak, A. S., Bhatia, S., & Agarwal, P. (2022). A novel framework for Arabic dialect chatbot using machine learning. *Computational Intelligence and Neuroscience*, *1844051*, 1–11. DOI: 10.1155/2022/1844051 PMID: 35310584

Almelhes, S. A. (2024). Gamification for teaching the Arabic language to non-native speakers: A systematic literature review. *Frontiers in Education*, *9*, 1371955. DOI: 10.3389/feduc.2024.1371955

Alsheddi, A. S., & Alhenaki, L. S. (2022). English and Arabic chatbots: A systematic literature review. *International Journal of Advanced Computer Science and Applications, 13*(8), 662–675. DOI: 10.14569/IJACSA.2022.0130876

Arabisard. (n.d.). Title of page. https://www.arabisard.com/site

Becheru, A., Calota, A., & Popescu, E. (2018). Analyzing students' collaboration patterns in a social learning environment using StudentViz platform. *Smart Learn. Environ., 5*(18), 1–18. DOI: 10.1186/s40561-018-0063-0

Belaid, L., & Ma a, L. (2024). Revolutionizing AI in education: A review of ethical challenges and frontiers. *Journal of Innovation in Psychology. Education and Didactics, 28*(2), 165–174.

Casebourne, I., Shi, S., Hogan, M., Holmes, W., Hoel, T., Wegerif, R., & Yuan, L. (2025). Using AI to Support Education for Collective Intelligence. *International Journal of Artificial Intelligence in Education, 35*(11), 1597–1629. DOI: 10.1007/s40593-024-00437-7

Chatzichristofis, S. A., Tsopozidis, A., Kyriakidou-Zacharoudiou, A., Evripidou, S., & Amanatiadis, A. (2025). Designing an AI-supported framework for literary text adaptation in primary classrooms. *AI, 6*(7), 150. DOI: 10.3390/ai6070150

Diglossia. (n.d.). Mubakkir. https://www.diglossia.net/mubakkir/

Dinnar, S. M., Dede, C., Johnson Dorley, E., Straub, C., & Korjus, K. (2021). Artificial intelligence and technology in teaching negotiation. *Negotiation Journal, 37*(2), 65–82. DOI: 10.1111/nejo.12351

Edwards, J., Nguyen, A., Lämsä, J., Sobocinski, M., Whitehead, R., Dang, B., Roberts, A.-S., & Järvelä, S. (2024). Human–AI collaboration: Designing artificial agents to facilitate socially shared regulation among learners. *British Journal of Educational Technology, 56*(2), 712–733. Advance online publication. DOI: 10.1111/bjet.13534

Elsayed, Y., Nabil, E., Torki, M., Faizullah, S., & Khalafallah, A. (2025). ZaQQ: A new Arabic dataset for automatic essay scoring via a novel human–AI collaborative framework. *Data, 10(9),* 148, 1–31.

Fernández-Herrero, J. (2024). Evaluating recent advances in affective intelligent tutoring systems: A scoping review of educational impacts and future prospects. *Education Sciences, 14*(8), 839. DOI: 10.3390/educsci14080839

Gini, F., Bassanelli, S., Bonetti, F., Mogavi, R. H., Bucchiarone, A., & Marconi, A. (2025). The role and scope of gamification in education: A scientometric literature review. *Acta Psychologica*, *259*, 105418. DOI: 10.1016/j.actpsy.2025.105418 PMID: 40850223

Hanandeh, A., Ayasrah, S., Kofahi, I., & Qudah, S. (2024). Artificial Intelligence in Arabic Linguistic Landscape: Opportunities, Challenges, and Future Directions. *TEM Journal*, *13*(4), 3137–3145. DOI: 10.18421/TEM134-48

Henriksen, D., Creely, E., Gruber, N., & Leahy, S. (2025). Social-emotional learning and generative AI: A critical literature review and framework for teacher education. *Journal of Teacher Education*, *76*(3), 312–328. DOI: 10.1177/00224871251325058

Klimova, B., & Pikhart, M. (2025). Exploring the effects of artificial intelligence on student and academic well-being in higher education: A mini-review. *Frontiers in Psychology*, *16*, 1498132. DOI: 10.3389/fpsyg.2025.1498132 PMID: 39963679

Kovari, A. (2025). A systematic review of AI-powered collaborative learning in higher education: Trends and outcomes from the last decade. *Social Sciences & Humanities Open*, *11*, 101335. DOI: 10.1016/j.ssaho.2025.101335

Létourneau, A., Deslandes Martineau, M., Charland, P., Karran, J. A., Boasen, J., & Léger, P. M. (2025*). A systematic review of AI-driven intelligent tutoring systems (ITS) in K-12 education. npj Science of Learning, 10*, 29, 1-13.

Marín, Y., Caro, O., Rituay, A., Llanos, K., Perez, D., Bardales, E., Tuesta, J., & Santos, R. (2025). Ethical Challenges Associated with the Use of Artificial Intelligence in University Education. *Journal of Academic Ethics*, *23*(4), 2443–2467. DOI: 10.1007/s10805-025-09660-w

Meddeb, O., Maraoui, M., & Zrigui, M. (2021). Personalized smart learning recommendation system for Arabic users in smart campus. *International Journal of Web-Based Learning and Teaching Technologies*, *16*(6), 1–21. DOI: 10.4018/IJWLTT.20211101.oa9

Merino-Campos, C. (2025). The Impact of Artificial Intelligence on Personalized Learning in Higher Education: A Systematic Review. *Trends in Higher Education*, *4*(2), 17. DOI: 10.3390/higheredu4020017

Mohammadinejad, H., & Mohammadhoseini, F. (2020). Privacy protection in smart cities by a personal data management protocol in blockchain. *I.J. Computer Network and Information Security*, *2020*(3), 44–52. DOI: 10.5815/ijcnis.2020.03.05

Mzwri, K., & Turcsányi-Szabó, M. (2025). The impact of prompt engineering and a generative AI-driven tool on autonomous learning: A case study. *Education Sciences, 15*(2), 199. DOI: 10.3390/educsci15020199

Outay, F., Jabeur, N., Bellalouna, F., & Al Hamzi, T. (2024). Multi-agent system-based framework for an intelligent management of competency building. *Smart Learn Environments, 11*(41), 1–18. DOI: 10.1186/s40561-024-00328-3

Pérez-Jorge, D., González-Afonso, M. C., Santos-Álvarez, A. G., Plasencia-Carballo, Z., & Perdomo-López, C. A. (2025). The impact of AI-driven application programming interfaces (APIs) on educational information management. *Information, 16*(6), 540, 1-31.

Qedear, A., Almatrafy, A., Al-Sowat, A., Saigh, A., & Alayed, A. (2024). Real-time air-writing recognition for Arabic letters using deep learning. *Sensors, 24(18),* 6098, 1-25.

Riar, M., Morschheuser, B., Zarnekow, R., & Hamari, J. (2022). Gamification of cooperation: A framework, literature review and future research agenda. *International Journal of Information Management, 67*, 102549. DOI: 10.1016/j.ijinfomgt.2022.102549

Salloum, S. A., Alomari, K. M., Alfaisal, A. M., Aljanada, R. A., & Basiouni, A. (2025). Emotion recognition for enhanced learning: Using AI to detect students' emotions and adjust teaching methods. *Smart Learning Environments, 12*(21), 1–17. DOI: 10.1186/s40561-025-00374-5

Samin, S. M., & Osman, R. A. (2024). Integrating artificial intelligence into the Arabic language teaching plan at higher education. *SHS Web of Conferences, 202*, 06010, 1-9.

Stade, E. C., Stirman, S. W., Ungar, L. H., Boland, C. L., Schwartz, H. A., Yaden, D. B., Sedoc, J., DeRubeis, R. J., Willer, R., & Eichstaedt, J. C. (2024). Large language models could change the future of behavioral healthcare: A proposal for responsible development and evaluation. *npj Mental Health Research, 3(1)*, 12, 1-12.

Subhash, S., & Cudney, E. A. (2018). Gamified learning in higher education: A systematic review of the literature. *Computers in Human Behavior, 87*, 192–206. DOI: 10.1016/j.chb.2018.05.028

Susnjak, T. (2023). Beyond predictive learning analytics modelling and onto explainable artificial intelligence with prescriptive analytics and ChatGPT. *International Journal of Artificial Intelligence in Education, 34*(2), 452–482. DOI: 10.1007/s40593-023-00336-3

Tabuenca, B., Uche-Soria, M., Greller, W., Hernández-Leo, D., Balcells-Falgueras, P., Gloor, P., & Garbajosa, J. (2024). Greening smart learning environments with Artificial Intelligence of Things. *Internet of Things : Engineering Cyber Physical Human Systems*, *25*, 101051. DOI: 10.1016/j.iot.2023.101051

Tan, S. C., Lee, A. V. Y., & Lee, M. (2022). A systematic review of artificial intelligence techniques for collaborative learning over the past two decades. *Computers and Education: Artificial Intelligence*, *3*, 100097. DOI: 10.1016/j.caeai.2022.100097

Torres-Toukoumidis, A., Merchan-Romero, J., Fernández, M. M., & Vega Ramírez, J. F. A. (2024). Gamification and artificial intelligence in the educational context: Analysis of scientific literature. *Lecture Notes in Computer Science*, **•••**, 349–354.

Xiao, F., Zhu, S., & Wen, X. (2025). Exploring the landscape of generative AI (ChatGPT)-powered writing instruction in English as a foreign language education: A scoping review. *ECNU Review of Education*, 1-19.

Xu, X. (2023). AI optimization algorithms enhance higher education management and personalized teaching through empirical analysis. *Scientific Reports, 15(1)*, 51057, 1-19.

Yin, Z., Chinta, S. V., Wang, Z., Gonzalez, M., & Zhang, W. (2025). FairAIED: Navigating fairness, bias, and ethics in educational AI applications. arXiv, 1, 1-59.

ZAI–Zayed Artificial Intelligence Center. (n.d.). *ZAI Home*. https://www.zu.ac.ae/main/en/zai/index

Zawya. (2025, March 10). Miqyas Al Dhad highlights role of Arabic reading scale in advancing literacy. https://www.zawya.com/en/press-release/companies-news/miqyas-al-dhad-highlights-role-of-arabic-reading-scale-in-advancing-literacy-nom82uft

Zhai, X., Chu, X., Chai, C. S., Jong, M. S. Y., Istenic, A., Spector, M., Liu, J.-B., Yuan, J., & Li, Y. (2021). A review of artificial intelligence (AI) in education from 2010 to 2020. *Education Research International*, *2021*, 8812542.

Zhai, Y., Nezakatgoo, B. (2025). Evaluating AI-Powered Applications for Enhancing Undergraduate Students' Metacognitive Strategies, Self-Determined Motivation, and Social Learning in English Language Education. *Sci Rep 15*, 35199 1-10.

Zhang, X., Ding, Y., Huang, X., Li, W., Long, L., & Ding, S. (2024). Smart classrooms: How sensors and AI are shaping educational paradigms. *Sensors (Basel)*, *24*(15), 5487. DOI: 10.3390/s24175487 PMID: 39275398

Zhang, Y., & Dong, C. (2024). Unveiling the dynamic mechanisms of generative AI in English language learning: A hybrid study based on fsQCA and system dynamics. *Behavioral Sciences (Basel, Switzerland)*, *14*(10), 1015. DOI: 10.3390/bs14111015 PMID: 39594315

Zhu, H., Sun, Y., & Yang, J. (2025). Towards responsible artificial intelligence in education: A systematic review on identifying and mitigating ethical risks. *Humanities & Social Sciences Communications*, *12*(1), 111. DOI: 10.1057/s41599-025-05252-6

Zhu, M., & Wang, C. (2014). A Systematic Review of Artificial Intelligence in Language Education from 2013 to 2023: Current Status and Future Implications. Available at *SSRN*: https://ssrn.com/abstract=4684304

Chapter 4

A Review of the Uses of Artificial Intelligence in English Language Teaching: Benefits and Challenges

Hanan Mohammad Mustafa
http://orcid.org/0009-0004-9123-6592
British University in Dubai, UAE

ABSTRACT

This paper presents a comprehensive review of the recent published literature on the uses of Artificial Intelligence in English Language Teaching, its benefits and challenges. The qualitative, narrative literature review design was employed to identify and analyze the articles published in the last five years on this topic. The researcher used most popular academic databases, namely Google Scholar, and screened the vast published literature between 2020 and 2025. Most studies that were searched presented systematic literature reviews; the researcher identified around 25 relevant papers on AI in ELT. The investigation of the literature has answered the three research questions on the topic of AI in ELT. Recent papers highlighted the benefits and useful application of AI tools in language education. While some papers revealed challenges and limitation of implementing AI in teaching and learning English Language. The researcher concludes the review by providing recommendations for future research.

DOI: 10.4018/979-8-2600-0328-2.ch004

1. INTRODUCTION

In recent years, AI has greatly impacted on all walks of life, from the applications that individuals have on their smart devices, tablets and computers to various sectors such as healthcare, transportation, finance and education. Artificial intelligence (AI) can be described as the process by which computers imitate human intelligence (Devasena, 2024). The effects of AI on the field of education have been gaining momentum, and AI has successfully introduced new paradigms in teaching and learning that are more efficient and personalized. Hence, educational reforms are being witnessed all around the globe and many educational institutions and policy makers are updating their policies to integrate AI in the educational practices. The main aim behind this is to facilitate teaching and learning and make it more effective.

As English language subject continues to be taught as a global lingua franca, teachers are increasingly exploring new innovative ways and tools to deliver their curriculums and enhance the learning outcomes. Taking into consideration that educators have to adapt with the change of the learners' learning styles and nowadays we have a generation that is digital native, teaching strategies and tools have to be innovative if we really want an effective learning. With the use of new technologies and digital platforms, teaching and learning English has become easier (Fitria, 2021). Traditional methods of teaching will definitely face challenges with regard to limited personalization and insufficient learner autonomy. Using AI technologies can enhance language skills. Most of the literature reviewed highlighted its positive impact on teaching skills and improving the learner's autonomy. Yang (2020) reiterated that AI not only provides automatic correction of composition, but also help educators select appropriate listening material that suit the learners' needs and abilities. In addition, the development of chatbot systems has enhanced opportunities to oral and written conversations and allowed more independent learning (Haristiani, 2019).

Hence, educators need to tailor instruction effectively and be smart to include AI technologies such as chatbots, intelligent tutoring programs that are introduced in ELT. There is a pressing need to examine how AI is currently being applied in ELT and find out what benefits and challenges it presents. This review of the vast literature on the use of AI in ELT will be limited to most recent articles published between 2020 and 2025. The main aim is to present the main applications of AI which can be a reference for educators and researchers in this field, and to identify the key strategies used, and evaluate their impact on the learning process and highlight the challenges encountered with their use. Thus, the significance of this study stems from its aim to obtain a clear picture of the dynamic research of AI in ELT.

The main research questions:

1- What are the current applications of AI in English Language teaching?

2- What are the benefits and limitations of using AI in ELT?

2. INTRODUCTION

This paper employs a qualitative research design through a literature review. This approach is well-suited for the aim of synthesizing current research, identify research gaps and mapping existing trends across the rapidly evolving field of AI in English Language Teaching. Literature reviews provide an overview of the existing knowledge that help in future research and policy makers (Zawacki-Richter et al., 2020). To ensure the reliability of the findings, the methodology prioritizes transparency and replicability.

For the main aim of collecting relevant literature, extensive research was carried out using academic databases including Google Scholar. The search included peer-reviewed journal article, research articles that were published between 2020 and 2025. This review followed mainly five phases: (1) planning and conducting the research using the keywords; (2) initial screening was done to remove irrelevant articles and the ones which were not in English and then identify the inclusion and exclusion criteria; (3) examine the articles based on the inclusion and exclusion criteria; (4) extract data and finally (5) the synthesis of the data collected.

During the first phase, the following keywords were used to refine the research:

- "Artificial Intelligence" AND "English Language Teaching"
- "AI in ELT" OR "AI for language learning"

These terms were used by the researcher in academic bases and the result was surprisingly over 20,000 articles and then the search was refined using the inclusion and exclusion conditions.

To ensure relevance and quality, some inclusion criteria were applied:

- Publications in English language.
- Empirical studies on AI applications in English Language Teaching.
- Sources published within the last five years (2020-2025).
- Studies that discuss AI tools or methodologies used in ELT settings.

Exclusion criteria included:

- Studies that focused on general educational technology, not mentioning AI.
- Papers that did not relate to English language education.
- Opinions or non-peer-reviewed papers.

After the initial screening, the researcher focused on the applications of AI in ELT and removed the duplicates and non-journal articles and any articles outside the scope and the researcher filtered around 30 articles articles with the main goal to look at useful applications of AI that will benefit English language educators.

A thematic analysis method was employed to synthesize the findings across the selected studies. Key themes were identified by coding literature of repeated patterns such as AI applications, language skill, and learner outcomes. These themes were grouped into broader categories to guide the analysis and the discussion. The findings were compared to identify knowledge gaps, consensus and contradictions in the existing literature.

3. LITERATURE REVIEW

3.1 Historical Development of AI in ELT

The historical advances of artificial intelligence in language teaching have evolved through several phases that reflected boarder advances in technology.

The emergence of computer-assisted instruction systems in the 1960s marked the early foundation of AI in English Language teaching. These systems which are known as Computer-Assisted Language Learning (CALL) allowed learners to be engaged with basic language and grammar exercises. While these systems offered limited feedback, they laid the basic groundwork for AI application and introduced individualized learning technologies (Deutschmann & Vu, 2015).

By the late 20th century, the further developments of AI had enabled the advances of Intelligent Tutoring Systems (ITS) that provided one-to-one instruction and adapted feedback and content to learners. Hence, they were more personalized. They applied data analytics and predictive models to monitor student progress and assist in developing lessons based on needs of learners (Kannan & Munday, 2018).

During 1960s and 1970s, Natural Language Processing (NLP) systems were developed and offered early chatbots like ELIZA. Kannan and Munday (2018) mentioned that these systems marked significant advances that enabled a natural interaction between machines and learners and added more conversation practice and instant feedback. NLP advanced enabled more language learning in grammar and interactive dialogue.

The 21st century has marked rapid progress and introduced new technologies and still continue evolving AI. The major improvement was the introduction of generative AI that provides more advanced chatbots and virtual tutors, realistic dialogues, immediate feedback and assessing writing and speaking skills, and many more. Generative AI still develops to introduce more advances that became essential for making language learning and teaching more effective and interactive and will continue to shape the future of ELT and education in general (Nah et al., 2023).

3.2 Key AI technologies used in ELT

It is evident the extent to which AI has significantly changed the way that English language is taught and learned through the technologies it provided. Fitria (2021) points out that one of the main advances is Natural Language Processing (NLP) that allows computers to analyze, comprehend and produce human language. It is applied in grammar and spell checkers and writing feedback tools. In addition, it powers conversational chatbots that allow learners to practice vocabulary, fluency and sentence structure.

Another vital technology is Speech Recognition that converts a spoken text into a written text. This can be useful to practice speaking and pronunciation since it enables students to talk into a device and then get instant feedback on the clarity and accuracy of their speech. Text-to-Speech (TTS) technologies enhances the students' pronunciation and listening skills and allows changing a written text into spoken audio (Shadiev & Liu, 2022).

Klimova et al. (2022) state that Machine Learning (ML) marks the foundation of personalized learning. These evaluate the learner's performance and modify instruction and content based on the learner needs. Hence students remain motivated and engaged in their learning. Another vital technology is Intelligent Tutoring Systems (ITS). These AI-driven tools guide students through lessons according to their individual learning styles and offer personalized feedback and support and help in scaffolding context and provide answer to questions.

Moreover, according to Huang et al. (2021) the AI-powered systems of chatbots are gaining popularity in ELT as they give the learners the chance to practice using language realistically without the stress of speaking to another human. These systems are able to correct grammar, recommend vocabulary and offer an enjoyable self-paced learning experience.

Currently, we are witnessing the development of ChatGPT and other Generative AI language models that have revolutionized English Language learning and teaching by offering dynamic instant feedback, creating writing tasks, stimulating real-life situations, preparing lesson plans and many more. Last but not least is the Sentiment Analysis tools which help in identifying the learner's emotional states in speech or text and these assist educators in maintaining a positive learning environment which is crucial in language learning.

Overall, these AI tools are transforming ELT and making it more effective, individualized and engaging.

3.3 Theoretical Frameworks on AI in ELT

One of the prominent theories for understanding learning is the digital age is the *Sociocultural Theory* that was advocated by the psychologist Lev Vygotsky. Learning according to this theory is first social and then individual. Learners build knowledge through interactions with others. This theory emphasizes how we contribute to each other's knowledge. With regard to second language learning, the theory highlights scaffolding and the Zone of Proximal Development. Language is much related to social, cultural and psychological aspects of humans. When learners interact with other participants through interactive activities, they can develop the second language (Zhou, 2020).

The study also investigates the theoretical concept of integrating technology which is the *Technological Pedagogical Content Knowledge (TPACK)* framework. This framework focuses on technological knowledge, pedagogical knowledge and content knowledge. These construct effective technology integration in education. Specific technological, when applied, can guide students toward a more effective understanding and learning. Hence educators can use technology to enhance teaching and learning (Koehler et al., 2009). In the field of English Language instruction, teachers' knowledge of teaching practices can be improved by integrating technology in their lesson plans and resources. "Teachers' technology integration tactics must be constantly adjusted to changing situations and contexts; hence these procedures are dynamic," according to Rahimi and Rezvani (2024, p. 78). Hence, AI tools can support teachers in creating AI-powered lessons that are meaningful, creative and more personalized.

3.4 Review of Literature

Based on the review and after investigating the literature, there appear to be vast applications of AI in ELT mainly in enhancing the skills of listening, speaking, reading and writing. That is in addition to developing translation skills and providing instant feedback. This paper will discuss some of these aspects.

The application of AI in English Listening and Speaking Teaching

According to Yang (2020), listening training is significant to learning a language and build basic English literacy. Many students struggle this skill due to its difficulty and the lack of appropriate teaching methods. Currently with the applications of AI that provide learners with listening materials that can help students match their learning needs and thus improve the learners' interest. These apps like Corpus can offer material that is suitable for students according to their age and English level.

Students can select the material based on their interests and plans for their future career plans. Artificial intelligence is able to make connections between life and listening practice.

In addition, the development of chatbot systems which are able to respond to human voice using speech recognition technology has provided tremendous opportunities for learning English speaking and listening as well. Chatbots allow learners to engage in oral and written intelligent conversations in any topic such as Lingo. Chatbots can be used as a tutor and as a personalized learning tool that enable learners to engage in both listening, speaking and reading activities. Chatbots have greatly improved the learning autonomy and reduce the anxiety of learning English in addition to availability of these tools any time and any place (Sharadgah & Sa'di, 2022).

The application of AI in English Writing Teaching

It is apparent how much AI has transformed the teaching and learning of the writing skill. Nowadays the vast developments in AI-powered applications such as ChatGPT and Gamma have provided chances for students to enhance their writing skill on any topic and are able to create PowerPoints in few seconds.

AI does assist students by brainstorming ideas and providing vocabulary that can help in their compositions. Not only that, but AI is also able to provide timely and effective feedback on students' writings and providing corrections of grammar and spelling and offer modifications. It is evident that the use of AI in writing has led students to have fun in writing and build self-confidence in their writing ability. Teachers also use AI writing applications to implement curriculum improvement by creating lesson plans and preparing assessments.

Albariqi (2024) highlights that the use of ChatGPT and other tools is useful for students who struggle with writing because they help foster creativity and building the foundation of the writing process by helping students in brainstorming and generating ideas. When students receive evaluation and actionable feedback, this will help students improve their writing. The feedback can assist students to discover their mistakes and use suggestions to rewrite and revise their writing.

In a case study conducted by Alam et al. (2023), that aims to improve ESL writing using Grammarly application. The researchers conducted experimental research that revealed an improvement in the learners' writing and proved the efficiency of an app like Grammarly to help ESL novel learners who are finding writing skills challenging.

Khalifa and Albadawy (2024) reported through the literature review they conducted that AI helps academic writing and research and facilitated the generation of ideas and creating designs and structures of research. AI tools ChatGPT can support editing and reviewing papers.

The application of AI in English Reading Teaching

Jendia and Ismail (2023) conducted a review to understand the developing personalized reading materials using ChatGPT. The findings indicated the importance of AI technologies and their role in enhancing teaching and learning English language. ChatGPT has the ability to create reading resources that align with the learners' interests and needs. Teachers can use ChatGPT to generate resources like dialogues and texts that are culturally relevant. By tailoring reading materials, this can enhance the reading motivation for students.

According to Hakim et al. (2024), the literature review that was conducted highlighted the significance of using technology-based apps to enhance the reading skill. The use of AI apps will help in generating interactive reading quizzes, visuals and animations and tailoring reading practice according to the level of students.

Hence, AI can help in offering personalized learning. Using adaptive reading platforms such as Epic has the ability to adapt the content of the reading task according to the learner's level. Moreover, the vast reading quizzes that can be auto-graded and easily accessed can help students in building their reading skill. Some apps like Grammarly can help students to create summaries or paraphrases to assist struggling readers.

Pedagogical Applications

AI has offered numerous pedagogical applications in English Language teaching that aim to support not only teachers but also learners and provide a more effective, engaging and personalized learning.

One major application is personalized and adaptive learning. After analyzing the learner performance, these AI systems tailor lessons' content to meet the learners' needs to ensure improvement in engagement and learning outcomes. Another application is the Interactive Language practice through chatbots that allow learners to drill speaking and pronunciation in real life situations and offering immediate feedback and reduce pressure. It allows for learners the chance to practice language outside the classroom (Ryoo & Winkelmann, 2021).

In a study conducted, it was proven that AI enhances assessments and offer personalized feedback and adaptive testing that caters to the learners' progress. Thus, AI makes language learning accessible and practical (AlAfnan, 2024).

In addition to that, Shi et al. (2024) confirm that automated assessment and feedback tools provide automatic feedback on writing, reading and speaking skills.

Also, these applications provide writing and reading guidance through grammar checking, editing and generating content. This supports the writing of students and help in correcting errors and recommend modifications of their writing. Besides, AI can offer appropriate reading texts and support comprehension by questioning.

Moreover, Shi et al. (2024) point that gamification and engagement are considered vital applications of AI in ELT. Many language apps include elements such as leaderboards and challenges which in turn enhances motivation and engagement in classrooms. The findings revealed that teachers rely on AI tools improve their teaching strategies and thus reiterated the benefits of AI in ESL teaching. The study concluded by suggesting to incorporate AI tools into the ELT process.

Hazaymeh et al. (2024) explored the perspectives of English as a foreign Language teachers' perspective who are working at universities across the UAE on the effectiveness of AI tools in their classrooms. Teachers managed to integrate AI applications according to their instructional goals and to support students learning. The quantitative study used a survey that investigated the teachers' opinions

To sum up, AI has successfully managed to expand learning beyond the classroom and offered the opportunity for learning English anywhere and anytime.

Impact on Learner Outcomes

Overall, most of the studies has reiterated a positive impact of AI on learners in ELT. AI offers personalized learning, increased motivation, improved self-learning and provided immediate feedback.

According to Wei (2023), AI provides a personalized learning experience and creates content and pacing based on the learner's needs. This means that students can focus on improvement. This definitely enhances motivation in particular for learners who struggle in regular classrooms. Furthermore, the instant feedback on grammar, vocabulary, pronunciation, and writing help reinforce the learning independently.

Chatbots and conversational tutors have offered flexibility and accessibility anytime and anywhere. This is significant as learning English is no longer limited in the classroom, but students can still practice the language outside their schools. Learners will thus be more comfortable and less anxious about making errors. This with no doubt will enhance confidence for learning a language. Gaming apps have become more accessible and provide learners the opportunities to learn English and remain engaged and enjoy learning (Wei, 2023).

Challenges and Limitations

Despite AI applications have offered tremendous benefits for ELT, still its implementation has some challenges and limitations. One major concern is the lack of human interaction. AI is not able to understand the cultural and emotional aspects of human interactions in real life. This can negatively impact the cultural appropriateness for language development and limits its understanding of the learner needs and provide empathy (Crompton et al., 2024).

Viktorivna et al. (2022) conducted a study using a survey that investigates the fears of using AI in language learning. The responses revealed a fear of the risk of losing personal life and losing the natural learning environment and their real emotions.

Another main challenge that was investigated by Krange et al. (2023) is the accurateness of the AI-generated feedback. Some corrections of grammar, spelling and writing may not be perfect in relation to advanced writing structures, and idiomatic expressions. In some instances, learners may receive incorrect or misleading corrections which can confuse them. Here we question the quality of the learning without the supervision of an expert like the teacher.

Avsheniuk et al. (2025) believe that the over reliance on AI has become a concern because learners may become dependent on AI for writing, feedback or answers. This can limit the critical thinking and creativity of learners. It also weakness the ability to solve learning tasks independently. Furthermore, Alshumaimeri and Alshememry (2023) posed the concern of privacy and data protection because most technologies request the sensitive data of teachers and students. Most apps ask for credentials or personal emails to access them and activate them.

In addition, Sadigzade (2025) highlights that while AI tools such as Grammarly can provide students with detailed instant feedback, there are concerns about the students' overreliance on AI and the quality of feedback, privacy and academic integrity. To implement these AI tools effectively, this requires student training in feedback literacy and teacher mediation as well.

4. DISCUSSION

Overall, theoretically speaking and thinking about the sociocultural theory and its implications in English language learning and teaching, learners are building knowledge through interacting with various AI tools such as chatbots. These can be like personal tutors that help students build the foundation of the language, when they are able to learn and practice the language without stress of making mistakes, this will motivate them to learn a second language such as English. In addition, learning should not only be limited to the classroom and to the English class time only, students have to practice the language using AI apps that they can easily access online on their mobile devices anytime and anywhere.

This review paper has the aim to explore current literature on the use of AI in English Language teaching. By investigating the vast literature published on this topic, it is evident that AI is applied widely in daily teaching practices whether in schools or universities. The key applications include using apps to enhance the skills of learners, provide personalized learning experience, increase motivation and engagement using games. AI has successfully managed to promote the effectiveness in teaching English; AI tools support educators to create supportive communication environment and thus encourage positive development among learners.

However, we can say nothing is perfect. Despite AI numerous benefits, it also poses some challenges and limitations. I think most importantly is the over-reliance on AI to do everything for us including thinking and solving anything. This can hinder creativity and critical thinking. Not forgetting to mention the loss of human touch. AI is simply a machine and when we are using it, we limit the human interaction. The use of AI tools cause issues in privacy and many ethical issues. One major concern is questioning the accuracy of information we get from AI technologies such the feedback we get from chatbots for instance.

The use of AI has become a necessity not an option as most countries have started already issuing policies to use AI in teaching. In the UAE, a resolution has been declared about the teaching Artificial Intelligence in all public schools for all grades. Not only the UAE, but also many countries like Singapore and Finland. Apparently, educators and policy makers are realizing the significance of AI and its role in education. Teachers should get training on how to incorporate AI in their teaching, our students who are digital natives are learning continuously all the time how to use AI and policy maker also should work on creating polices that regulate the use of AI.

Some suggested future research recommend would be measuring the impact of AI on teaching English and all subjects. Most research discuss the use and applications of AI in teaching English language but little research that really measures the true impact of it on learners. In addition, it is suggested on working on creating an international policy for AI in education that is implemented in all educational institutions. It is also significant to create a database for teachers to spread knowledge about how to use AI effectively. Currently this is a personal effort and educators find it hard to try new apps without considering their limitations. What we usually receive is mostly posts on social media, and there should be reliable resources and research papers that provide useful apps that support teachers who are teaching English language in all educational institutions.

5. CONCLUSION

To sum up, this paper presented a literature review of the use of AI in ELT in the recent five years. Overall, most literature highlights that the future of AI is promising.

Generally, AI has positive impacts in terms of teaching reading, writing, listening, speaking, feedback and motivation. This can be evident by noticing the noticeable increase in the number of research papers conducted recently. Overall, when integrating AI in language education, it is important to use it wisely by educators and learners as well. That is why policies can help in regulating its use. Teachers should keep up with the trend of times to update their teaching and use AI technology to improve the experience of English learning. Therefore, educational institutions hold a big responsibility in providing training for language teachers on how to integrate AI in their teaching practices. More training programs should be provided for students as well on how to use AI ethically in their learning process. It is also suggested that policies on the use of AI should be applied by everyone; teachers and students, to make sure we are getting the best out of this new technology. In addition, research on most effective applications should be conducted and provided for educators to assist them in integrating these technologies successfully.

REFERENCES

AlAfnan, M. A. (2024). Artificial Intelligence and Language: Bridging Arabic and English with Technology. *Journal of Ecohumanism*, *3*(8). Advance online publication. DOI: 10.62754/joe.v3i8.4961

Alam, S., Usama, M., Alam, M. M., Jabeen, I., & Ahmad, F. (2023). Artificial Intelligence in Global World: A case study of Grammarly as e-Tool on ESL Learners' writing of Darul Uloom Nadwa. *International Journal of Information and Education Technology (IJIET)*, *13*(11), 1741–1747. DOI: 10.18178/ijiet.2023.13.11.1984

Albariqi, Z. (2024). A systematic review exploring the use of artificial intelligence in developing writing skills. *Journal of Critical Studies in Language and Literature*, *5*(6), 59–64. DOI: 10.46809/jcsll.v5i6.308

Alshumaimeri, Y. A., & Alshememry, A. K. (2023). The extent of AI applications in EFL learning and teaching. *IEEE Transactions on Learning Technologies*, *17*, 653–663. DOI: 10.1109/TLT.2023.3322128

Avsheniuk, N., Seminikhyna, N., Ruban, L., & Sviatiuk, Y. (2025). Exploring overreliance on AI tools in English for specific purposes Courses: Challenges and implications for learning and academic integrity. *Arab World English Journal*, *1*(1), 3–20. DOI: 10.24093/awej/AI.1

Crompton, H., Edmett, A., Ichaporia, N., & Burke, D. (2024). AI and English language teaching: Affordances and challenges. *British Journal of Educational Technology*, *55*(6), 2503–2529. DOI: 10.1111/bjet.13460

Deutschmann, M., & Vu, M. T. (2015). Computer assisted language learning in language education: an overview of theories, methods, and current practices. In Lindgren, E., & Enever, J. (Eds.), *Språkdidaktik: researching language teaching and learning* (pp. 43–60). Department of Language Studies, Umeå University., http://urn.kb.se/resolve?urn=urn:nbn:se:umu:diva-106898

Devasena, R. (2024). Artificial intelligence in Education: An alternative to Traditional learning. *Journal of English Language Teaching*, *66*(1), 13–14. DOI: 10.66121/45wnfw13

Fitria, T. N. (2021). THE USE TECHNOLOGY BASED ON ARTIFICIAL INTELLIGENCE IN ENGLISH TEACHING AND LEARNING). *ELT Echo the Journal of English Language Teaching in Foreign Language Context*, *6*(2). Advance online publication. DOI: 10.24235/eltecho.v6i2.9299

Hakim, A., & Wahyuni, S. Postgraduate of State Institute of Islamic Studies of Kediri, Indonesia, & Postgraduate of State Institute of Islamic Studies of Kediri, Indonesia. (2024). A Critical review: Technology as Learning Media in Teaching Reading. *J-SHMIC : Journal of English for Academic, 11*(1). https://journal.uir.ac.id/index.php/jshmic

Haristiani, N. (2019). Artificial Intelligence (AI) Chatbot as Language Learning Medium: An inquiry. *Journal of Physics: Conference Series, 1387*(1), 012020. DOI: 10.1088/1742-6596/1387/1/012020

Huang, W., Hew, K. F., & Fryer, L. K. (2021). Chatbots for language learning—Are they really useful? A systematic review of chatbot-supported language learning. *Journal of Computer Assisted Learning*, *38*(1), 237–257. DOI: 10.1111/jcal.12610

Jendia, J., & Ismail, H. H. (2023). Developing personalised reading materials for Malaysian primary school pupils using ChatGPT: A review. *International Journal of Academic Research in Business & Social Sciences, 13*(12). Advance online publication. DOI: 10.6007/IJARBSS/v13-i12/20172

Kannan, J., & Munday, P. (2018). New Trends in Second Language Learning and Teaching through the lens of ICT, Networked Learning, and Artificial Intelligence. *Círculo de Lingüística Aplicada a la Comunicación*, *76*, 13–30. DOI: 10.5209/CLAC.62495

Khalifa, M., & Albadawy, M. (2024). Using artificial intelligence in academic writing and research: An essential productivity tool. *Computer Methods and Programs in Biomedicine Update*, *5*, 100145. DOI: 10.1016/j.cmpbup.2024.100145

Klimova, B., Pikhart, M., Benites, A. D., Lehr, C., & Sanchez-Stockhammer, C. (2022). Neural machine translation in foreign language teaching and learning: A systematic review. *Education and Information Technologies*, *28*(1), 663–682. DOI: 10.1007/s10639-022-11194-2

Koehler, M. J., Mishra, P., Mishra, P., & Koehler, M. J. (2009). What is Technological Pedagogical Content Knowledge? In Judi Harris & Matt Koehler (Eds.), *Contemporary Issues in Technology and Teacher Education* (Vol. 9, Issue 1, pp. 60–70). https://www.citejournal.org/wp-content/uploads/2016/04/v9i1general1-1.pdf

Krange, I., Segaran, M., Gamlem, S., Moltudal, S., & Engeness, I. (2023). A triple challenge: Students' identification, interpretation, and use of individualized automated feedback in learning to write English as a foreign language. *Deleted Journal*, *59*(59), 37–61. DOI: 10.55612/s-5002-059-001

Nah, F. F.-H., Zheng, R., Cai, J., Siau, K., & Chen, L. (2023). Generative AI and ChatGPT: Applications, challenges, and AI-human collaboration. *Journal of Information Technology Case and Application Research, 25*(3), 277–304. DOI: 10.1080/15228053.2023.2233814

Rahimi, S., & Rezvani, R. Corresponding Author. (2024). Enhancing English instructors' TPACK through AI: Exploring its role in Language Education. *Iranian Journal of English for Academic Purposes, 13–3*, 76–97. https://journalscmu.sinaweb.net/article_212184.html

Ryoo, J., & Winkelmann, K. (Eds.). (2021). Innovative Learning Environments in STEM Higher Education: Opportunities, challenges, and looking forward. In *SpringerBriefs in Statistics* [Book]. https://library.oapen.org/bitstream/handle/20.500.12657/47325/1/9783030589486.pdf#page=31

Sadigzade, Z. (2025). AI-Powered Feedback in ESL writing Classes: Pedagogical opportunities and ethical concerns. *Journal of Azerbaijan Language and Education Studies., 2*(4), 5–17. DOI: 10.69760/jales.2025004000

Shadiev, R., & Liu, J. (2022). Review of research on applications of speech recognition technology to assist language learning. *ReCALL, 35*(1), 74–88. DOI: 10.1017/S095834402200012X

Sharadgah, T. A., & Sa'di, R. A. (2022). A systematic review of research on the use of artificial intelligence in English language teaching and learning (2015-2021): What are the current effects? *Journal of Information Technology Education, 21*, 337–377. DOI: 10.28945/4999

Shi, H. Yantai University, Chinese University of Hong Kong, Aryadoust, V., & National Institute of Education, Nanyang Technological University, Singapore. (2024). A systematic review of AI-based automated written feedback research. In *ReCALL* (Vols. 36–2, pp. 187–209). https://doi.org/DOI: 10.1017/S0958344023000265

Viktorivna, K. L., Oleksandrovych, V. A., Oleksandrivna, K. I., & Oleksandrivna, K. N. (2022). Artificial Intelligence in Language Learning: What Are We Afraid of. *Arab World English Journal, 8*(8), 262–273. DOI: 10.24093/awej/call8.18

Wei, L. (2023). Artificial intelligence in language instruction: Impact on English learning achievement, L2 motivation, and self-regulated learning. *Frontiers in Psychology, 14*, 1261955. Advance online publication. DOI: 10.3389/fpsyg.2023.1261955 PMID: 38023040

Yang, G. (2020). The application of Artificial intelligence in English teaching. *International Journal of Frontiers in Sociology*, *2*(3). Advance online publication. DOI: 10.25236/ijfs.2020.020309

Zawacki-Richter, O., Kerres, M., Bedenlier, S., Bond, M., & Buntins, K. (2020). *Systematic reviews in educational research.* https://library.oapen.org/bitstream/handle/20.500.12657/23142/1007012.pdf?sequenc#page=22

Zhou, W. (2020). Sociocultural Theory and its implications in college English teaching and learning in the age of artificial Intelligence. *Journal of Physics: Conference Series*, *1646*(1), 012142. DOI: 10.1088/1742-6596/1646/1/012142

Chapter 5
Academic Integrity in the Age of Generative AI:
Risks and Institutional Responses

Mustafa Kayyali
http://orcid.org/0000-0003-3300-262X
Maaref University of Applied Sciences, Syria

ABSTRACT

Generative AI has entered MENA classrooms faster than institutional cultures and regulations can catch up. This chapter examines how tools that can instantly generate essays, solutions, and code unsettle long-standing ideas of originality, authorship, and effort. It maps the emerging risk landscape—from invisible outsourcing of assignments to the gradual erosion of students' confidence in their own thinking—while situating these dynamics within the socio-economic pressures and exam-centred traditions of MENA education systems. Rather than framing AI only as a threat, the chapter explores how universities and schools can respond through coherent policy, imaginative assessment design, and sustained staff and student development. Drawing on regional examples, it argues for a shift from policing misconduct to cultivating a shared culture of integrity, where AI is used transparently, critically, and in ways that deepen, rather than replace, human learning.

INTRODUCTION

In many universities across the MENA region, the story now begins with a dimly lit screen. A student sits in a crowded apartment in Casablanca, Amman, or Aleppo, juggling family obligations, part-time work, and the silent weight of expectations. The deadline for a research paper is hours away. One tap opens an AI chatbot; an-

DOI: 10.4018/979-8-2600-0328-2.ch005

other tap pastes the assignment prompt. Within seconds, a polished, fluent response appears—far more fluent than the student feels in that moment. The cursor blinks, inviting a decision: copy, edit, adapt, or close the tab and struggle alone.

This scene is neither dystopian fantasy nor isolated misbehaviour. It captures a new ordinary in academic life, where generative AI systems capable of composing essays, solving equations, writing code, or summarizing dense articles coexist with fragile cultures of academic integrity. For educators and policymakers, the question is no longer whether students *might* use such tools, but how this ubiquitous presence reshapes what it means to learn honestly, to demonstrate one's own understanding, and to trust the value of educational credentials.

Academic integrity has traditionally been framed through relatively familiar categories: plagiarism, contract cheating, collusion, data fabrication, exam misconduct (Johnson, 2023). Underneath these categories lies a moral and relational fabric: respect for knowledge, fairness towards peers, accountability to one's community, and the basic promise that grades reflect genuine effort and achievement. Integrity is not only about rules; it is about the sort of person a learner becomes while engaging with knowledge, and the kind of institution a university chooses to be in the eyes of its students and society.

Generative AI does not erase this fabric, but it pulls at the threads in unexpected ways. Unlike earlier technologies—calculators, translation tools, search engines—these systems do not simply retrieve information or automate narrow tasks (Kayyali, 2025 C). They imitate the visible surface of human thinking: the paragraph, the argument, the structured explanation. They can respond in Arabic or English, echoing disciplinary jargon and even approximating certain academic styles. As a result, the line between "using a tool" and "outsourcing the cognitive core of the task" becomes dangerously blurred.

What does it mean to submit "one's own work" if an AI system drafted the first version, organized the structure, and suggested the key arguments? Is the student merely editing, curating, and making judgments, or are they substituting automation for understanding? When the output looks convincing, should educators trust it? And when they don't, should they trust their students?

These dilemmas are sharpened by the particular realities of MENA education systems (Boudihaj & Sahli, 2022). Many countries in the region still carry strong legacies of high-stakes examinations, competitive placement mechanisms, and large classes where personal feedback is scarce. Students often experience education as a series of hurdles, not as an extended conversation about ideas. Parents, facing economic uncertainty and political instability, may perceive a degree as a lifeline rather than a journey of intellectual growth. Under such pressure, "getting the grade" can easily overshadow "owning the learning."

At the same time, institutions themselves face complex constraints. Digital infrastructure is uneven; some universities are experimenting with AI-enabled platforms and analytics, while others struggle with basic connectivity. Faculty members, especially in public systems, are overloaded with teaching, administrative duties, and sometimes external work to supplement their income. Few have the luxury of redesigning assessments from the ground up. Policy frameworks—where they exist—are often imported, translated, or loosely adapted from global templates, without fully grappling with how generative AI interacts with local cultural norms, languages, and power relations (Kulesz, 2024).

In such a landscape, it is tempting for institutions to respond defensively: to announce bans, to purchase AI-detection software, to treat generative AI primarily as a new kind of plagiarism machine. Yet this instinct, understandable as it is, risks missing the wider picture. Detection tools are fallible and can produce false accusations, especially for students writing in additional languages. Blanket prohibitions are often unenforceable and can push AI use underground, deepening mistrust between students and staff. Most importantly, a narrow focus on "catching cheaters" overlooks the deeper curricular and pedagogical questions that AI brutally exposes.

Generative AI forces educators to confront long-standing weaknesses in assessment design: overreliance on generic essay prompts, predictable assignments, and tasks that reward surface reproduction rather than critical engagement. When a machine can produce passable responses to such tasks in seconds, the underlying problem is not simply that students *can* cheat more easily; it is that the tasks themselves may no longer be robust indicators of learning. AI does not merely create a new form of misconduct; it reveals how fragile some of our old assumptions have always been.

Within the MENA region, these challenges are entangled with multilingual realities. Many students navigate Arabic (standard and dialect), English, and sometimes French as part of their educational journeys. Generative AI tools can, at least superficially, ease these transitions by helping with translation, paraphrasing, or drafting in a target language (Balaji et al, 2025). Used thoughtfully, they can support language learning and inclusion; used uncritically, they can mask underlying language gaps and reduce opportunities to struggle productively with expression and meaning. Institutions thus face not only ethical questions about authorship but also pedagogical questions about language, identity, and voice.

Yet it would be misleading to frame this chapter around risk alone. The same tools that threaten to hollow out academic effort can also be harnessed to strengthen integrity if embedded within a culture of transparency and critical reflection. For example, educators might invite students to use AI to generate initial ideas or alternative explanations, while making the process visible and assessable. Institutions might reorient from secret surveillance toward explicit guidance: clarifying when

AI is allowed, how it should be acknowledged, and what kinds of learning outcomes must always be demonstrated through human performance.

This chapter takes seriously both sides of the equation: the genuine dangers generative AI poses to academic integrity and the potential it offers to rethink what honest, meaningful learning can look like in MENA education systems. It begins by unpacking how generative AI reshapes the conceptual terrain of integrity, moving beyond simplistic notions of "copying" to consider accountability, authorship, and the erosion or strengthening of student agency. It then maps the emerging risk landscape, from invisible outsourcing of assignments to subtle dependencies that undermine confidence and autonomy.

Building on this analysis, the chapter turns to the specific dynamics of the MENA context: social and economic pressures, institutional hierarchies, linguistic complexities, and the lived realities of students and faculty who must adapt to AI with limited resources and uneven support. In the final sections, it explores institutional responses—from policy and governance to assessment design and professional development—and sketches pathways toward a culture of trustworthy learning in AI-rich classrooms.

Ultimately, the central question is not whether AI will remain in education (it will), but what kind of moral and institutional ecosystem will grow around it. Will generative AI deepen shortcuts, cynicism, and inequality, or will it become an occasion to renew commitments to honesty, responsibility, and shared intellectual labour? The answer depends less on the technology itself and more on the choices that institutions, educators, and students make together in the years ahead.

GENERATIVE AI AND THE CHANGING MEANING OF ACADEMIC INTEGRITY

For a long time, academic integrity sounded relatively straightforward. Students were expected to do their own work, acknowledge the sources they used, resist the temptation to copy, and avoid paying others to complete assignments (Tolman & Kremling, 2023). The moral vocabulary was familiar: honesty, fairness, responsibility, respect, trust. Even when violations occurred, the underlying picture was still binary. Either the student produced the work, or someone else did. Either the words were original, or they were copied. The rules were not always followed, but they felt conceptually clear.

Generative AI quietly unsettles that clarity. It does so not by introducing a new type of calculator or spell-checker, but by intruding on the very activity that assessment is supposed to reveal: the act of thinking through a problem and expressing that thinking in language, code, or design (Betz, 2025). When a student feeds a prompt into an AI system and receives a coherent answer, the result is neither fully "stolen" nor fully "their own." It emerges from a statistical model trained on vast quantities of human expression, then tailored through the student's prompts, edits, and choices. In other words, the boundary between author and tool is no longer a simple line; it becomes a gradient.

This gradient is where academic integrity starts to feel less like a checklist and more like a moving landscape. Consider a common scenario in MENA universities today: a student struggling with academic English or French, anxious about grades, asks an AI system to "rephrase" a paragraph to sound more formal. The tool returns a polished version that preserves the overall meaning but changes structure and vocabulary. Has the student plagiarized? Some would say no: the ideas are still theirs, just better expressed. Others would argue that the student has outsourced a crucial part of the intellectual labour—crafting argument through language—and that something essential has been hollowed out.

Now stretch this scenario a little further. The same student asks the AI to "draft an introduction based on these points," and the model produces several paragraphs that the student then rearranges, trims, and augments with a few personal sentences. At what point does assistance become substitution? How much editing transforms an AI-generated draft into "the student's own work"? Traditional definitions of plagiarism, focused on copying from identifiable human sources, were never designed to answer these questions. Yet institutions are already being forced to take a stance, sometimes in a hurry, sometimes with contradicting signals across departments.

Another layer complicates matters: generative AI does not simply help students *express* what they know; it can help them *simulate* knowing (Borge et al, 2024). In exam-based systems, shortcuts existed, but they usually required coordination: copying from peers, purchasing essays, smuggling notes into exam halls. With AI, a student can sit alone in a quiet room and produce an apparently competent answer to a question they barely understand. The surface text may look perfectly acceptable—grammatical, coherent, even sprinkled with references that sound plausible. To the untrained eye, or to the tired marker with a heavy load, nothing looks suspicious. Yet beneath the polished language, there may be almost no genuine engagement, no internal wrestling with the material, no mental re-structuring of ideas.

Academic integrity, then, can no longer be reduced to "did this person physically type these sentences?" It has to grapple with deeper questions: Did the assessment provide an opportunity for the student to think? Did the student actually take that opportunity, or did they let the machine perform a kind of cognitive performance on their behalf? Integrity becomes tied less to the material origin of the text and more to the authenticity of the learning process that produced it.

From this angle, generative AI reveals something uncomfortable. Even before AI, many assessments in the region—and globally—rewarded surface performance more than deep understanding (Yan et al, 2024). Formulaic essays, memorized definitions, recycled project templates: these existed long before the first chatbot appeared in a browser. AI did not create superficial academic work; it simply made its production less time-consuming and more widely accessible. When a routine assignment can be completed in seconds by a model, the problem may not lie only in students' moral weakness but also in the design of the task itself.

Table 1. AI Use Scenarios and Integrity Categories

AI Use Scenario	Description	Integrity Category	Suggested Policy Stance
Grammar and clarity editing of a student-written draft	Student drafts the text and uses AI to tidy language while preserving their own structure and argument.	Generally acceptable support (if disclosed where required).	Allowed with guidance; encourage disclosure and attention to preserving student voice.
Translation support between Arabic, English, and French	Student uses AI to move between languages, then checks meaning and revises for accuracy and style.	Conditionally acceptable support (depends on task and disclosure).	Allowed where language scaffolding is an outcome; clarify limits for language-intensive assessments.
Idea generation and alternative explanations for a concept	Student prompts AI for examples, outlines, or ways to understand a topic before writing independently.	Potentially acceptable learning aid if followed by independent work and acknowledgment.	Encourage as part of critical engagement with AI; require students to document how they used the tool.
Generating draft paragraphs then heavily revising them	AI produces initial wording for sections that the student then rewrites, re-structures, and sources properly.	Grey zone; may be acceptable only under strict conditions and explicit transparency.	Treat cautiously; require process evidence and explicit acknowledgment of AI's role.
Generating a complete assignment and submitting it as own work	Student relies on AI to produce most or all of the text, with minimal human understanding or contribution.	Clear academic misconduct; constitutes outsourcing of core intellectual work.	Prohibited; communicate as equivalent to contract cheating or ghostwriting.
Using AI to fabricate citations, quotations, or data	AI is prompted to invent references, page numbers, or datasets that do not actually exist.	Clear fabrication and serious breach of academic integrity.	Prohibited; classify as research and academic fraud with appropriate sanctions.
Using AI tools during a closed-book or in-class exam without permission	AI is accessed on a device to obtain answers during an exam where only human memory and notes are allowed.	Clear exam misconduct and violation of assessment conditions.	Prohibited; address within existing exam misconduct frameworks and communicate clearly to students.

Still, the moral dimension cannot be dismissed. Education involves a promise: that the grades attached to a student's name represent their own effort and growth. When generative AI is used clandestinely to manufacture assignments, that promise is broken. Not just because rules are violated, but because the student opts out of the formative struggle that genuine learning requires. One might say that the student "cheats themselves," yet this phrase risks sounding sentimental. In systems where a degree may mean access to employment, migration opportunities, or social recognition, the incentive to cut corners is not purely individual; it is structured by economic and social pressures. Integrity, under such conditions, becomes an act of resistance as much as compliance.

Generative AI also challenges the meaning of originality. In academic discourse, originality has often been romanticized: the lone student crafting a unique argument, the researcher discovering an insight no one else has seen (Garcia, 2025). AI-generated text, by contrast, is derived from patterns in existing data. It does not "create" in a human sense; it recombines. Yet human writing also builds on prior language and ideas, consciously or not. No student writes in a vacuum; everyone leans on phrases heard in lectures, formulations from articles, expressions circulating in their linguistic environment. What generative AI does is make that recombination hyper-efficient, stripping away the slow, sometimes messy process of reading, digesting, misinterpreting, and eventually rephrasing. The student who uses AI to generate a literature review may still produce something technically "new," in the narrow sense that no identical paragraph exists elsewhere, but that novelty can feel hollow—like a mosaic assembled by someone who has never seen the original tiles up close.

Figure 1. Illustrative Patterns of Student Use of Generative AI in Coursework

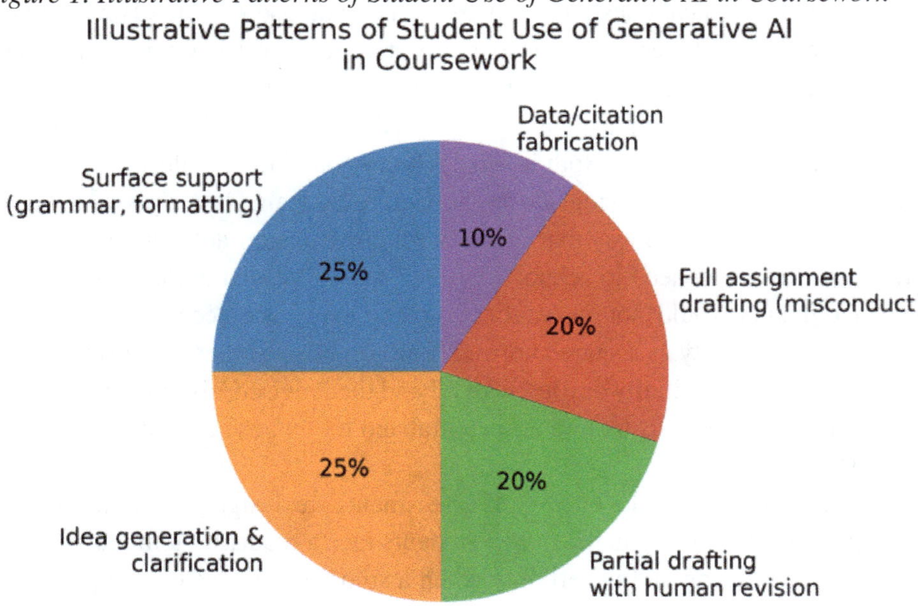

In the MENA context, where multilingualism is common and academic writing often takes place in a second or third language, generative AI can appear as a lifeline rather than a threat. Students use it to clean up grammar, find transitional phrases, or check whether a paragraph "sounds academic enough." Some educators quietly encourage such use, seeing it as a form of scaffolding. Others fear that heavy reliance on AI will stunt the development of genuine linguistic competence and critical thinking in languages of instruction. Integrity, then, stops being a simple rule about copying and becomes entangled with broader questions about linguistic justice, equity, and the purpose of language learning in higher education.

At institutional level, the meaning of integrity is shifting in another way. Universities are beginning to recognize that integrity is not just the student's burden (Christensen Hughes, 2022). When institutions adopt AI tools—for automatic grading, plagiarism detection, or "learning analytics"—they also introduce new forms of opacity and potential unfairness. A student accused of AI-based misconduct may find it difficult to defend themselves if the accusation rests on a proprietary detection algorithm whose inner workings are hidden. What does integrity look like when the very tools used to enforce it are partially inscrutable, possibly biased, and sometimes wrong? The moral conversation cannot remain at the level of student behaviour; it has to include institutional responsibility for the technological ecosystems being deployed.

All of this points toward a broader redefinition: academic integrity in the age of generative AI becomes less about policing specific forbidden acts and more about cultivating a relationship to knowledge and tools that is honest, self-aware, and accountable. The ethical question shifts from "Did you use AI?" to "How did you use it, and why?" A student who transparently states that an AI system was used to generate illustrative examples, but then critically evaluates those examples, engages in a very different act from a student who secretly submits an AI-written essay as their own (Kayyali, 2025 A). Both involve AI; only one involves deception.

This shift suggests that integrity might need to be framed partly as a practice of disclosure. In the same way that scholars acknowledge co-authors, editors, and funders, students may need to acknowledge the role AI played in their work. Such acknowledgments would not automatically make every use acceptable, but they would recenter honesty as a shared norm. A culture where students feel safe to say, "This paragraph was initially drafted with AI and then revised," is already different from a culture where AI is treated as a contraband tool whose use must be hidden at all costs.

Yet disclosure alone is not enough. If assessments are designed such that almost any AI-generated answer can pass, then students face a recurring temptation: why wrestle with confusion and uncertainty when a smooth response can be produced instantly? That temptation is not a sign of moral collapse; it is a human reaction to misaligned incentives (Akbar, 2025). To protect integrity, tasks must be reshaped so that genuine understanding, personal engagement, and context-specific reasoning are not optional extras but necessary conditions for success. This could mean more oral examinations, reflective journals tied to personal experience, in-class synthesis tasks, or problems grounded in local realities that AI models trained mostly on global data may struggle to handle meaningfully.

Underneath the policy debates and technical fixes, an older question re-emerges: what is education for? If the primary purpose is credentialing—producing certificates that unlock jobs—then the rise of AI will almost inevitably erode integrity, because the fastest route to the credential will often run through technological shortcuts. If, however, institutions insist that education is about cultivating judgment, discernment, critical imagination, and moral agency, then AI becomes a demanding test of that claim (Saltman, 2022). It forces universities in the MENA region and beyond to decide whether they are prepared to align their assessment practices, curricula, and support systems with that deeper purpose, rather than merely declaring it in mission statements.

In that sense, generative AI functions like a stress test. It presses on contradictions already present in academic life: between rhetoric and reality, between the ideal of independent thinking and the routine of formulaic assignments, between the language of ethics and the pressures of survival. Academic integrity, once a relatively contained concept referring to cheating and plagiarism, now stretches to cover how communities of learners and educators negotiate their shared dependence on powerful tools.

The meaning of integrity is changing, not because the underlying values are obsolete, but because the conditions under which those values are enacted have shifted dramatically (Kirby, 2022). Honesty, accountability, and respect for knowledge do not disappear when an AI system enters the classroom. They become harder to perform lazily. They demand new forms of transparency, new conversations about authorship, and new forms of courage—both from students who choose to learn honestly when dishonesty is easy, and from institutions that choose to reimagine assessment when complacency would be simpler.

RISK LANDSCAPES: AUTOMATION, AUTHORSHIP, AND THE TEMPTATION TO OUTSOURCE THINKING

The emergence of generative AI has not simply added another tool to the student's digital toolbox; it has rearranged the entire terrain on which risk, responsibility, and temptation live. What used to be a relatively narrow question—"Did this student copy from somewhere?"—has expanded into a messier inquiry: "Who actually did the thinking here?" The answer is no longer obvious, even to the student.

Automation sits at the heart of this new landscape. At first glance, much of what AI does looks harmless, even helpful. It tidies grammar, proposes headings, suggests synonyms, formats references, generates quick summaries of dense articles. Tasks that used to devour hours now shrink into a few prompts. For a student juggling lectures, part-time work, family commitments, and the emotional residue of political or economic instability, such relief can feel less like luxury and more like oxygen. Why spend an entire evening drafting an introduction when a system can produce a fluent one in twenty seconds?

Yet automation rarely stays politely in its corner. Once a student has seen how easily an AI model can produce a clear paragraph from a vague idea, the temptation steadily creeps upwards: from editing to drafting, from drafting to structuring, from structuring to composing an entire assignment (Nabilla et al, 2024). The slope is not experienced as a dramatic fall but as a series of small, reasonable decisions: "Let it generate a first version, I'll improve it later"; "Let it suggest three arguments, I'll pick the best"; "Let it answer this section, I don't have time to read all the sources anyway." At each step, the student is still present, still making choices, yet the proportion of genuine cognitive effort quietly shrinks.

This is where the risk becomes subtle. Academic dishonesty in the past often required a clear, conscious crossing of a line: buying a paper, copying from a classmate, sneaking notes into an exam (Kayyali, 2026 A). In the age of automation, the boundary can feel fuzzy even to the person crossing it. A student who starts with the intention of "only using AI for ideas" might end up handing in a text in which most of the original language, structure, and argument emerged from the model. They may not experience themselves as cheating in the classic sense; they feel they have worked, because they selected, edited, and adapted. Yet the heavy lifting—the intellectual wrestling that assignments are supposed to provoke—has been outsourced.

The cost of that outsourcing is not only ethical; it is cognitive and emotional. Learning, especially in demanding fields and additional languages, is often uncomfortable. It involves sitting with confusion, testing hypotheses, revising misunderstandings, and gradually building confidence in one's own capacity to make sense of complex material. When automation steps in too early and too strongly, it interrupts this process. The student gets the outcome (a plausible text, a solved problem set, a working piece of code) without building the inner architecture of understanding that such outcomes are meant to represent. Over time, this can erode something deeper than skill: a sense of intellectual self-trust.

The MENA region, with its crowded classrooms, exam-driven cultures, and uneven access to high-quality schooling, provides particularly fertile ground for this erosion. Many students carry a quiet narrative that they are "not good enough" in the language of instruction, or that theoretical material is too abstract to be truly grasped. Generative AI can act as a seductive ally to that narrative: a silent voice whispering, "Don't struggle; let me handle this." When that whisper aligns with social pressure to get high grades quickly, or with family expectations that leave little room for failure, automation becomes more than a convenience (Rettberg, 2024). It becomes a psychological crutch.

Authorship, in this environment, starts to fragment. Traditional academic culture assumes a reasonably clear chain: a human mind engages with sources, interprets them, and produces a text whose authorship can be attributed to that mind, even if supported by peers or supervisors (Schorske & Bender, 2021). With generative AI involved, the authorship chain becomes braided. The model contributes patterns, phrases, and connections drawn from its training data; the student contributes prompts, edits, and contextual decisions. Who, then, is the author? Is the text "by" the student, "by" the model, or some hybrid that our current categories do not yet properly capture?

In some cases, the answer might be straightforward: a short AI-suggested phrase inserted into an otherwise human-written essay hardly undermines authorship. Yet when a model generates entire paragraphs, examples, and even citations, the situation grows murkier. The student may not fully know how the model arrived at its suggestions, what sources underlie them, or whether the references are even real. They are asked to sign their name under a document whose internal logic and provenance they only partially understand. Authorship turns into a kind of performance: the student appears as the visible face of a collaborative process in which the invisible partner (the AI) has done a disproportionate share of the intellectual labour.

This has ethical weight. Academic authorship has never been purely about who typed the words; it has been about who stands behind the claims, who takes responsibility for the accuracy of citations, who accepts the consequences if errors or fabrications are later uncovered (Panjaitan et al, 2024). When generative AI is heavily involved, that responsibility can feel oddly diffused. If the model invented a source, is the student guilty of fabrication, or merely careless? If the model blended several authors' ideas into a single seamless paragraph, has the student plagiarized, even if no single original passage was copied? Institutions are only beginning to grapple with such questions, but students face them daily in a very immediate way, often without clear guidance.

The risk landscape does not end with explicit misconduct. There is also automation bias: the tendency to trust machine-generated output simply because it appears confident and well-structured. In many cases, especially for students who feel insecure in their subject knowledge, AI responses can acquire an aura of authority (Gao, 2025). The tone is polished, the language academic, the structure tidy. It "sounds right." Under such conditions, students may accept AI-produced content with minimal scrutiny, simply because they assume the machine must know better. This can lead to the spread of inaccuracies, oversimplifications, or culturally skewed interpretations that go unnoticed, then reappear in assignments, presentations, and even research proposals.

For the MENA context, the issue of cultural and epistemic bias is not trivial. Many generative models are trained predominantly on English-language data, often reflecting Western-centric perspectives and assumptions. When students rely heavily on such systems to shape their understanding of local issues—education reforms, social movements, regional histories—the risk is not only academic but epistemological. The model may subtly universalize certain viewpoints while marginalizing others, and the student, trusting the confident tone, may internalize these perspectives as neutral truth. Outsourcing thinking in this case does not just affect grades; it influences how young people understand their own societies.

Another layer of risk touches the relationship between students and educators. As more assignments exhibit the eerie fluency and stylistic sameness typical of AI-generated text, suspicion can seep into classroom dynamics. Teachers who were already under pressure to grade quickly may start to read with an investigative eye, searching for traces of AI rather than engaging with the substance of students' ideas (Shah, 2023). Some will turn to detection tools, which offer probability scores and risk assessments that feel scientific but remain fallible. False accusations become a real possibility, especially for students who write in unexpectedly sophisticated ways or who use unusual phrasing due to multilingual backgrounds. The risk here is not just unfair punishment; it is the slow poisoning of trust.

At the same time, educators themselves face a temptation parallel to the students'. AI can summarize readings, generate quiz questions, design lesson plans, and even provide feedback suggestions. Under heavy workloads, the lure of automation can be strong. If a teacher routinely relies on AI to craft assignments, there is a chance that some of those tasks will be easily answerable by similar systems, reinforcing the cycle where both sides—student and teacher—lean on tools rather than on their own creative pedagogy or authentic engagement. The entire educational ecosystem risks slipping into a strange simulation, where human beings supervise a conversation largely conducted between machines.

Contract cheating, once a relatively visible phenomenon involving external ghostwriters, also shifts shape. Generative AI can function as an in-house ghostwriter, available around the clock, cost-free after initial access, and capable of producing many variations of the same assignment. Services are already emerging that combine AI with human editing, blurring the line further between paid cheating and "legitimate" editing support. The risk profile becomes more distributed: instead of a small number of students using external essay mills, a much larger group may quietly automate substantial portions of their work.

Yet the most pervasive risk may not be dramatic misconduct so much as a gradual change in students' relationship to effort. When every moment of difficulty can be bypassed with a prompt, the tolerance for ambiguity, frustration, and slow thinking can start to thin out. A generation already accustomed to instant information through search engines now encounters a tool that offers instant *formulated* responses. The habit of pausing, wondering, sketching out rough ideas, or trying to recall a concept before looking it up can easily be replaced by a pattern of "ask, paste, submit." The visible harm may be delayed—grades might stay high—but the invisible harm accumulates in quieter ways: diminished curiosity, fragile confidence when AI is unavailable, a sense that one's own mind is always slightly inferior to the machine.

None of these risks arise in a social vacuum. They intersect with economic inequality, digital divides, language hierarchies, and the broader politics of knowledge (Helsper, 2021). Students in under-resourced institutions may rely on free, public models with fewer safeguards and higher hallucination rates, while students in elite universities use licensed tools integrated into learning platforms, with better support and clearer guidelines. Those with strong preparatory education may use AI as a supplement, while those with weaker foundations may depend on it as a substitute. Over time, this can deepen existing inequities under the guise of technological progress.

Figure 2. Shifting Integrity Risk Profile Before and After Generative AI

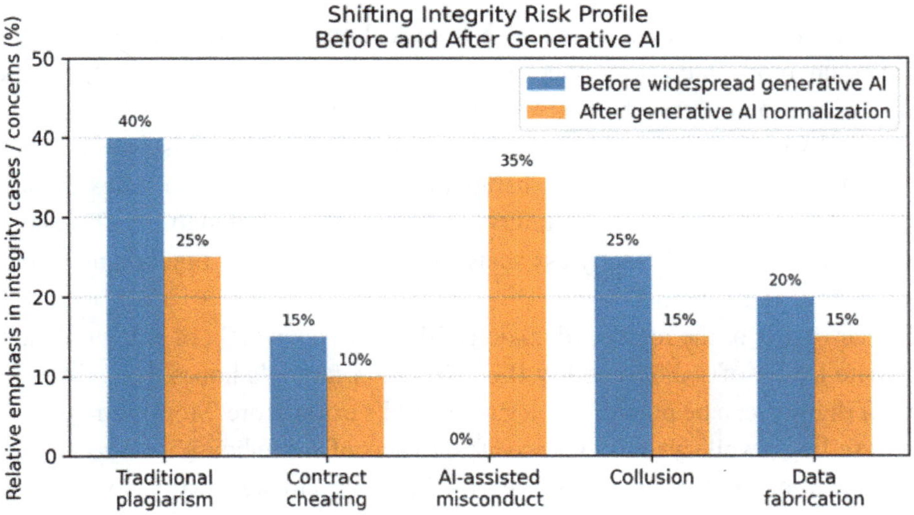

Mapping this risk landscape is not about demonizing automation or romanticizing pre-digital learning. The point is to recognize how easily generative AI can slide from assistant to surrogate thinker, and how quickly the meaning of authorship can be hollowed out when that slide goes unexamined. When assignments become mere prompts to be fed into a system, and when the main human action is copy–paste, the educational project loses its soul, even if the surface remains shiny and efficient.

The challenge for institutions, especially in the MENA region, is to walk a narrow path. Denying students access to AI altogether is unrealistic and, frankly, educationally unwise in a world where such tools will shape future work and civic life (Cabrera et al, 2024). Embracing automation without limits, on the other hand, risks cultivating graduates who carry impressive transcripts but fragile intellectual autonomy. Between these extremes lies a more demanding route: acknowledging the realities of automation, naming the temptations to outsource thinking, and redesigning tasks, policies, and conversations so that students are nudged back, again and again, toward genuine engagement.

In that sense, risk is not purely a technical problem to be solved with better detection or stricter rules. It is an ethical and pedagogical problem that exposes what kind of thinking universities truly value, and whether they are prepared to defend that kind of thinking when shortcuts become almost irresistibly easy.

THE MENA EDUCATIONAL CONTEXT: CULTURAL NORMS, PRESSURES, AND DIGITAL HABITS

Talking about generative AI in the abstract is almost too easy. The conversation becomes far more interesting once it drops into specific streets, languages, and family living rooms across the MENA region. Academic integrity here doesn't float in a neutral vacuum; it is braided with social expectations, long histories of exam culture, and very particular digital habits that have emerged in societies marked by youth bulges, economic uncertainty, and uneven political stability. The same chatbot that appears as a "study assistant" in one country may function as a quiet survival strategy in another.

In many parts of the region, education still carries the weight of being the main legitimate ladder of social mobility (Lee, 2022). A family's hopes, sometimes its sense of dignity, can be poured into a single child's exam score. Stories circulate of parents selling jewellery to pay for private tutoring, of entire households reorganizing daily routines around high-stakes tests—the baccalaureate, tawjihi, concours, or university entrance exams. Under this pressure, learning easily shifts from a journey of discovery to a narrow tunnel with one bright opening at the end: a particular degree, a specific faculty, a small set of prestigious professions. When the stakes are that high and the route so tightly scripted, it's not surprising that students start to see grades as a kind of currency and everything that boosts those grades, ethically or not, as part of the same economy.

Cultural norms reinforce this gravitational pull. In collectivist settings, success is rarely experienced as purely individual; it reflects on the entire family, sometimes on the extended kin network. A "good mark" is not just personal satisfaction; it's something that relatives mention at visits, neighbours hear about, and elders interpret as a sign that sacrifices were worthwhile. Failure, conversely, is not just a private disappointment. It can feel like letting people down, like mishandling a trust. When generative AI appears as a tool that can quickly remove obstacles—language difficulties, time pressure, unfamiliar genres—it steps into a moral terrain already saturated with obligations and unspoken debts (King, 2024).

This doesn't mean that students in the region lack ethical awareness. Many feel deeply uncomfortable about what they themselves call "shortcuts," yet they also inhabit systems where cutting corners is normalized in other domains of life: bureaucratic workarounds, informal payments, "wasta" networks that grease the wheels. If a young person sees adults navigate a world where rules are frequently bent to cope with dysfunction, the boundary between clever adaptation and dishonesty can blur. Academic integrity then becomes one more arena where the tension between ideals and lived reality plays out (Davis, 2023). Generative AI intensifies that tension by offering a perfectly legal, socially acceptable way to bend the spirit of educational expectations while technically staying hidden (Kayyali, 2025 B).

Language adds another twist. Across MENA, students move between dialectal Arabic, Modern Standard Arabic, and often English or French as languages of academic instruction. The emotional home is usually the dialect; the language of exams and textbooks is something more distant, formal, sometimes experienced as cold or intimidating. A lot of students never feel fully at home in the language of assessment. They may understand content but struggle to wrap it in the right register, the right academic tone. Generative AI promises to bridge that gap instantly. A rough paragraph written in hesitant English can be transformed into a polished, idiomatic text at the click of a button; an abstract can be generated in French even if the student thinks through the topic internally in Arabic (Srivastava & Kumar, 2025).

On the surface, this looks like pure support for inclusion. Yet the effect on integrity is complicated. When the model rewrites a student's text so thoroughly that syntax, vocabulary, and rhythm no longer resemble the original, the question emerges: whose voice is now speaking? Students often describe a strange disconnection when reading AI-polished work that they're supposed to "own"—they recognize the ideas but not the sound. Over time, this can create a habit of outsourcing not just grammar but self-expression, a habit that is strengthened by the fact that many teachers, under pressure and with limited training in writing pedagogy, tend to reward polished surface over honest, imperfect attempts.

Add to this the digital environment in which all of this unfolds. MENA youth are overwhelmingly smartphone natives. The device in the pocket is the primary gateway not only to social media but also to study materials, lecture recordings, and entire informal knowledge networks (Snoussi, 2024). WhatsApp or Telegram "study groups" operate as parallel classrooms where lecture notes, past exam papers, screenshots of solved exercises, and sometimes entire assignments circulate freely. These groups can be supportive spaces of peer teaching, but they also normalize a kind of continuous, low-level academic copying: "Send me the answer," "Forward the file," "Share your report, I'll change it a bit." When generative AI is added into this ecosystem, it doesn't arrive as a solemn academic resource; it appears as one more clever trick shared in the group: "Ask the bot to write it for you," "Paste the question here and see what happens."

Digital habits formed on social media also shape how AI tools are used. Short attention spans, multitasking across dozens of chats, the constant presence of notifications—the mental environment is already fractured. Switching from a meme on Instagram to a prompt in an AI app and back again feels natural. The idea of sitting quietly with a dense article for an hour, a pen in hand, taking notes, feels much less natural. When AI can summarize that article in a few lines, the pre-existing preference for quick consumption over deep reading gets reinforced (Srinivasan, 2022). Students may start with good intentions—"I'll use it just to get the main idea"—but the convenience quietly displaces the slower forms of engagement that academic integrity implicitly assumes: wrestling with original texts, checking references, forming independent judgments.

Regional inequalities sharpen these patterns. In some Gulf universities, for instance, students might have access to institutionally licensed AI platforms integrated into learning management systems, with guidelines, workshops, and relatively clear policies. In conflict-affected or under-resourced contexts, students rely on free public models accessed via unstable internet connections, often without any structured conversation about ethics or limitations. For those who have lived through displacement, economic hardship, or disrupted schooling, AI may feel less like a controversial novelty and more like an overdue form of compensatory support: a way to catch up quickly in systems that rarely slowed down for them. It is hard to preach about the dangers of "outsourcing thinking" to students who feel that the world has rarely given them a fair chance to think in peace.

Teacher–student dynamics carry their own cultural and institutional imprint. In many MENA universities, the classroom is still marked by strong hierarchy. The professor is expected to embody authority; challenging that authority in public can be risky or simply unimaginable. At the same time, students know that some assessments are recycled year after year, that some faculty rely heavily on dictated notes or imported PowerPoint slides, that curricula sometimes lag behind real-world change by a decade or more (David, 2025). This mixture of respect and quiet disillusionment creates a peculiar atmosphere: students may admire individual teachers while holding a more cynical view of the system as a whole. In such an environment, the moral force of exhortations about academic integrity depends heavily on whether students perceive their educators as intellectually engaged and ethically consistent, or as merely enforcing tired rules.

When generative AI enters this fragile relationship, it can either deepen mistrust or open a new channel of collaboration. In settings where teachers react primarily with suspicion—accusations, threats, heavy reliance on detection tools—students may retreat into defensive secrecy. In settings where educators acknowledge their own uncertainty, invite students into shared exploration, and discuss when AI use is legitimate and when it undermines learning, a different culture can begin to form. The challenge is that such open dialogue requires time and institutional support, two resources that are often in short supply, especially in public systems overwhelmed by numbers and bureaucracy.

Another dimension that cannot be ignored is the region's experience of surveillance and control. In societies where state monitoring is a familiar reality, students may already feel watched in multiple domains of life. Introducing AI detection tools that claim to "discover" whether a text is machine-generated may inadvertently echo those broader patterns of surveillance, even if the intentions are purely academic. For some, this will reinforce compliance; for others, it will cultivate a deeper desire to outsmart the system. Both reactions shape how generative AI is used: either carefully hidden or defiantly playful.

Gender dynamics also intersect with digital habits. In some contexts, young women encounter restrictions on physical mobility yet enjoy relatively greater freedom in online spaces (Harding & Smith, 2022). For them, digital tools—including AI—become crucial instruments of self-education, networking, and academic support. At the same time, they may face specific pressures to excel academically as a way to secure autonomy or negotiate family expectations. The temptation to use AI aggressively to maintain high performance while juggling domestic responsibilities can be particularly intense, and conversations about integrity need to recognize this without collapsing into stereotypes.

Under all these layers lies a deeper historical rhythm. For decades, MENA education systems have been subjects of reform rhetoric: calls for "critical thinking," "student-centered learning," "innovation," often imported in policy documents and donor-funded projects, sometimes with little translation into everyday classroom life. Generative AI arrives into this landscape not as a carefully planned reform, but as a disruptive outsider, adopted bottom-up by students and, increasingly, by some faculty. It exposes the gap between slogans about creativity and the routine reality of rote assessments. In a sense, AI becomes a mirror: if an assignment can be answered convincingly by a model with minimal adaptation, then perhaps the assignment was never designed to measure what ministries and universities claim to value.

All of this means that academic integrity in the MENA region cannot be addressed by technology-neutral policies. Cultural norms around family obligation, communal honour, and coping with systemic dysfunction; the lingering dominance of high-stakes exams; multilingual navigation between local and colonial languages; habitual patterns of digital use shaped by smartphones and social media—these elements form the soil into which generative AI sinks its roots (Antia, 2021). Some of that soil is fertile for genuine innovation; some of it is saturated with anxiety and survival-mode thinking.

Responding to AI ethically, then, is not just a matter of importing guidelines from elsewhere and translating them into Arabic or French. It requires listening to how students in Beirut, Cairo, Tunis, Riyadh, Rabat, Sana'a, or Erbil actually live their educational lives: where they study, who pressures them, what they fear, what they dream of, how they already negotiate small acts of resistance or compliance every day. Only in that textured, sometimes uncomfortable space can institutional strategies around AI and integrity resonate as something more than abstract rules.

REBUILDING A CULTURE OF TRUSTWORTHY LEARNING IN AI-RICH CLASSROOMS

Rebuilding a culture of trustworthy learning in AI-rich classrooms starts with a fairly uncomfortable admission: the old culture, in many places, was already fragile before generative systems ever appeared on students' screens. Trust was often thin, built on ritual rather than relationship—students trusting that if they memorised enough, something good might happen; teachers trusting that if they set a certain number of assignments, the learning would somehow occur. Into this already delicate ecosystem walks a new presence: an invisible collaborator that can write, solve, summarise, translate, and sometimes bluff its way through tasks better than tired humans at midnight.

In that sense, the task is not simply to "restore" some lost golden age of integrity, because that age was partly imagined. The more realistic goal is to rebuild from the ground up, making trust and truthfulness explicit rather than accidental. AI is not going away, so the question becomes: what kind of classroom culture can live alongside it without being hollowed out?

Trustworthy learning begins with the way difficulty is framed. In many MENA classrooms, students have been socialised to treat struggle as a sign of weakness or failure, something to be covered up rather than explored (Abdulhadi, 2024). If a learner cannot produce a fluent paragraph in English or cannot immediately see the solution to a statistics problem, shame can arrive very quickly. Generative AI offers a tempting escape from that discomfort. One prompt, and the shame disappears behind a polished answer. Rebuilding a different culture means telling a different story about effort: that confusion is not a personal defect but part of serious thinking, that the classroom is a place where it is permitted—even expected—to be uncertain.

This sounds soft, but it is deeply practical. A teacher who openly narrates their own process, including false starts and revisions ("This was my first draft of the question; it didn't work, so here's how I changed it") creates a small crack in the façade of perfection. Students who are invited to share not only correct solutions but also failed attempts begin to see thinking as an evolving path, not a single jump to the "right" answer. Once that atmosphere is established, the conversation about AI shifts. The question becomes less "Did you use it?" and more "At which point in your struggle did you bring it in, and what did it do to your understanding?"

Transparency is the second pillar. In many institutions, AI use now lives in the shadows: students experiment privately, teachers suspect privately, administrators worry privately (Salla et al, 2024). Everyone feels that something significant is happening, and almost no one talks about it in the open. A culture of trustworthy learning asks for the opposite. AI should be named in the syllabus, discussed in the first weeks of the course, folded into the learning outcomes as something to be navigated, not smuggled.

Table 2. Institutional Response Framework for AI & Integrity

Institutional Domain	Key Action Area	Example Measures in MENA Universities	Indicative Indicators
Policy & governance	Clarify acceptable and unacceptable AI uses; embed AI in integrity codes.	Issue bilingual AI guidance; align faculty handbooks and student charters; involve student councils in drafting norms.	Existence of publicly available AI policy; staff and student awareness survey results.
Assessment design	Redesign tasks to emphasise process, reflection, and local context that AI cannot easily simulate.	Introduce oral defences, in-class synthesis tasks, reflective journals, and community-anchored projects.	Proportion of courses using AI-resilient assessment formats; student reports of meaningful learning.
Teaching & learning culture	Build classroom norms of transparency, dialogue, and shared responsibility for integrity.	Run facilitated conversations about AI in first-year seminars; model ethical use in teaching materials.	Survey measures of trust and openness; classroom observations of student participation.
Student support & AI literacy	Equip students with critical AI literacy and coping strategies for pressure and time scarcity.	Offer workshops on prompt design, verification of AI output, and healthy digital study habits.	Participation rates in AI literacy programmes; self-reported confidence in ethical AI use.

continued on following page

Table 2. Continued

Institutional Domain	Key Action Area	Example Measures in MENA Universities	Indicative Indicators
Technology & infrastructure	Choose and configure AI tools, LMS integrations, and detection systems responsibly.	Provide campus access to vetted tools; avoid overreliance on opaque detection; invest in secure networks.	Inventory of adopted tools; audits of detection tool usage and false-positive rates.
Integrity processes & justice	Ensure fair, educative handling of AI-related misconduct allegations.	Develop clear appeal routes; publish anonymised case summaries; train panels on AI-specific nuances.	Number and outcomes of AI-related cases; student perceptions of fairness and consistency.
Regional collaboration & knowledge sharing	Share MENA-specific cases, policies, and research on AI and integrity across institutions.	Create regional consortia, webinars, and Arabic-language resources on AI-integrity practices.	Joint policy statements; co-authored research; number of regional events and shared toolkits.

One concrete practice is to co-create a set of AI norms with students. Instead of dictating a long list of "thou shalt not" clauses, an educator can ask: in this course, given our goals, where might AI help you think, and where might it replace your thinking in ways we want to avoid? Students can propose categories—brainstorming, grammar checking, quick illustrations—as well as red lines—complete assignment generation, using AI to fabricate data, copying references without checking them. The final rules will still have to align with institutional policy, but the process of co-creation matters. It signals that integrity is a shared project, not an external policing mechanism. In MENA settings where young people often feel decisions are made far above them, that shared authorship is not trivial.

Trust in an AI-rich classroom also depends on making process visible (Omirali et al, 2025). For written work, this might mean students keeping a brief "process note" with each assignment: a short, honest account of how they worked, which tools they used (including AI), what they revised, what they still do not understand. For group projects, it might involve individual reflections on how the group decided whether and how to employ generative tools. These notes do not have to be elaborate; even a few sentences can reveal whether a student simply pasted a prompt into a model and accepted the first answer, or whether they engaged critically—comparing outputs, cross-checking with other sources, integrating AI suggestions with their own ideas.

In classes that thrive, AI becomes both object and tool of inquiry. Students can be asked to feed the same prompt to a model, then collectively analyse the outputs: Which arguments appear? Which voices are missing? Are any facts subtly wrong? What assumptions about the region, about language, about gender or religion are embedded in the text? When learners see that AI can be biased, superficial, or simply bizarre, the aura of infallibility begins to crack. The machine stops being a magical oracle and becomes a fallible partner. This demystification is itself a form of integrity education: it teaches that reliance on tools, human or digital, must be accompanied by judgment.

For language learners, especially in Arabic–English or Arabic–French programmes, this critical engagement can be woven into writing pedagogy. A student might be invited to draft an essay in their own words, then generate an AI version based on the same outline, and finally write a short reflection comparing the two. Which sentences in the AI text sound impressive but empty? Where does the student's own draft feel clumsy yet more honest? Such exercises can be uncomfortable—they highlight gaps in proficiency—but they also dignify the student's voice. Trustworthy learning grows when students sense that teachers value their authentic attempts, not just machine-smooth surface.

Another ingredient is the way feedback is given. In many systems, feedback is scarce, late, or purely judgmental. Comments often arrive as red marks and numbers, with little explanation. Under such conditions, it is easy for students to conclude that what matters is the grade, not the conversation. AI makes that conclusion even more tempting: if the grade is everything, and AI can help boost it, why not quietly use it? Rebuilding culture means changing what feedback feels like. When comments engage with students' reasoning, acknowledge their efforts, and pose questions rather than only corrections—"Why did you choose this example? How does this connect to your experience?"—students have a reason to bring their own minds to the task.

Figure 3. Growth of Institutions Adopting Explicit Generative AI Academic Integrity Policies

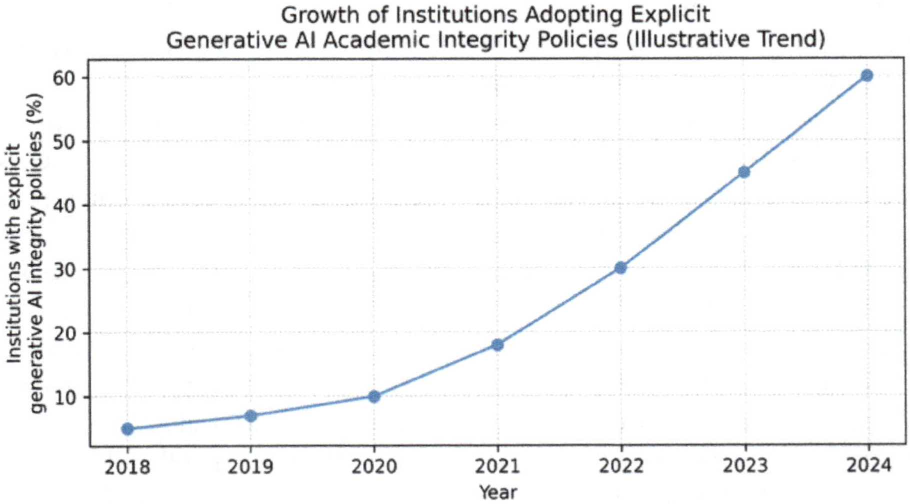

Time is a constraint, of course. In crowded MENA universities, one instructor may face hundreds of students (Daou & El Hajj, 2023). Handcrafted feedback on every piece of work is not realistic. Yet AI itself can be harnessed in careful ways to make feedback more frequent without losing the human core. For instance, an educator might use a model to generate a first set of generic comments on common issues, then personalise a subset of those comments for each student. Or students could be trained to use AI for peer-review support, with clear rubrics: they submit their peer's paper and ask the tool to highlight only certain features—cohesion, argument structure, clarity of thesis—before adding their own, human reflections. The point is not to hand feedback entirely to the machine, but to use it as a scaffold that frees human attention for the most nuanced parts.

Rebuilding trust also has a quieter, interpersonal side. In many AI debates, students are portrayed as potential cheaters, teachers as detectives, institutions as courts (Mita, 2022). That adversarial framing damages everyone. An alternative image treats the classroom as a small learning community facing a common challenge: how to grow intellectually in an era when ready-made answers are always available. When teachers share their own explorations with AI—what they find useful, what worries them, where they have decided not to use it—they model the kind of reflective stance they want students to adopt. When they admit uncertainty ("This technology is moving fast; we're figuring it out together") they invite students into a more adult conversation.

In the MENA region, where authority distances can be large, such vulnerability may feel risky for educators who have been trained to maintain a certain formality. Yet a carefully calibrated openness can strengthen rather than weaken legitimacy. Students are more likely to trust rules about AI when they sense that those rules are being crafted by people who are also wrestling with the same tools, not by remote officials who have never typed a prompt in their lives.

The physical and digital configuration of learning spaces also matters. AI-rich classrooms are not just rooms with laptops; they are environments where screens, networks, and human bodies are in constant negotiation (Beale, 2025). Simple practices can send powerful signals: moments where devices are deliberately put away to allow for screen-free dialogue; structured small-group discussions that cannot be outsourced; check-ins where students talk about how they are managing their digital habits, including AI use. On the other side, intentionally AI-on moments can be designed: a ten-minute segment where everyone experiments with a model, followed by collective debrief. The alternation between AI-off and AI-on practices helps students experience that they, not the tool, set the rhythm of their learning.

Trustworthy learning also requires that students see some consequences for honesty beyond the absence of punishment (Stitzlein, 2023). In high-stakes systems, where future opportunities hang on a few grades, telling students "learn honestly because it's good for your soul" rarely carries enough weight by itself. They need visible examples of how genuine engagement actually helps them later. Alumni testimonies, internships where shallow understanding quickly gets exposed, capstone projects that demand integration of prior knowledge—these can make the benefits of real learning concrete. When graduates say, "The courses where I couldn't hide behind copy–paste or AI are the ones that prepared me for work or further study," younger students start to connect integrity with survival, not just virtue.

For all of this to take root, institutional signals must align. If a university praises integrity in speeches but rewards departments solely on the basis of pass rates and enrolment numbers, students and staff quickly detect the contradiction. Rebuilding culture means adjusting incentives, even modestly. Recognising programmes that experiment seriously with assessment redesign, valuing educators who invest in mentoring and dialogue, tracking not just academic performance but indicators of student engagement and belonging—these are structural choices that either support or undercut classroom-level efforts.

None of this is a quick fix. Trust grows slowly, often invisibly, and it can be damaged overnight by a scandal, a perceived injustice, or a poorly handled misconduct case. In some MENA contexts, where trust in institutions is already fragile due to wider political and economic factors, the task is even heavier (Akacem et al, 2023). Yet AI, strangely, offers a kind of opportunity. It has exposed with brutal clarity the limitations of an education model built on rote, formula, and surveillance. If machines can now perform that kind of education more efficiently, humans are forced to ask: what remains that is truly ours?

A culture of trustworthy learning in AI-rich classrooms will probably look less tidy than the old, exam-centered order. There will be messy discussions, experiments that fail, disagreements about where to draw lines. Students will use AI in ways teachers did not anticipate; teachers will discover uses students had not considered. Integrity, in such a world, stops being a static rulebook and becomes a habit of mind and heart: a way of showing up to learning with honesty, curiosity, and a willingness to own both the effort and the outcome.

In the end, rebuilding this culture is not about nostalgia for a pre-digital past. It is about refusing to let automation define what counts as education. AI can generate sentences, but it cannot care. It can synthesise arguments, but it cannot choose what is worth struggling for. Classrooms that remember this—where the goal is not just correct answers but the cultivation of judgment, courage, and a sense of shared intellectual life—will remain trustworthy, even with powerful machines humming quietly in the background.

CONCLUSION

Standing at the end of this inquiry, academic integrity in the age of generative AI looks far less like a technical puzzle and far more like an ongoing negotiation about the meaning of education itself. The appearance of AI systems capable of drafting essays, solving assignments, or simulating expertise has not created the desire to bypass effort—that desire has always existed, shaped by pressure, fear, and opportunity. What AI has done is radically lower the practical barriers: the shortcut is now always within reach, on every device, in every language, at all hours.

Within MENA education systems, where youth populations are large, resources are stretched, and social mobility still hinges heavily on credentials, this shift is particularly acute. AI has become both a quiet accomplice and a potential ally. Students can lean on it to survive overwhelming workloads or compensate for uneven schooling, but they can also rely on it to avoid confronting gaps in understanding, to escape the discomfort of not knowing. Educators, in turn, can experience AI as an invisible competitor that threatens their authority, or as a catalyst that forces overdue conversations about what they truly value when they say a student has "learned."

The arguments developed in this chapter point toward a simple but uncomfortable conclusion: generative AI magnifies whatever integrity culture already exists. Where trust is thin, communication is weak, and assessments are mainly ritualistic hurdles, AI will easily become a tool for quiet evasion. Where ethics are treated as a list of prohibitions rather than a shared commitment to honest learning, students will navigate around the rules rather than internalize them. Conversely, where institutions cultivate open dialogue, explain the "why" behind academic expectations, and design tasks that genuinely require engagement, AI is more likely to be integrated as a visible, bounded, and reflective partner in the learning process.

For institutions in the MENA region, this demands more than a new paragraph in the plagiarism policy. It calls for a deliberate rethinking of several intertwined domains.

First, assessment must be reconsidered with courage, not nostalgia. Assignments that can be completed adequately by an AI with minimal human intervention are no longer reliable measures of learning, whatever their tradition or convenience. This does not mean abandoning written work, projects, or take-home tasks. It means reshaping them: embedding iterative drafts, personal reflection, oral defenses, in-class synthesis, and contextualized problems that hinge on local realities and lived experiences. When students must connect knowledge to their own contexts, critique AI outputs, or build on them thoughtfully, the space for integrity widens, not shrinks.

Second, policy needs to move from reactive prohibition to clear, nuanced guidance. Students and staff deserve unambiguous answers to practical questions: When is AI use acceptable? For which parts of an assignment? How should it be acknowledged?

What counts as excessive reliance? In multilingual MENA classrooms, these questions intersect with translation, paraphrasing, and accessibility tools. Ambiguity here is dangerous: it breeds either paralysis ("better not use anything and hope for the best") or quiet opportunism ("if no one explains the rules, anything goes").

Third, faculty support is non-negotiable. Expecting educators to "manage" AI while carrying exhausting teaching loads and lacking training is unrealistic and unfair. Institutions that treat the AI challenge as an individual teacher's problem will likely see fragmented, inconsistent practices that confuse students and undermine integrity. In contrast, when universities provide shared guidelines, professional development, spaces for experimentation, and time for redesigning courses, educators can move from defensive policing to creative leadership.

Fourth, technological responses—especially AI-detection tools—should be approached with caution and humility. Detection may play a limited role in investigating suspicious cases, but it cannot serve as the backbone of an integrity strategy. False positives risk harming precisely those students who already face linguistic and socio-economic barriers. Overreliance on surveillance can quietly erode the trust that academic integrity is meant to protect. The more institutions communicate that they fundamentally distrust their students, the less reason students have to act in good faith.

Fifth, the broader culture of academic life needs attention. Integrity is not formed only in examination halls; it is shaped in daily interactions: how teachers speak about grades, how supervisors discuss research, how administrators respond to pressure from families or officials, how role models handle their own citations and acknowledgements. In MENA systems where some students have seen adults navigate a world of informal favours, shortcuts, and bureaucratic workarounds, universities have an opportunity—and a responsibility—to model a different kind of public ethics. If AI is to be integrated responsibly, it must be nested within this wider commitment to fairness and honesty.

This chapter has also suggested that there is an opportunity hidden inside the disruption. Generative AI can be used to illustrate the very principles of integrity it threatens. Students can be invited to experiment with AI, compare its outputs to their own, critique its biases, and reflect on how it shapes their understanding. They can practice acknowledging AI contributions, just as they acknowledge human sources. They can learn to see AI not as a secret accomplice, but as a visible tool whose use must be justified and whose limits must be recognized. In this sense, AI becomes a mirror: it reveals something about students' values, teachers' expectations, and institutional priorities.

Looking ahead, the MENA region stands at a crossroads. It can choose to import ready-made AI policies that treat local contexts as an afterthought, or it can craft its own responses grounded in regional realities, languages, and aspirations. It can cling to assessment forms that AI has quietly hollowed out, or it can experiment with new, more authentic ways of demonstrating learning. It can invest energy primarily in policing, or it can channel that energy into building communities of practice, student partnerships, and cross-institutional collaborations that share resources, evidence, and stories of what works.

There is no final, stable solution on offer. AI systems will continue to evolve; new tools will emerge; clever workarounds will always exist. Integrity in this environment cannot be a static set of rules pinned to a noticeboard. It has to be a living conversation, revisited frequently, involving students as co-authors rather than passive recipients. It has to be tied to a larger vision of education where the point is not merely to obtain a degree but to grow in judgment, responsibility, and the capacity to contribute meaningfully to one's community.

For MENA education systems, carrying the weight of history, conflict, resilience, and hope, this is not a small ambition. It means insisting that academic work still matters, that effort still matters, and that truthfulness in learning is not a luxury but a form of dignity. Generative AI, with all its risks and seductions, tests the seriousness of that insistence.

If institutions respond with fear alone, they will likely end up chasing students through an ever-shifting technological maze. If, however, they respond with reflection, courage, and a willingness to redesign the conditions under which learning takes place, AI can become something else: a demanding partner that forces everyone—students, teachers, leaders—to clarify what they stand for.

In the end, academic integrity in the age of generative AI is not simply about what students do when no one is watching. It is about what universities choose to value when a powerful new technology makes both shortcuts and possibilities more visible than ever. The choices made now, across classrooms and campuses in the MENA region, will quietly shape not only how degrees are perceived, but also what kind of moral and intellectual character future graduates carry into a world where human and machine intelligence are increasingly intertwined.

REFERENCES

Abdulhadi, S. (2024). Uprooted but Unbroken: Exploring the Experiences of Yemeni Students at Yemeni Schools in Cairo.

Akacem, M., Faulkner, J. L., & Miller, D. D. (2023). Oil MENA's Challenges and the Policy Response: Addressing the Institutional and Trust Deficits. *Journal of South Asian and Middle Eastern Studies, 46*(4), 1–32. DOI: 10.1353/jsa.2023.a899953

Akbar, M. S. (2025). Beyond Detection: Designing AI-Resilient Assessments with Automated Feedback Tool to Foster Critical Thinking. arXiv preprint arXiv:2503.23622.

Antia, B. E. (2021). Multilingual examinations: Towards a schema of politicization of language in end of high school examinations in sub-Saharan Africa. *International Journal of Bilingual Education and Bilingualism, 24*(1), 138–153. DOI: 10.1080/13670050.2018.1450354

Balaji, M. T. M., & Balajiraja, N. UMA, M. P., & Nair, M. S. P. (2025). Generative AI Tools: Concepts, Applications, and Innovations. Academic Guru Publishing House.

Beale, R. (2025). The Revolution Has Arrived: What the Current State of Large Language Models in Education Implies for the Future. arXiv preprint arXiv:2507.02180.

Betz, H. C. (2025). AI and Writing: Where Are We Now? (Doctoral dissertation, The Florida State University).

Borge, M., Smith, B. K., & Aldemir, T. (2024). Using generative ai as a simulation to support higher-order thinking. *International Journal of Computer-Supported Collaborative Learning, 19*(4), 479–532. DOI: 10.1007/s11412-024-09437-0

Boudihaj, A., & Sahli, M. (2022). Education in the MENA Region. In World Education Patterns in the Global South: The Ebb of Global Forces and the Flow of Contextual Imperatives (pp. 19-41). Emerald Publishing Limited. DOI: 10.1108/S1479-36792022000043B002

Cabrera, I., Vilca, J., Oliva, E., García, K., Rojas, R., Casaverde, M., & Colonia, C. U. (2024). *Artificial intelligence in the ethics of education.* Editorial Mar Caribe. DOI: 10.70288/emc.9789915970646

Christensen Hughes, J. (2022). Academic integrity across time and place: Higher education's questionable moral calling. In *Academic integrity in Canada: An enduring and essential challenge* (pp. 25–59). Springer International Publishing. DOI: 10.1007/978-3-030-83255-1_2

Daou, L., & El Hajj, C. (2023). Challenges and Opportunities Faced by the Students and Faculty Members. Governance in Higher Education: Global Reform and Trends in the MENA Region, 89-105.

David, J. O. (2025, May). Redefining assessment for sustainability: A reflective approach to curriculum transformation in environmental education. []. Frontiers Media SA.]. *Frontiers in Education*, *10*, 1553999. DOI: 10.3389/feduc.2025.1553999

Davis, A. (2023). Academic integrity in the time of contradictions. *Cogent Education*, *10*(2), 2289307. DOI: 10.1080/2331186X.2023.2289307

Gao, R. (2025). The Erosion and Reconstruction of Teachers' Authority in the Context of Artificial Intelligence. *Journal of Theory and Practice in Education and Innovation*, *2*(2), 26–33.

Garcia, M. B. (2025). The paradox of artificial creativity: Challenges and opportunities of generative AI artistry. *Creativity Research Journal*, *37*(4), 755–768. DOI: 10.1080/10400419.2024.2354622

Harding, S., & Smith, L. M. (2022). Freedom through constraint: Young women's embodiment, space and wellbeing during lockdown. *Wellbeing, Space and Society*, *3*, 100101. DOI: 10.1016/j.wss.2022.100101 PMID: 35990881

Helsper, E. (2021). The digital disconnect: The social causes and consequences of digital inequalities.

Johnson, C. (2023). *Understanding academic integrity and plagiarism in the digital age: can digital forensics techniques help prevent and detect academic misconduct?* University of South Wales.

Kayyali, M. (2025 A). Ethical Implications of Generative AI in Education: Privacy, Bias, and Integrity. In Transformative AI Practices for Personalized Learning Strategies (pp. 185-218). IGI Global Scientific Publishing.

Kayyali, M. (2025 B). Generative AI and Education: Transforming Teaching and Learning Through Collaborative Intelligence. In Humans and Generative AI Tools for Collaborative Intelligence (pp. 25-52). IGI Global Scientific Publishing.

Kayyali, M. (2025). C). The Evolution of AI in Education From Concept to Classroom. In *Navigating Barriers to AI Implementation in the Classroom* (pp. 325–368). IGI Global Scientific Publishing. DOI: 10.4018/979-8-3373-1827-1.ch013

Kayyali, M. (2026). A). AI in higher education: The risk of excluding vulnerable learners. In *AI and New Forms of Exclusion* (pp. 57–82). IGI Global Scientific Publishing.

King, D. (2024). *Legal & Humble AI: Addressing the Legal, Ethical, and Societal Dilemmas of Generative AI.* Ingene Publishers.

Kirby, N. (2022). Institutional integrity: Its meaning and value. *Ethical Theory and Moral Practice*, *25*(5), 809–834. DOI: 10.1007/s10677-022-10330-8

Kulesz, O. (2024). Artificial Intelligence and International Cultural Relations: Challenges and Opportunities for Cross-Sectoral Collaboration.

Lee, S. (2022). A social ladder or a glass floor? The role of higher education in intergenerational social mobility: Empirical evidence from South Korea. *Higher Education Policy*, *35*(4), 969–998. DOI: 10.1057/s41307-021-00241-1

Mita, S. (2022). AI proctoring: Academic integrity vs. student rights. *The Hastings Law Journal*, *74*, 1513.

Nabilla, C., Apriani, E., & Gusmuliana, P. (2024). Promoting Students' Writing Critical Thinking By Using Paragraph Writing Ai Technology (Doctoral dissertation, Institut agama islam negeri curup).

Omirali, A., Kozhakhmet, K., & Zhumaliyeva, R. (2025). Digital Trust in Transition: Student Perceptions of AI-Enhanced Learning for Sustainable Educational Futures. *Sustainability (Basel)*, *17*(17), 7567. DOI: 10.3390/su17177567

Panjaitan, A. O., Novelyn, S., & Angreni, F. (2024). The impact of proper citation on academic integrity and scholarship. *Asian Journal of Advanced Research and Reports*, *18*(10), 192–201. DOI: 10.9734/ajarr/2024/v18i10766

Rettberg, J. W. (2024). How generative AI endangers cultural narratives. *Issues in Science and Technology*, *40*(2), 76–79. DOI: 10.58875/TJOD6844

Salla, S., Pasumarthy, A., Tadikonda, D., Parsha, T., & Mandal, S. K. (2024). Private AI in Education: Critical Challenges and Aspects of Enhancement Strategies. In Sustainable Development Using Private AI (pp. 109-131). CRC Press.

Saltman, K. J. (2022). *The alienation of fact: Digital educational privatization, AI, and the false promise of bodies and numbers*. MIT Press. DOI: 10.7551/mitpress/14387.001.0001

Schorske, C. E., & Bender, T. (2021). American academic culture in transformation: Fifty years, four disciplines.

Shah, P. (2023). *AI and the Future of Education: Teaching in the Age of Artificial Intelligence*. John Wiley & Sons.

Snoussi, T. (2024). LMS VS. SOCIAL MEDIA USE FOR LEARNING IN THE MENA REGION BEFORE THE COVID-19 PANDEMIC. Social Media, Youth, and the Global South: Comparative Perspectives, 169.

Srinivasan, V. (2022). AI & learning: A preferred future. *Computers and Education: Artificial Intelligence*, *3*, 100062.

Srivastava, S., & Kumar, M. A. S. M. V. (2025). *Unlocking Generative AI: A Beginner's Guide*. Perfect Writer Publishing.

Stitzlein, S. (2023). Teaching Honesty and Improving Democracy in the Post-Truth Era. *Educational Theory*, *73*(1), 51–73. DOI: 10.1111/edth.12565

Tolman, A. O., & Kremling, J. (Eds.). (2023). *Why students resist learning: A practical model for understanding and helping students*. Taylor & Francis.

Yan, L., Greiff, S., Teuber, Z., & Gašević, D. (2024). Promises and challenges of generative artificial intelligence for human learning. *Nature Human Behaviour*, *8*(10), 1839–1850. DOI: 10.1038/s41562-024-02004-5 PMID: 39438686

KEY TERMS AND DEFINITIONS

Academic Integrity: — the shared commitment to honesty, fairness, responsibility, and respect for knowledge in teaching, learning, and assessment, now challenged by invisible AI assistance.

AI-Assisted Misconduct: — forms of cheating where generative AI is used to draft, solve, or fabricate substantial parts of academic work that are then submitted as if produced by the student alone.

AI-Resilient Assessment: — assessment designs (e.g., oral defences, process portfolios, local case work) that still validly capture student learning even when generative AI is widely available.

Automation Bias: — the tendency of students and staff to over-trust fluent AI output and accept it with minimal scrutiny, even when it contains errors, bias, or fabricated references.

Disclosure-Based Integrity: — an emerging norm where students are expected to be transparent about *how* they used AI tools, distinguishing legitimate support from deceptive outsourcing.

Generative AI in Higher Education: — large language models and related tools that can automatically produce text, code, or media, reshaping how students complete assignments and how integrity is judged.

MENA Academic Ecosystem Pressures: — the mix of high-stakes exams, economic precarity, multilingual demands, and large classes in the MENA region that intensify temptation to rely on AI shortcuts.

Chapter 6
Artificial Intelligence in Higher Education:
Applications, Ethical Challenges, and Strategic Pathways for Institutional Transformation

Zeina Hojeij
http://orcid.org/0000-0002-7417-6610
Zayed University, UAE

Areej ElSayary
http://orcid.org/0000-0002-5554-0069
Zayed University, UAE

ABSTRACT

Artificial Intelligence (AI) is rapidly transforming higher education, reshaping pedagogical practices, administrative operations, and institutional strategies. This literature review synthesizes recent scholarship (2023–2025) to examine how AI, particularly generative tools such as ChatGPT, is being integrated across global higher education contexts. Findings highlight dual pathways of adoption: pedagogically, AI supports personalized and adaptive learning, intelligent tutoring, content creation, and collaborative learning environments; administratively, it enables data-driven decision-making, resource optimization, and student lifecycle management. While offering significant opportunities, AI adoption raises critical ethical concerns, including academic integrity, data privacy, algorithmic bias, and risks to human development and social interaction. Institutional strategies for effective AI integration emphasize the importance of responsible leadership, robust governance frameworks, faculty development, and infrastructure investment. Student perspectives reveal widespread adoption of AI tools, driven by efficiency and work-

DOI: 10.4018/979-8-2600-0328-2.ch006

load pressures, but tempered by concerns about reliability, autonomy, and social consequences. Global analyses underscore disparities in adoption across regions, with most research originating from high-income countries, leaving gaps in understanding cross-cultural and equity-focused implications. The review concludes that AI in higher education is not merely a technological shift but a systemic transformation requiring balanced approaches that align innovation with ethics, efficiency with equity, and automation with human values. Recommendations are offered for institutional leaders, faculty, students, and researchers to guide responsible and sustainable AI implementation in higher education.

1. INTRODUCTION

Artificial Intelligence (AI) has emerged as a transformative force in higher education, reshaping traditional teaching, learning, administration, and research approaches. The rapid evolution of AI technologies, particularly the advent of generative AI tools like ChatGPT, has accelerated this transformation, presenting unprecedented opportunities and complex challenges for higher education institutions worldwide. This literature review examines the current role of AI in higher education, synthesizing findings from scholarly research to provide a comprehensive understanding of how AI is being integrated across various domains of higher education and the implications of this integration.

The significance of AI in higher education has grown exponentially in recent years, driven by technological advancements, changing educational paradigms, and the need for institutions to adapt to an increasingly digital world. Ahmed (2024) observes that increasing AI adoption in higher education correlates with greater acknowledgment of its capacity to improve educational methods and results. This observation is further supported by Khairullah et al. (2025), who note that AI provides increasingly sophisticated tools for administrative and academic functions. The emergence of sophisticated AI tools, particularly large language models like ChatGPT, has further accelerated this trend. Ansari et al. (2023) report that educators and students are widely adopting these tools as convenient tools to assist teachers, students, and researchers in various tasks.

The COVID-19 pandemic has significantly accelerated the adoption of AI technologies in higher education (Crawford et al., 2024). This acceleration aligns with broader technological shifts identified by Zekaj (2023), who notes that pandemic-related disruptions created urgent needs for digital solutions. This spurt has created both opportunities and challenges as institutions navigate the integration of these powerful tools into their educational frameworks. Recent empirical studies have demonstrated that AI technologies influence students' critical, reflective, and creative thinking skills (Essel et al., 2023) while also revealing potential negative consequences such as procrastination, memory loss, and decreased academic performance when used without proper guidance (Abbas et al., 2024).

Research has identified that while AI may enhance certain aspects of student performance, it can harm achievement when social support, psychological well-being, and a sense of belonging are considered (Crawford et al., 2024). These findings align with concerns raised by Joseph (2024) regarding the social costs of excessive AI reliance in educational contexts. These findings emphasize the importance of responsible strategic leadership in AI implementation to balance innovation with ethical considerations (Khairullah et al., 2025). Recent studies distinguish between AI tools designed for academic support, such as ChatGPT, and those designed for social support and companionship (Crawford et al., 2024), highlighting the diverse applications of AI in educational contexts. Furthermore, empirical findings have revealed that students' use of AI tools is often driven by specific factors such as academic workload and time pressure (Abbas et al., 2024), providing valuable insights into the motivations behind AI adoption in higher education.

1.1 An Integrated Framework for AI in Higher Education

To move beyond a thematic description and provide a more integrative synthesis, this chapter proposes a conceptual framework that illustrates the dynamic relationships between the core domains of AI in higher education. As shown in Figure 1, this framework positions Strategic & Institutional Transformation as the central driver, influencing the three key operational domains: Pedagogical Applications, Administrative Leadership, and the Student Experience. These domains are, in turn, governed by a layer of Ethical Considerations and situated within a broader context of Global Perspectives.

Figure 1. An Integrated Framework for AI in Higher Education

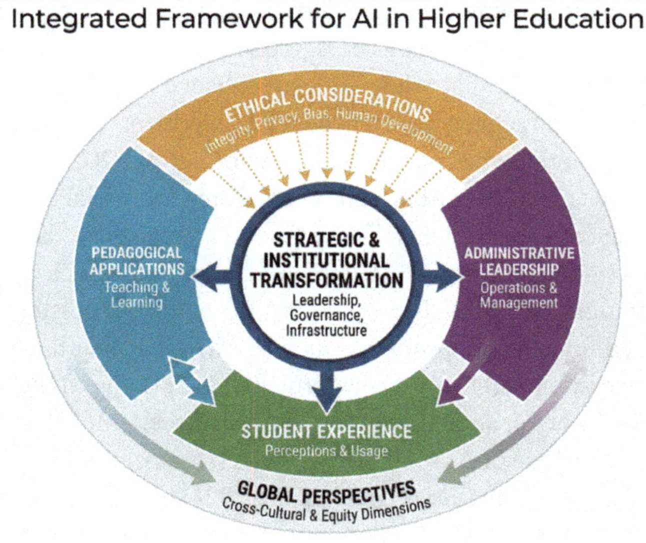

This model serves as the chapter's central argument, proposing that effective AI integration is not merely a technological challenge but a systemic one that requires a holistic approach. It posits that institutional strategy is the engine of change, directly shaping how AI is used in teaching, learning, and administration. Furthermore, it highlights the bidirectional relationship between pedagogical practices and the student experience, while also acknowledging that all AI-related activities must be continuously evaluated through an ethical lens. By using this framework as an organizing structure, this review aims to connect findings across disparate domains and provide a more coherent understanding of the systemic nature of AI's impact on higher education.

2. RESEARCH QUESTIONS

This literature review aims to analyze the current state of research on AI in higher education, identifying key themes, trends, and gaps in the literature. Specifically, this review seeks to address the following research questions:

1. What are the primary applications of AI in higher education, both pedagogical and administrative?
2. What ethical considerations and challenges are associated with AI implementation in higher education?
3. How are higher education institutions strategically approaching AI integration?

4. How do students perceive and utilize AI tools in higher education settings?

This review is structured to provide a comprehensive examination of these questions through the lens of the integrated framework presented in Figure 1. By synthesizing current research on AI in higher education, this review aims to contribute a deeper understanding of how AI is redesigning the higher education environment and provide insights that can inform policy, practice, and future research in this rapidly evolving field.

3. METHODOLOGY

This study aims to summarize the current state of artificial intelligence in higher education through an analysis of relevant published studies. The chapter employed an integrative literature review methodology, which is designed to synthesize diverse literature to create new frameworks and perspectives (Torraco, 2005). While not a formal systematic review, the process was guided by principles of transparency and replicability, adapting key stages from the PRISMA framework to identify, select, and analyze scholarly articles, guided by specific selection rules and criteria to ensure comprehensive coverage while focusing on quality, relevant sources.

3.1 Selection Rules and Criteria

Articles were included in the review based on several criteria. First, relevance was considered, with priority given to articles directly addressing AI's role, implementation, or impact in higher education contexts. Second, recency was emphasized, with priority given to recent publications (from 2023-2025) to capture the rapidly evolving landscape of AI in education, particularly following the transformative impact of the COVID-19 pandemic and the subsequent release of advanced generative AI tools like ChatGPT in late 2022. Third, thematic coverage was considered, with articles selected to represent diverse aspects of AI in higher education, including pedagogical applications, administrative functions, ethical considerations, institutional transformation, student experiences, and global perspectives. Fourth, all materials must be initially written in English or officially translated into English. Fifth, the topic of each work must explicitly connect to both artificial intelligence and higher education contexts. Finally, methodological diversity was sought, with a mix of empirical studies (both quantitative and qualitative) included in the analysis.

Specific inclusion and exclusion criteria were established to refine the selection process further. For inclusion, studies needed to (a) present an analysis of empirical data; (b) be published in peer-reviewed journal articles; (c) address how AI influences one or more aspects of higher education curriculum, instruction, and assessment, such as curriculum design, instructional planning, delivery, assessment, or evaluation. For exclusion, studies were eliminated if they (a) discussed higher education curriculum, instruction, and assessment but were unrelated to how AI impacts them; (b) presented broad perspectives on AI (such as benefits, weaknesses, or preparation) rather than its specific impact on higher education curriculum, instruction, and assessment; or (c) focused on the impact of AI on non-higher education curriculum, instruction, or assessment contexts, such as K-12 school settings.

3.2 Research Procedure

This review employed a systematic three-phase research procedure designed to ensure comprehensive coverage and methodological transparency.

Phase 1: Keyword Identification and Refinement. The researcher began the initial phase with a structured brainstorming and keyword identification stage. To generate an initial broad range of potential search terms, the researcher employed ChatGPT as an exploratory tool to obtain information about AI applications in academia and to extract candidate keywords from this content. This approach was used as a supplementary first step to identify diverse terminology and conceptual areas. The researcher employed ChatGPT to obtain information about AI applications in academia and to extract key search terms from this content. The researcher then evaluated and refined the AI-generated keywords, selecting terms including personalized education, adaptive learning platforms, intelligent learning assistants, tutoring systems, intelligent assessment and feedback, enhanced resource recommendation, literature review, information retrieval, automated manuscript writing and summarization, data analysis, interpretation, and visualization. This refinement process ensured that the final keyword set was grounded in established academic discourse rather than relying solely on AI-generated suggestions.

Phase 2: Literature Search and Retrieval. The refined keywords were used to locate relevant academic literature in the second phase of the research process. The search was conducted through two parallel methods to maximize comprehensiveness and reduce platform-specific bias. The researcher first used Consensus AI with the refined keywords to rapidly identify keyword-relevant research, using the search strings. Following this initial search, the researcher repeated the entire process on Google Scholar using the same refined keywords and search strings to ensure complete coverage and identify any additional relevant studies not captured by the first platform. This two-platform strategy strengthened the comprehensiveness of the literature search process.

Phase 3: Analysis and Synthesis. The third and final phase thoroughly examined all materials that satisfied the selection criteria and contained the identified keywords. Each selected study underwent detailed individual analysis to determine its methodology, strengths, weaknesses, recommendations, constraints, and conclusions. Studies were categorized by research methodology (empirical quantitative, empirical qualitative, theoretical/conceptual, or mixed-methods) and by thematic domain (pedagogical, administrative, ethical, strategic/institutional, student experience, or global perspectives). After individual assessment, findings across articles were integrated to recognize shared themes, patterns, inconsistencies, and research gaps. This thematic integration provided the organizational framework for the review's results section.

4. LIMITATIONS

This literature review has several limitations that should be acknowledged. While efforts were made to include diverse perspectives, the review is not exhaustive and may not capture all relevant literature on AI in higher education. The review primarily includes published scholarly articles, which may introduce publication bias by excluding unpublished studies or those with negative findings. Given the rapidly evolving nature of AI technologies and their applications in higher education, some recent developments may not be fully captured in the published literature. As noted in one of the systematic reviews analyzed (Ansari et al., 2023), most research on AI in higher education comes from high-income countries (77%), potentially limiting the global perspective. The review includes a mix of empirical studies, theoretical frameworks, and reviews, each with methodological limitations that may affect the reliability and generalizability of findings. Despite these limitations, this review provides a comprehensive synthesis of current research on AI in higher education, offering valuable insights into the current state of the field and directions for future research.

5. RESULTS

The following sections present the findings from the literature, organized according to the key operational and governing domains of the integrated framework (Figure 1). Additionally, below is the master synthesis of key literature on AI in higher education (see Table 1).

Table 1. Master Synthesis of Key Literature on AI in Higher Education

Author(s) & Year	AI Application Type	Key Finding/Argument	Methodology	Domain(s)
Abbas et al. (2024)	Generative AI (ChatGPT)	AI use is linked to procrastination and memory loss; driven by workload and time pressure.	Empirical (Quantitative)	Ethical, Student Exp.
Ahmed (2024)	General AI	AI adoption improves educational methods; ethical considerations are crucial for positive outcomes.	Conceptual	Ethical, Institutional
Ajuwon et al. (2024)	Administrative AI	AI enables data-driven decisions but raises significant data privacy and bias concerns.	Review	Admin., Ethical
Almassaad et al. (2024)	Generative AI (ChatGPT)	Students widely use AI for efficiency but worry about reliability and learning autonomy.	Empirical (Quantitative)	Student Exp.
Ansari et al. (2023)	Generative AI (ChatGPT)	AI adoption is widespread for convenience; research is dominated by high-income countries.	Systematic Review	Pedagogical, Global
Bannister et al. (2023)	Generative AI	Cultural values and language shape AI perception and use in transnational education.	Empirical (Qualitative)	Global
Barnes & Huston (2024)	General AI	Effective AI integration requires visionary leadership that balances innovation with ethics.	Conceptual	Institutional
Crawford et al. (2024)	General AI / Chatbots	AI has a net negative effect on achievement when social factors (loneliness, belonging) are considered.	Empirical (Quantitative)	Student Exp., Ethical
Cotton et al. (2024)	Generative AI (ChatGPT)	AI blurs the line between legitimate learning assistance and academic misconduct.	Conceptual	Ethical
Essel et al. (2023)	Generative AI (ChatGPT)	AI can enhance critical and reflective thinking but requires proper integration to avoid negative effects.	Empirical (Mixed-Methods)	Pedagogical, Student Exp.
Foung et al. (2024)	Generative AI (ChatGPT)	Institutions should reinvent assessments to focus on higher-order skills that AI cannot replicate.	Conceptual	Pedagogical, Ethical
Joseph (2024)	General AI / Chatbots	Over-reliance on AI can lead to social costs like loneliness, harming student success and retention.	Conceptual	Student Exp., Ethical
Katsamakas et al. (2024)	General AI	AI implementation is a systemic institutional transformation, not just a technological change.	Conceptual	Institutional
Khairullah et al. (2025)	General & Admin. AI	Responsible strategic leadership is essential to unlock AI's potential and manage ethical risks.	Review	Admin., Institutional

continued on following page

Table 1. Continued

Author(s) & Year	AI Application Type	Key Finding/Argument	Methodology	Domain(s)
Strzelecki (2024)	Generative AI (ChatGPT)	Student adoption of AI is driven by performance/effort expectancy and social influence.	Empirical (Quantitative)	Student Exp.
Yusuf et al. (2024)	Generative AI	AI presents a dual challenge to academic integrity, offering benefits while posing significant threats.	Review	Ethical, Global

5.1 Pedagogical Applications of AI in Higher Education

Artificial Intelligence has significantly transformed pedagogical approaches in higher education, offering innovative tools and methods to enhance teaching and learning processes. As the framework in Figure 1 illustrates, these pedagogical applications represent a core operational domain directly influenced by institutional strategy and, in turn, shaping the student experience. The literature reveals several key applications of AI in pedagogical contexts, including personalized education, intelligent tutoring systems, content creation and curation, and collaborative learning environments. A significant application of AI in higher education is the development of personalized and adaptive learning systems. These systems employ AI algorithms to examine student performance data and customize instructional content to address individual learning requirements. AI-powered adaptive learning platforms can analyze students' learning patterns, identify knowledge gaps, and create personalized learning paths (Abbas et al., 2024). Beyond generative AI, this includes learning analytics dashboards that provide students and instructors with real-time feedback on progress and engagement. This personalization capability enables more efficient and effective learning experiences tailored to each student's needs.

Zekaj (2023) further emphasizes that AI-powered adaptive learning systems can provide immediate feedback, adjust difficulty levels based on student performance, and offer additional resources when needed. This adaptive approach has shown promise in improving educational outcomes by addressing the diverse learning needs of students in higher education settings. The emergence of sophisticated AI chatbots and virtual assistants has created new opportunities for providing on-demand learning support to students. Ansari et al. (2023) find that ChatGPT is a convenient tool to assist teachers, students, and researchers in various tasks, with students increasingly using these tools as personal tutors for various learning purposes. These AI tutors can answer questions, explain concepts, and provide guidance outside traditional classroom hours.

The ability of AI systems to simulate human-like interactions makes them particularly valuable as learning assistants. As Zekaj (2023) notes, these systems can engage students in natural language conversations, answer questions, and provide explanations that mimic human tutoring. This capability is especially beneficial in higher education contexts where instructor availability may be limited. AI tools are increasingly used for content creation and curation in higher education. Khalifa and Albadawy (2024) highlight how AI can facilitate idea generation, improve content structuring, and support literature review processes. These capabilities enable educators and students to develop and organize educational content more efficiently.

Generative AI tools like ChatGPT have expanded these capabilities further. Almassaad et al. (2024) find that students primarily use these tools to define or clarify concepts, translate, generate ideas in writing, and summarize academic literature. This suggests that AI is becoming an integral part of the content creation process in higher education, serving as a collaborative partner in developing educational materials. AI technologies are also enhancing collaborative learning environments in higher education. Islam & Arifeen (2024) describe how AI tools can facilitate virtual teamwork, collaborative learning, and group projects by providing platforms for communication, coordination, and shared content creation. These tools are particularly valuable in supporting remote and hybrid learning environments, which have become increasingly common in higher education.

Integrating AI in collaborative learning contexts also helps prepare students for professional environments where AI-enhanced collaboration is becoming the norm. Islam & Arifeen (2024) note that these tools help prepare students for professional world challenges and develop digital competencies that are increasingly valued in the workforce. The practical implementation of AI in teaching and learning processes varies across institutions and disciplines. Almahasees et al. (2024) provide insights into implementation strategies, highlighting the importance of faculty training, infrastructure development, and alignment with educational objectives. The study emphasizes that successful implementation requires a thoughtful approach considering technological capabilities and pedagogical goals. Ansari et al.'s (2023) systematic review of 69 studies on ChatGPT use in higher education reveals that while specific uses vary, the underlying motivation remains consistent: seeking personal benefits and reducing academic burdens. This suggests that educators and students are drawn to AI tools primarily for their efficiency and convenience in educational contexts.

Recent empirical research has provided valuable insights into how AI affects students' cognitive development. Essel et al. (2023) conducted a mixed-methods study with 125 undergraduate students in Ghana, finding that incorporating ChatGPT significantly influences students' critical, reflective, and creative thinking skills. The study reveals that ChatGPT's conversational format encourages students to exchange questions and answers, promoting deeper personal reflection through scaffolding learning. Additionally, the ability to answer follow-up questions encourages students to challenge and clarify information, facilitating synthesis with actual knowledge.

AI-powered adaptive learning systems can create personalized learning paths that complement each student's unique learning preferences and aptitudes. Khairullah et al. (2025) highlight that these systems can sort through large volumes of data to develop customized learning routes, significantly improving the educational experience. Furthermore, AI-powered intelligent tutoring solutions provide students with immediate feedback and assistance, enabling them to understand different subjects better and attain learning objectives. Virtual learning assistants can enhance student engagement by providing prompt support when needed and creating more interactive learning environments.

These pedagogical applications have particular relevance in specific educational contexts. In STEM disciplines, AI tools provide specialized support for complex problem-solving and visualization (Falebita & Kok, 2024), while in humanities and social sciences, AI assists with textual analysis and language learning (Khalifa & Albadawy, 2024). Professional programs like business, medicine, and law benefit from AI-powered simulations and case-based learning that prepare students for real-world scenarios (Ajuwon et al., 2024). Distance and online education programs leverage AI to create more engaging and responsive virtual learning environments, addressing the unique challenges of remote instruction (Islam & Arifeen, 2024).

5.2 Administrative and Leadership Applications

Beyond pedagogical applications, AI is increasingly significant in administrative and leadership functions within higher education institutions. The literature identifies several key areas where AI is applied administratively, including data-driven decision-making, resource optimization, student lifecycle management, and leadership approaches to AI integration.

AI systems enhance decision-making processes in higher education administration by analyzing large datasets to identify patterns, trends, and insights. As shown in the integrated framework (Figure 1), these administrative applications are a key operational domain driven by institutional strategy. The literature identifies several key administrative applications of AI, including predictive analytics for student success, resource allocation optimization, and automated student support services. For example, institutions are increasingly using predictive models for student success to identify at-risk students and provide timely interventions, moving beyond the common focus on generative AI. Ajuwon et al. (2024) highlight how AI enables data-driven decision-making by processing and analyzing institutional data more efficiently and accurately than traditional methods. This capability allows administrators to make more informed decisions based on comprehensive data analysis.

Sain et al. (2024) further emphasize that AI-powered analytics can provide insights into student enrollment, engagement, and retention, helping administrators identify factors affecting student success and implement targeted interventions. These data-driven approaches are particularly valuable for addressing complex challenges in higher education management.

AI-driven predictive analytics offers powerful tools for administrative decision-making. According to Khairullah et al. (2025), these analytics help academic institutions spot patterns and trends for data-driven decisions about resource allocation, budgeting, and focused interventions that boost student achievement. This capability is particularly valuable regarding limited resources and increasing demands on higher education institutions. AI also optimizes resource allocation and management in higher education institutions. Ajuwon et al. (2024) describe how AI systems can analyze resource utilization patterns to identify inefficiencies and recommend optimal allocation strategies.

The literature also highlights the role of AI in student lifecycle management, from recruitment and admissions to retention and career services. Sain et al. (2024) note that AI tools can support personalized communication with prospective students, automate administrative processes, and provide targeted support for at-risk students. These applications can enhance operational efficiency and student experiences throughout their educational journey. Khairullah et al. (2025) emphasize that AI can streamline administrative tasks by enhancing admissions and enrollment processes, academic records management systems, and financial aid and scholarship processes. By automating mundane and monotonous tasks, AI allows staff and faculty members to concentrate more on responsibilities and strategic initiatives that require focused attention.

Leadership approaches to AI integration emerge as a critical factor in successful implementation. Barnes and Huston (2024) emphasize the importance of visionary leadership, strategic planning, and stakeholder engagement in guiding AI implementation in higher education. They highlight that effective leaders balance innovation with ethical considerations, ensuring AI adoption aligns with institutional values and educational goals. Strategic leadership plays a crucial role in successful AI implementation in administrative contexts. Khairullah et al. (2025) emphasize that responsible strategic leadership is key to unlocking the significant potential of AI in higher education institutions.

The literature also identifies several challenges in administrative AI implementation, including data quality issues, integration with existing systems, staff training needs, and ethical concerns. Ajuwon et al. (2024) note that addressing these challenges requires a comprehensive approach that considers the technical, organizational, and ethical dimensions of AI implementation. This multifaceted approach is essential for realizing the potential benefits of AI in higher education administration while mitigating potential risks. Integrating AI into administrative procedures can usher in a new age of efficient and data-driven decision-making, with far-reaching impacts on higher education management and leadership.

5.3 Ethical Considerations and Challenges

Implementing AI in higher education raises significant ethical considerations and challenges that institutions must navigate. These concerns form the governing layer of our conceptual framework (Figure 1), highlighting the need for ethical oversight across all AI applications in higher education. The literature identifies several key ethical dimensions, including academic integrity concerns, data privacy and security, algorithmic bias and fairness, and impacts on human development and social interaction. Academic integrity emerges as a primary ethical concern in the literature, particularly with the advent of generative AI tools like ChatGPT. Yusuf et al. (2024) examine the fundamental question of whether generative AI threatens academic integrity or reformation in higher education. Their study explores perspectives from diverse global contexts, finding that while generative AI tools offer significant educational benefits, they simultaneously present substantial challenges to academic integrity.

The literature identifies several academic integrity challenges, including plagiarism, cheating, and blurring boundaries between legitimate assistance and academic misconduct. This creates a central pedagogical tension: AI tools can serve as a powerful scaffold for learning, but they can also become a shortcut that undermines the development of critical cognitive skills and encourages procrastination (Abbas et al., 2024). Cotton et al. (2024) examine the dual nature of chatting and cheating in the era of ChatGPT, highlighting how the same tools that can enhance learning can also facilitate academic misconduct. Their study emphasizes that the line between legitimate assistance and cheating has become increasingly blurred, creating significant challenges for students navigating ethical use and institutions developing appropriate policies.

Data privacy and security represent another significant ethical concern in AI implementation. Ajuwon et al. (2024) highlight data privacy, cybersecurity, and algorithmic bias as significant ethical considerations in administrative AI applications. The study emphasizes that as institutions increasingly rely on AI systems for decision-making and student support, the volume and sensitivity of data being processed create substantial privacy risks. These concerns are particularly relevant given the sensitive nature of educational data, which may include academic performance and personal characteristics, behaviors, and even biometric information in some applications. Algorithmic bias and fairness emerge as critical ethical considerations in the literature. Ajuwon et al. (2024) specifically identify algorithmic bias as a concern in administrative applications, highlighting the risk that AI systems may perpetuate or amplify existing inequities if not carefully designed and monitored. The study notes that AI systems trained on historical data may replicate and amplify existing patterns of bias and discrimination, potentially disadvantaging already marginalized student populations. This concern is particularly relevant in higher education contexts, where historical inequities related to race, gender, socioeconomic status, and other factors are well-documented.

The literature also raises concerns about the potential impacts of AI on human development and social interaction in educational contexts. Ansari et al. (2023) note concerns about potential negative effects on cognitive and social development associated with AI use in educational contexts. Their systematic review finds that these concerns are consistently highlighted in many studies, suggesting widespread recognition of the potential risks to student development posed by uncritical or excessive AI use. The review emphasizes that while AI tools can enhance certain learning aspects, they may undermine the development of important cognitive and social skills if not thoughtfully integrated into educational practices.

Moreover, there are several approaches to addressing ethical challenges in AI implementation. Ahmed (2024) highlights the importance of incorporating ethical considerations in the administrative implementation of AI systems, including robust data governance frameworks that address privacy and security concerns. Similarly, Barnes and Huston (2024) emphasize the role of leadership in navigating ethical challenges through clear vision, values-based decision-making, and inclusive governance processes. These approaches recognize that addressing ethical challenges requires technical solutions, organizational structures, and cultural norms supporting responsible AI use.

Recent studies have revealed the ethical implications of AI usage in higher education. Abbas et al. (2024) conclude that ChatGPT usage is associated with tendencies for procrastination and memory loss and negatively impacts students' academic performance. Their study, which used a three-wave time-lagged design with 494 university students, provides concrete evidence of potential negative consequences that must be addressed through ethical frameworks and policies.

Institutional concerns about AI tools have led to varied responses. Abbas et al. (2024) note that some academic institutions in the United States have prohibited ChatGPT due to concerns about academic cheating, highlighting the conflict between innovation and academic integrity. This tension is particularly evident in developing countries like Ghana, which lack standard policies governing the integration of AI-based models into educational institutions (Essel et al., 2023).

The implementation of AI in higher education also raises significant concerns about biases in AI systems. Khairullah et al. (2025) identify questions about accountability, transparency, privacy, and security as critical ethical challenges that must be addressed. Robust data governance, informed consent, and cybersecurity measures are essential for guaranteeing the privacy and security of student data in AI-driven systems.

5.3.1 Operationalizing Ethical Governance

Addressing these ethical challenges requires institutions to move beyond theoretical discussion to implement concrete operational mechanisms. The literature suggests that effective ethical governance involves mapping principles to specific institutional practices. As shown in Table 2, this involves creating clear policies and procedures for data privacy, algorithmic bias, and human development to ensure that ethical considerations are embedded in the entire lifecycle of AI implementation.

Table 2. Framework for Operationalizing Ethical Governance in AI Implementation

Ethical Principle	Operational Mechanism
Data Privacy & Security	• Enforce comprehensive data governance policies. • Implement secure procurement processes with vendor vetting. • Establish clear protocols for data consent, storage, and access.
Algorithmic Bias & Fairness	• Conduct regular, independent audits of AI tools for bias. • Mandate transparency reports from AI vendors. • Create appeal processes for students affected by algorithmic decisions.
Human Development & Well-being	• Invest in mandatory AI literacy programs for all students and staff. • Develop faculty training on ethical AI pedagogy. • Preserve human-in-the-loop decision-making for high-stakes issues.

This structured approach ensures that ethical principles are not merely aspirational but are translated into accountable, transparent, and actionable institutional processes.

5.4 Institutional Transformation and Strategic Implementation

AI is revolutionizing higher education institutions fundamentally, necessitating comprehensive strategic frameworks for effective implementation and integration across organizational structures. This includes organizational change processes, strategic planning frameworks, faculty development initiatives, and infrastructure requirements for effective AI integration. Katsamakas et al. (2024) examine how AI is redesigning institutional structures, processes, and cultures through a systems approach. The study emphasizes that AI implementation is not merely a technological change but a transformative process that affects all aspects of institutional functioning, from teaching and learning to administration and research.

The literature identifies several strategic frameworks for guiding AI implementation in higher education. Barnes and Huston (2024) present a comprehensive framework that addresses AI implementation's technological, organizational, and ethical dimensions. The model emphasizes aligning AI initiatives with institutional mission and values, engaging diverse stakeholders in implementation processes, and developing appropriate governance structures to guide responsible AI use. This strategic approach recognizes that successful AI implementation requires careful planning and coordination across multiple institutional domains.

Faculty development emerges as a critical component of successful AI implementation. Mah and Groß (2024) explore artificial intelligence in higher education. They find that faculty require significant support to develop the knowledge and skills to integrate AI effectively into their teaching and research practices. The study emphasizes that faculty development initiatives should address technical skills, pedagogical approaches, and ethical considerations related to AI use. This approach to faculty development is essential for ensuring that AI tools enhance rather than undermine educational quality and integrity.

Infrastructure requirements for AI implementation are also highlighted in the literature. Almahasees et al. (2024) emphasize the importance of developing appropriate technological infrastructure, data management systems, and support services for effective AI use. Their study notes that educational goals and users should guide infrastructure development needs rather than be driven solely by technological capabilities. This user-centered approach to infrastructure development helps ensure that AI systems effectively support institutional priorities and stakeholder needs.

Substantial challenges hinder institutional transformation and strategic AI implementation, including persistent resistance to change, significant resource limitations, and complex coordination issues that divide efforts across diverse institutional units. Katsamakas et al. (2024) emphasize the importance of change management approaches that address these challenges through clear communication, stakeholder engagement, and phased implementation strategies. These approaches recognize that successful institutional transformation requires technological innovation and organizational and cultural change. Responsible strategic leadership is essential for successful institutional transformation through AI integration. Khairullah et al. (2025) emphasize that strategic leadership requires aligning AI integration goals with the strategic mission of higher education institutions, fostering an environment ready to embrace innovation, and ensuring that the required accountability and governance frameworks are in place for AI integration and usage. This comprehensive approach recognizes that successful AI implementation requires technological innovation and organizational and cultural change.

The balance between innovation and addressing implementation challenges is critical to institutional transformation. Khairullah et al. (2025) identify several challenges, including biases in AI systems, questions about accountability, transparency, privacy and security, and concerns about job displacement. Addressing these challenges requires a multifaceted approach that considers the technical, organizational, and ethical dimensions of AI implementation. The post-pandemic context has accelerated institutional transformation through technology. Crawford et al. (2024) position AI as potentially the 'new-new-norm' in a post-pandemic learning environment, noting that COVID-19 accelerated the introduction of online technologies in higher education. This acceleration has created opportunities and challenges for institutional transformation, requiring thoughtful leadership and strategic planning.

Furthermore, a comprehensive view of institutional transformation requires broadening the stakeholder analysis beyond faculty and students. The integration of AI profoundly impacts the roles and workloads of professional and support staff. Learning technologists and instructional designers are tasked with supporting faculty in adopting new pedagogical tools and redesigning curricula. Librarians are developing new methods for information literacy in an AI-driven landscape, while IT and security staff face new challenges in data governance, procurement, and infrastructure management. Quality assurance departments must also adapt their processes to evaluate AI-integrated programs. Acknowledging the critical role of these staff members is essential for a holistic, systems-level understanding of the organizational change required for successful AI adoption.

5.5 Student Experience and Outcomes

Research provides insights into how AI affects student experiences and outcomes in higher education, including student perceptions and adoption patterns, impacts on learning processes and outcomes, and implications for student development and well-being. Student perceptions and adoption patterns are a significant focus in the literature. Almassaad et al. (2024) find that 78.7% of students in their study frequently use generative AI tools, with ChatGPT being the most popular (86.2%). The study identifies everyday use cases, including defining or clarifying concepts, translating, generating writing ideas, and summarizing academic literature. These findings suggest the widespread adoption of AI tools among students for diverse academic purposes.

In addition, the literature identifies several factors that influence student adoption of AI tools. Strzelecki (2024) examines students' acceptance of ChatGPT in higher education through an extended unified theory of acceptance and use of technology. The study finds that performance expectancy, effort expectancy, social influence, and facilitating conditions significantly affect students' intentions to use AI tools. These findings highlight the complex interplay of technological, social, and contextual factors that shape student adoption patterns. Student perceptions of AI tools reveal both perceived benefits and concerns. Almassaad et al. (2024) found that students perceive several benefits of AI tools, including ease of access, time-saving, and instant feedback. However, they also express concerns about subscription costs, unreliable information, plagiarism, reduced human-to-human interaction, and impacts on learning autonomy. This perspective suggests that students are aware of both the potential advantages and limitations of AI tools in educational contexts.

Emerging empirical research explores AI's impact on learning processes and outcomes, revealing promising but still-developing evidence in this critical area. Essel et al. (2023) explore ChatGPT's effects on undergraduate students' cognitive skills, finding that AI-based conversational large language models can enhance certain aspects of learning while potentially undermining others. Their study emphasizes the importance of thoughtful integration of AI tools into educational practices to maximize benefits while mitigating potential negative effects on learning. Implications for student development and well-being are also addressed in the literature. Joseph (2024) examines when artificial intelligence substitutes humans in higher education, focusing on the cost of loneliness, student success, and retention. The study highlights the potential social costs of excessive reliance on AI, noting that human connection and relationship remain essential components of effective education, particularly for supporting student well-being and persistence. This perspective emphasizes that while AI can enhance certain aspects of education, it cannot fully replace the human dimensions of teaching and learning.

Various research-based strategies emerge for optimizing student experiences with AI. Foung et al. (2024) propose reinventing assessments with ChatGPT and other online tools, arguing for AI-empowered assessment practices that leverage rather than prohibit AI tools. This approach involves redesigning assessments to focus on higher-order thinking skills, creative application, and critical evaluation rather than content reproduction. Similarly, Nayak (2024) advocates for inclusive learning and assessment in the era of AI, emphasizing the need for assessment approaches that maintain integrity while accommodating diverse learning needs and technological realities.

When it comes to the factors driving students' use of AI tools, Abbas et al. (2024) find that when students face higher academic workload and time pressure, they are more likely to use ChatGPT. Their study reveals that students use AI as a coping mechanism when faced with high workload and time pressure, looking for shortcuts to manage stressful academic situations. Interestingly, in their study, students who were sensitive to rewards were less likely to use ChatGPT, suggesting complex motivational factors at play in AI adoption. Moreover, the social impact of AI on student experience is a critical consideration. Crawford et al. (2024) find that while AI may be associated with student performance, when social support, psychological well-being, loneliness, and sense of belonging are considered, AI has a negative effect on achievement. Their research examines the consequences when students choose to seek support from AI rather than humans (e.g., librarians, professors, or student advisors), highlighting potential negative social outcomes. This finding is particularly significant given the importance of the sense of belonging for student motivation, achievement, attention, engagement, retention, resilience, self-esteem, and enjoyment of learning. The impact of AI on cognitive skills has also been investigated. Essel et al. (2023) find that incorporating ChatGPT influences students' critical, reflective, and creative thinking skills. Their study, which uses a mixed-methods approach with 125 undergraduate students, provides evidence that AI tools can enhance certain aspects of cognitive development when properly integrated into educational contexts.

Distinct patterns emerge in how AI impacts various student populations according to studies. First-generation students often benefit from AI-powered learning support but may face technology access barriers (Opesemowo & Adekomaya, 2024). International students use AI tools for language support and cultural navigation, though language-specific limitations affect non-English speakers (Ansari et al., 2023). Students with disabilities leverage AI for accessibility enhancements, while graduate students employ more sophisticated AI applications for research and complex analysis than undergraduates (Almassaad et al., 2024). Socioeconomic factors create digital divides in AI access and utilization patterns, reinforcing the need for equity-focused implementation strategies (Falebita & Kok, 2024).

5.6 Global and Cross-Cultural Perspectives

The literature provides insights into how AI implementation in higher education varies across different global contexts, including regional adoption patterns, cultural factors influencing AI use, and implications for global educational equity. Significant variations in AI implementation across different global contexts are evident in regional adoption patterns. Ansari et al. (2023) find in their systematic review that most research on ChatGPT in higher education comes from high-income countries (77%), with limited representation from low- and middle-income countries. This finding highlights a potential gap in our understanding of how AI is being implemented and experienced in diverse global contexts.

Several factors contributing to regional variations in AI adoption are also identified in the literature, including technological infrastructure, regulatory frameworks, educational traditions, and economic resources. Falebita and Kok (2024) examine strategic goals for artificial intelligence integration among STEM academics and undergraduates in African higher education, highlighting how resource constraints and infrastructure limitations affect AI implementation in these contexts. Their study emphasizes the importance of context-sensitive AI implementation approaches considering local conditions and needs. Cultural factors influencing AI use are also addressed as Bannister et al. (2023) explore transnational higher education cultures and generative AI, presenting a nominal group study for policy development in English medium instruction. They highlight how cultural values, educational traditions, and linguistic factors shape perceptions and uses of AI in different cultural contexts. These findings emphasize the importance of culturally sensitive approaches to AI implementation that respect diverse perspectives and practices. Yusuf et al. (2024) present evidence from multicultural perspectives on generative AI and the future of higher education, highlighting the benefits of sharing insights and approaches across different cultural contexts. They emphasize that cross-cultural collaboration can enrich the understanding of both the opportunities and challenges associated with AI in higher education and support the development of more inclusive and effective implementation strategies.

Implications for global educational equity are also examined in the literature. Opesemowo and Adekomaya (2024) explore harnessing artificial intelligence for advancing sustainable development goals in South Africa's higher education system, emphasizing the potential of AI to address educational inequities while also acknowledging the risk of exacerbating existing disparities if not thoughtfully implemented. Their study highlights the importance of equitable approaches to AI implementation that prioritize access, inclusion, and capacity building in underserved contexts. Finally, among the challenges identified in global AI implementation are language barriers, cultural misalignments, and resource disparities. Ansari et al. (2023) note that language-specific challenges are particularly significant for non-English speaking contexts, as most AI tools are developed primarily for English language use. These challenges highlight the importance of developing AI tools and implementation approaches that accommodate linguistic and cultural diversity in global higher education.

6. DISCUSSION

This literature review synthesizes findings from scholarly articles on the current role of AI in higher education, revealing a complex landscape of applications, challenges, and emerging practices. The discussion examines key patterns, contradictions, and gaps identified across the literature and considers implications for practice and future research. A clear pattern emerging from the literature is the rapid adoption of AI technologies across diverse domains of higher education, from teaching and learning to administration and research. This widespread adoption reflects growing recognition of AI's potential to enhance educational processes and outcomes, though the specific applications and implementation approaches vary significantly across different contexts and institutions.

6.1 RQ1 - Primary Applications of AI in Higher Education

The findings reveal dual tracks of AI implementation in higher education. Pedagogically, AI serves as a personalized learning facilitator, intelligent tutor, content creator, and collaborative learning enabler across diverse disciplines and educational contexts (Zekaj, 2023; Almassaad et al., 2024). These applications leverage AI's capabilities to adapt to individual learning needs, provide immediate feedback, generate educational content, and facilitate collaborative learning experiences. The effectiveness of these applications varies across different educational contexts, with some studies showing promising results in improving student engagement and learning outcomes while others caution about potential limitations. Administratively, AI functions as a data analyst for decision-making, resource optimizer, and student lifecycle manager, with particular strengths in predictive analytics and process automation (Ajuwon et al., 2024; Khairullah et al., 2025). Higher education institutions increasingly use AI to analyze large datasets for strategic planning, optimize resource allocation, and manage various aspects of the student lifecycle, from recruitment to alumni engagement. These administrative applications demonstrate AI's potential to enhance operational efficiency and effectiveness, though their implementation often requires significant organizational change and capacity building.

Despite the widespread adoption of AI across these domains, a notable gap exists between theoretical potential and empirical evidence of effectiveness. While many studies highlight AI's potential benefits in enhancing educational experiences and outcomes, rigorous empirical research demonstrating these benefits remains limited. This gap is particularly evident in discussions of learning outcomes, where claims about AI's potential to improve educational effectiveness often outpace empirical evidence. As Ansari et al. (2023) note in their systematic review, more rigorous empirical research is needed to examine AI's actual impacts on teaching, learning, and administrative processes in higher education. The quality of existing empirical studies varies considerably, with many relying on small samples, short-term interventions, or self-reported data that may not capture the full complexity of AI's educational impact.

6.2 RQ2 - Ethical Considerations and Challenges

The literature identifies several critical ethical concerns associated with AI implementation in higher education. Academic integrity issues emerge prominently, with studies demonstrating the conflict between AI as a learning aid and a potential facilitator of misconduct (Yusuf et al., 2024; Cotton et al., 2024). This is particularly evident in discussions of generative AI tools like ChatGPT, which can be used for legitimate educational purposes but also to circumvent traditional assessment approaches. The research suggests that addressing these concerns requires ethical guidelines and fundamental rethinking of assessment approaches to emphasize skills and processes that AI cannot easily replicate.

Data privacy and security concerns grow as institutions collect and process increasingly sensitive student information (Ajuwon et al., 2024). AI systems often require extensive data to function effectively, raising questions about data ownership, consent, and protection. The literature suggests that institutional approaches to these concerns vary significantly, with some institutions developing comprehensive data governance frameworks while others struggle to address these issues systematically.

Algorithmic bias threatens to perpetuate or amplify existing inequities if not carefully addressed (Ajuwon et al., 2024). Research demonstrates that AI systems can inherit biases from their training data or design processes, potentially disadvantaging certain student groups. Ahmed's (2024) finding that ethical considerations moderate the relationship between AI usage and academic achievement provides evidence of this contradiction, suggesting that ethical considerations cannot be treated as an afterthought but must be integrated into implementation strategies. This research represents a significant contribution to understanding the ethical dimensions of AI in education, as it moves beyond theoretical concerns to empirically demonstrate the relationship between ethical implementation and educational outcomes.

Additionally, research reveals concerning impacts on student development, including procrastination tendencies and memory challenges (Abbas et al., 2024). The social dimensions of AI use in education also require careful consideration. Crawford et al. (2024) find that individuals who lack human companionship are more vulnerable to developing AI relationships in place of human-human relationships. Their research raises concerns about dependency on AI chatbots, noting that participants may develop dependencies that potentially lower their capacity and confidence in building new human relationships over time. This finding suggests a relationship between AI and student agency, which depends significantly on how AI tools are implemented and used in specific educational contexts.

Foung et al. (2024) argue in their exploration of reinventing assessments with ChatGPT and other online tools that addressing these ethical tensions requires fundamentally rethinking educational practices rather than simply applying ethical constraints to existing approaches. This perspective suggests that the most effective responses to ethical challenges may involve reimagining educational practices that align with both technological possibilities and ethical principles. The quality of this argument is strengthened by its recognition of the systemic nature of ethical challenges, which cannot be addressed through isolated interventions but require comprehensive institutional responses.

6.3 RQ3 - Institutional Strategic Approaches to AI Integration

The literature reveals multifaceted implementation frameworks for AI integration in higher education. Successful approaches align AI initiatives with institutional mission and values while engaging diverse stakeholders in implementation processes (Barnes & Huston, 2024). This alignment ensures that AI implementation serves institutional priorities rather than being driven solely by technological possibilities. The research suggests that institutions that develop clear connections between AI initiatives and their core educational and organizational goals are more likely to achieve meaningful and sustainable implementation.

Comprehensive faculty development initiatives address technical skills, pedagogical approaches, and ethical considerations (Mah & Groß, 2024). These initiatives recognize that effective AI implementation requires technical capacity, pedagogical innovation, and ethical awareness. Mah and Groß's (2024) exploration of faculty use, self-efficacy, distinct profiles, and professional development needs represents an important contribution to understanding these dimensions. However, more research is needed to evaluate the effectiveness of different faculty development approaches across diverse institutional contexts.

Infrastructure development follows user-centered principles rather than being driven solely by technological capabilities (Almahasees et al., 2024). This approach emphasizes the importance of developing AI infrastructure that responds to actual user needs and contexts rather than implementing technologies because they are available. The research suggests that user-centered approaches are more likely to result in sustainable and effective implementation, though they may initially require more time and resources.

Strategic leadership emerges as essential, balancing innovation with ethical considerations through clear vision, values-based decision-making, and inclusive governance (Khairullah et al., 2025). The literature suggests that leadership approaches vary significantly across institutions, with some adopting top-down approaches while others emphasize distributed leadership and stakeholder engagement. The effectiveness of different leadership approaches appears to depend on institutional context, culture, and capacity, suggesting the need for context-sensitive approaches rather than universal models.

These findings demonstrate that successful AI implementation requires coordinated efforts across technological, organizational, and ethical domains. The literature suggests that institutions that address these multiple integrated dimensions are more likely to achieve meaningful and sustainable AI implementation. However, the specific approaches that work best may vary across different institutional contexts.

6.4 RQ4 - Student Perceptions and Utilization of AI Tools

The findings reveal widespread adoption of AI tools among students with attitudes toward their benefits and limitations. Research demonstrates high adoption rates (78.7%), with ChatGPT being the most popular (86.2%), used primarily for defining concepts, translation, idea generation, and summarizing literature (Almassaad et al., 2024). This high adoption rate suggests that AI tools have quickly become part of the educational landscape, but the specific uses and perceptions vary across different student populations.

Student adoption is influenced by multiple factors, including performance expectancy, effort expectancy, social influence, and facilitating conditions (Strzelecki, 2024). This multi-layered adoption model suggests that students consider both the perceived benefits of AI tools and the ease of using them and social and contextual factors that enable or constrain their use. This research provides a more sophisticated understanding of student adoption than earlier studies that focused primarily on technological factors.

Students perceive both benefits and challenges associated with AI use. Benefits include time-saving and instant feedback, while concerns encompass reliability, plagiarism, and reduced human interaction (Almassaad et al., 2024). Almassaad et al.'s finding that students express concerns about impacts on learning autonomy highlights conflicts from the student perspective. This research suggests a complex relationship between AI and student agency, which depends significantly on how AI tools are implemented and used in specific educational contexts.

Usage patterns vary significantly across diverse student populations, with different benefits and challenges for first-generation students, international students, students with disabilities, and graduate versus undergraduate students (Opesemowo & Adekomaya, 2024; Ansari et al., 2023; Falebita & Kok, 2024). This variation suggests that AI implementation strategies must be sensitive to different student populations' diverse needs and contexts rather than assuming universal experiences or approaches. The research on these differences is still emerging, with most studies focusing on specific populations rather than comparative analyses, suggesting the need for more comprehensive research in this area.

These findings highlight the need for specific, equity-focused implementation strategies that recognize and respond to the diverse ways in which students perceive and use AI tools. The research suggests that one-size-fits-all approaches are unlikely to be effective, given the significant variation in student experiences and needs. Instead, institutions need to develop flexible and responsive approaches that can adapt to different student contexts and evolve as student needs and uses change over time.

7. CROSS-CUTTING THEMES, CONTRADICTIONS, AND GAPS

Several important cross-cutting themes, contradictions, and gaps emerge from the literature on AI in higher education. One significant theme is the discord between innovation and ethical considerations in AI implementation. While the literature consistently acknowledges AI's potential benefits in higher education, it also highlights significant ethical challenges related to academic integrity, data privacy, algorithmic bias, and impacts on human development. This is evident in discussions of both pedagogical and administrative applications, suggesting that it is a fundamental aspect of AI implementation rather than a domain-specific concern. Another important theme is the relationship between AI and human agency in educational contexts. The literature reveals contradictory perspectives on how AI affects student agency. Some studies suggest that AI tools can enhance student agency by providing personalized support and removing barriers to learning. Others emphasize the risk of creating dependency and undermining students' development of independent thinking and problem-solving skills. This contradiction suggests a complex relationship between AI and student agency, which depends significantly on how AI tools are implemented and used in specific educational contexts.

The literature also reveals contrasting viewpoints on institutional approaches to AI, particularly generative AI tools like ChatGPT. Some perspectives suggest that prohibiting certain AI uses may be necessary in some contexts. Others advocate for integration approaches that acknowledge the reality of AI tools and focus on guiding their responsible use. This reflects different assessments of the balance between risks and benefits of AI in educational contexts and different institutional capacities for managing these risks. It also highlights the challenge of developing ethically sound and practically effective approaches in real educational environments, where complete prohibition may be difficult to enforce. It may create new ethical challenges related to surveillance and punishment.

The limited representation of diverse global perspectives on AI in higher education is a significant gap in the current literature. Ansari et al. (2023) note in their systematic review that most research on ChatGPT in higher education comes from high-income countries (77%), limiting our understanding of how AI is implemented and experienced in diverse global contexts. This gap is particularly notable given the global nature of both higher education and AI development and the potential for cultural differences to shape perceptions and uses of AI in educational contexts. Another major gap is the limited empirical evidence on the long-term impacts of

AI on cognitive development, educational outcomes, and social dynamics in higher education. While many studies raise concerns about potential negative effects on critical thinking, creativity, and interpersonal skills, longitudinal research examining these effects over time is notably scarce. This gap is particularly important given the potentially profound implications of AI for how students learn, think, and interact in educational contexts.

While student perspectives on AI are increasingly well-represented in the literature, faculty perspectives remain relatively underexplored.

The empirical evidence on AI's impact on higher education presents a complex picture with contradictory findings. Abbas et al. (2024) note that existing studies provide contradictory evidence on whether ChatGPT is helpful or harmful for students. Their research identified that most prior studies consist of theoretical discussions, commentaries, or reviews, with limited empirical research on the factors driving ChatGPT usage among university students. This gap in empirical research highlights the need for more rigorous studies examining the actual impacts of AI on teaching, learning, and administrative processes in higher education.

8. IMPLICATIONS FOR PRACTICE

The literature suggests several implications for practice in AI implementation in higher education. First, there is a need for comprehensive institutional frameworks that address multiple dimensions of AI implementation, including technological, pedagogical, ethical, and organizational aspects. These frameworks should be developed through inclusive processes involving diverse stakeholders and integrated into broader institutional strategies and governance structures. The research suggests that such frameworks are more likely to result in sustainable and effective implementation than approaches that focus primarily on technological adoption without addressing broader organizational and ethical considerations.

Second, there is a need for faculty and student development initiatives that build capacity for effective and responsible AI use. These initiatives should address technical skills, ethical awareness, critical thinking, and pedagogical approaches that leverage AI to enhance rather than undermine educational quality and integrity. The research suggests that such initiatives are essential for ensuring that AI implementation enhances rather than diminishes the quality and integrity of higher education. More research is needed to identify the most effective approaches to such development across different institutional contexts.

Third, there is a need for assessment approaches that acknowledge the reality of AI tools while maintaining academic standards and promoting meaningful learning. This may involve redesigning assessments to focus on higher-order thinking skills, creative application, and critical evaluation rather than content reproduction. The research suggests that such redesign is essential for addressing academic integrity concerns associated with AI despite the need for significant pedagogical innovation and institutional support.

Fourth, there is a need for ethical governance structures that guide responsible AI implementation while allowing for innovation and adaptation. These structures should involve diverse stakeholders in decision-making processes and should be grounded in clear ethical principles while maintaining flexibility to respond to rapidly evolving technological landscapes. The research suggests that such governance is essential for navigating the ethical challenges of AI implementation, even though effective governance approaches may vary across different institutional contexts and cultures.

9. RECOMMENDATIONS

Based on the findings of this review, several recommendations can be offered for different stakeholders in higher education:

9.1 For Institutional Leaders and Administrators

1. Develop comprehensive strategic frameworks that address multiple dimensions of AI implementation, including technological, pedagogical, ethical, and organizational aspects (Khairullah et al., 2025; Barnes & Huston, 2024). These frameworks should be developed through inclusive processes involving diverse stakeholders and integrated into broader institutional strategies and governance structures.
2. Invest in infrastructure, resources, and professional development needed to support effective and responsible AI implementation, recognizing that successful implementation requires both technological innovation and organizational and cultural change (Mah & Groß, 2024; Almahasees et al., 2024).
3. Balance technological innovation with preserving human interaction. Crawford et al. (2024) found that AI has a net negative effect on achievement when social factors are considered, highlighting the importance of maintaining human connections in educational contexts. This suggests that AI should complement rather than replace human interaction in teaching, learning, and student support.
4. Address the factors driving students' use of AI tools. Abbas et al. (2024) found that academic workload and time pressure increase students' likelihood of using ChatGPT, suggesting that managing these factors could help guide more appropriate AI use. Additionally, institutions should develop clear policies and

ethical frameworks for AI integration, particularly in contexts currently lacking such guidance (Essel et al., 2023).

5. Develop robust data governance and cybersecurity measures to address privacy concerns and potential biases in AI systems (Ajuwon et al., 2024). These measures should protect sensitive student information while enabling appropriate data use for educational improvement.

9.2 For Faculty and Educational Developers

1. Develop both technical understanding of AI capabilities and limitations and pedagogical approaches that use AI to enhance teaching and learning (Mah & Groß, 2024). This requires ongoing professional development that addresses AI implementation's technological and pedagogical dimensions.
2. Redesign educational practices, particularly assessment approaches, to acknowledge the reality of AI tools while maintaining academic standards and promoting meaningful learning (Foung et al., 2024). This involves focusing on skills and processes that AI cannot easily replicate, such as critical thinking, creativity, and collaborative problem-solving.
3. Explore the ethical dimensions of AI in specific disciplinary and pedagogical contexts, recognizing that ethical considerations may vary across different educational settings (Ahmed, 2024; Yusuf et al., 2024). This requires ongoing dialogue and reflection on the ethical implications of AI use in different educational contexts.

9.3 For Students

1. Develop critical AI literacy that enables responsible and effective use of AI tools (Almassaad et al., 2024). This includes technical skills for using AI and ethical awareness of the implications of AI use for learning, development, and academic integrity.
2. Use AI tools in ways that enhance rather than diminish agency and development, maintaining a balance that supports the development of critical thinking, creativity, and other essential skills (Abbas et al., 2024). This requires reflective and intentional approaches to AI use rather than uncritical adoption.

9.4. For Researchers

1. Conduct empirical studies examining the actual impacts of AI on teaching, learning, and administrative processes in higher education (Ansari et al., 2023). This includes longitudinal studies tracking the effects of AI implementation over

time, comparative studies examining different implementation approaches and their outcomes, and mixed-methods research combining quantitative measures of effectiveness with qualitative insights into user experiences and perceptions.

2. Explore how AI implementation varies across different disciplinary, institutional, and cultural contexts, addressing the limited representation of diverse global perspectives in the current literature (Ansari et al., 2023). This includes studies examining AI implementation in low- and middle-income countries, research on culturally specific perceptions and uses of AI, and cross-cultural comparative studies that illuminate both commonalities and differences in AI implementation across diverse contexts.
3. Investigate faculty experiences and perspectives on AI in higher education, addressing the relative underrepresentation of faculty voices in the current literature (Mah & Groß, 2024). This includes studies examining faculty attitudes, concerns, and professional development needs related to AI, research on how faculty integrate AI into their teaching and research practices, and investigations of how AI affects faculty roles and identities in higher education.
4. Develop and evaluate practical frameworks and tools for guiding responsible AI implementation in higher education. This includes studies developing and testing ethical frameworks, governance structures, assessment approaches, and faculty development models that support effective and responsible AI use in diverse educational contexts. Such research would help connect theoretical discussions of AI potential with practical implementation in real educational environments.
5. Finally, it is crucial to acknowledge the high-income dominance in the current body of literature as a significant limitation of the available evidence. While this review synthesizes the existing research, the scarcity of studies from low- and middle-income contexts (LMICs) means that our understanding is incomplete. The challenges faced in these regions are likely to be distinct and more acute, extending beyond the issues identified in high-income countries. Hypothesized challenges for LMICs include prohibitive infrastructure and data costs, the risk of data colonialism where local data is exploited without commensurate local benefit, a lack of AI models trained on local languages and cultural contexts, and a potential brain drain as local talent is recruited by global tech firms. Future research must prioritize context-sensitive studies in these regions to develop a truly global and equitable understanding of AI in higher education.

10. CONCLUSION

This literature review examined AI's role in higher education across four key research questions: primary applications, ethical considerations, institutional strategic approaches, and student perceptions and utilization. The findings reveal a rapidly evolving environment characterized by widespread adoption of AI technologies, significant ethical challenges, diverse implementation approaches, and complex student experiences. The review makes three significant contributions: it provides a comprehensive synthesis of current knowledge about AI applications, revealing both the breadth of implementation and limited empirical evidence of effectiveness; it illuminates the complex ethical dimensions of AI implementation, demonstrating that ethical considerations must be integrated into implementation strategies; and it identifies significant gaps in current research, particularly regarding diverse global perspectives, long-term impacts, and faculty experiences.

These findings have profound implications for higher education. AI is not merely a technological addition but a transformative force challenging fundamental assumptions about teaching, learning, and knowledge creation. While offering substantial benefits for educational access and effectiveness, successful implementation requires ethical frameworks that balance innovation with responsibility, efficiency with equity, and technological capabilities with human values. As AI integration deepens, institutions must develop context-sensitive approaches that are aligned with their specific missions, student populations, and resources—approaches grounded in ethical principles while maintaining flexibility to adapt to evolving technologies. By approaching these challenges with critical awareness and creative vision, higher education can shape a future where AI enhances educational experiences while preserving the human relationships and values at the heart of meaningful education.

REFERENCES

Abbas, M., Jam, F. A., & Khan, T. I. (2024). Is it harmful or helpful? Examining the causes and consequences of generative AI usage among university students. *International Journal of Educational Technology in Higher Education*, *21*, 10. Advance online publication. DOI: 10.1186/s41239-024-00444-7

Ahmed, H. (2024). Institutional integration of artificial intelligence in higher education: The moderation effect of ethical consideration. *International Journal of Educational Reform*. Online publication. DOI: 10.1177/10567879241247551

Ajuwon, O. A., Animashaun, E. S., & Chiekezie, N. R. (2024). Integrating AI and technology in educational administration: Improving efficiency and educational quality. *Open Access Research Journal of Science and Technology*, *11*(2), 116–127. DOI: 10.53022/oarjst.2024.11.2.0102

Almahasees, Z., Al Awabdeh, A., & Mahmoud, S. (2024). ChatGPT and higher education: A pathway to unprecedented progress. *Journal of Higher Education Theory and Practice*, *24*(5). Advance online publication. DOI: 10.33423/jhetp.v24i5.7004

Almassaad, A., Alajlan, H., & Alebaikan, R. (2024). Student perceptions of generative artificial intelligence: Investigating utilization, benefits, and challenges in higher education. *Systems*, *12*(10), 385. DOI: 10.3390/systems12100385

Ansari, A. N., Ahmad, S., & Bhutta, S. (2023). Mapping the global evidence around the use of ChatGPT in higher education: A systematic scoping review. *Education and Information Technologies*, *29*(9), 1–41. DOI: 10.1007/s10639-023-12223-4

Bannister, P., Alcalde Peñalver, E., & Santamaría Urbieta, A. (2023). Transnational higher education cultures and generative AI: A nominal group study for policy development in English medium instruction. *Journal for Multicultural Education*, *18*(4). Advance online publication. DOI: 10.1108/JME-10-2023-0102

Barnes, E., & Huston, J. (2024). Strategic integration of AI in higher education and industry: The AI8-point model. *Advances in Social Sciences and Management*, *2*(6), 39–52. DOI: 10.63002/assm.26.520

Crawford, J., Allen, K. A., Pani, B., & Cowling, M. (2024). When artificial intelligence substitutes humans in higher education: The cost of loneliness, student success, and retention. *Studies in Higher Education*, *49*(5), 883–897. DOI: 10.1080/03075079.2024.2326956

Cotton, D. R. E., Cotton, P. A., & Shipway, J. R. (2024). Chatting and cheating: Ensuring academic integrity in the era of ChatGPT. *Innovations in Education and Teaching International, 61*(2), 228–239. DOI: 10.1080/14703297.2023.2190148

Essel, H. B., Vlachopoulos, D., Essuman, A. B., & Amankwa, J. O. (2023). ChatGPT effects on cognitive skills of undergraduate students: Receiving instant responses from AI-based conversational large language models. *Computers and Education: Artificial Intelligence, 6*(1), 100198. DOI: 10.1016/j.caeai.2023.100198

Falebita, O. S., & Kok, P. J. (2024). Strategic goals for artificial intelligence integration among STEM academics and undergraduates in African higher education: A systematic review. *Discover Education, 3*, 151. Advance online publication. DOI: 10.1007/s44217-024-00252-1

Foung, D., Lin, L., & Chen, J. (2024). Reinventing assessments with ChatGPT and other online tools: Opportunities for GenAI-empowered assessment practices. *Computers and Education: Artificial Intelligence, 6*, 100250. DOI: 10.1016/j.caeai.2024.100250

Islam, A., & Arifeen, S. H. (2024). Empowering virtual collaboration: Harnessing AI for enhanced teamwork in higher education. *Educational Technology Quarterly, 2024*(3), 337–359. DOI: 10.55056/etq.746

Katsamakas, E., Pavlov, O. V., & Saklad, R. (2024). Artificial intelligence and the transformation of higher education institutions: A systems approach. *Sustainability, 16*(14), 6118. DOI: 10.3390/su16146118

Khairullah, S. A., Harris, S., Hadi, H. J., Sandhu, R. A., Ahmad, N., & Alshara, M. A. (2025). Implementing artificial intelligence in academic and administrative processes through responsible strategic leadership in higher education institutions. *Frontiers in Education, 10*, 1548104. Advance online publication. DOI: 10.3389/feduc.2025.1548104

Khalifa, M., & Albadawy, M. (2024). Using artificial intelligence in academic writing and research: An essential productivity tool. *Computer Methods and Programs in Biomedicine Update, 5*, 100145. DOI: 10.1016/j.cmpbup.2024.100145

Mah, D.-K., & Groß, N. (2024). Artificial intelligence in higher education: Exploring faculty use, self-efficacy, distinct profiles, and professional development needs. *International Journal of Educational Technology in Higher Education, 21*, 58. Advance online publication. DOI: 10.1186/s41239-024-00466-8

Nayak, R., Yassin, H., Ramesh, G., & Godiishala, A. G. (2024). Inclusive learning and assessment in the era of AI. *SN Computer Science*, *5*(8), 975. Advance online publication. DOI: 10.1007/s42979-024-03346-7

Opesemowo, O., & Adekomaya, V. (2024). Harnessing artificial intelligence for advancing sustainable development goals in South Africa's higher education system: A qualitative study. *International Journal of Learning. Teaching and Educational Research*, *23*(3), 67–86. DOI: 10.26803/ijlter.23.3.4

Sain, Z. H., Hina, S., & Serban, R. (2024). Implementing artificial intelligence in educational management systems: A comprehensive study of opportunities and challenges. *Asian Journal of Managerial Science*, *13*(1), 23–31. DOI: 10.70112/ajms-2024.13.1.4235

Strzelecki, A. (2024). Students' acceptance of ChatGPT in higher education: An extended unified theory of acceptance and use of technology. *Innovative Higher Education*, *49*, 223–245. DOI: 10.1007/s10755-023-09686-1

Torraco, R. J. (2005). Human resource development transcends disciplinary boundaries. *Human Resource Development Review*, *4*(3), 251–253.

Yusuf, A., Pervin, N., & Román-González, M. (2024). Generative AI and the future of higher education: A threat to academic integrity or reformation? Evidence from multicultural perspectives. *International Journal of Educational Technology in Higher Education*, *21*, 21. Advance online publication. DOI: 10.1186/s41239-024-00429-z

Zekaj, R. (2023). AI language models as educational allies: Enhancing instructional support in higher education. *International Journal of Learning. Teaching and Educational Research*, *22*(8), 120–134. DOI: 10.26803/ijlter.22.8.7

Chapter 7

Evaluating the Efficacy of AI-Based Formative Assessment in Promoting Student Learning in Secondary Education

Kingsley Asante
http://orcid.org/0009-0000-4346-0494
The British University in Dubai, UAE

Khawla Alshehhi
http://orcid.org/0009-0000-9372-7572
Higher Colleges of Technology, Ras Al Khaimah, UAE

ABSTRACT

Using Constructivist Learning Theory by Vygotsky and Piaget and Feedback Theory by Hattie & Timperley as theoretical frameworks, this study evaluates how Artificial Intelligence (AI)-based formative assessments improve student learning outcomes and engagement in secondary education. Emphasising feedback quality, progress monitoring, and general learning impact, the study critically contrasts AI-based assessments such as interactive quizzes and Learning Management Systems (LMS) with traditional approaches. The findings suggest that AI tools have significant benefits such as real-time, adaptive feedback, customised learning experiences, and higher student motivation. These advantages align with Constructivist ideas and the Feedback Theory. The study also points out difficulties, including teacher readiness, infrastructure constraints, and the requirement of a balanced integration

DOI: 10.4018/979-8-2600-0328-2.ch007

with conventional approaches. Recommendations underline professional growth for teachers, funding of technological infrastructure, and the encouragement of fair access to resources.

INTRODUCTION

With the introduction of computers in classrooms, many supporters of technologies said they would drastically change instruction and learning (Fauville et al., 2014). They believed that it could change teaching and learning dramatically (Fauville et al., 2014). The assertions encompassed that technology would (a) improve communication between learners and educators; (b) improve motivation among learners; (c) broaden the number of educational materials available; (d) enable learners to become skilled in actively searching for information rather than passive obtaining facts; (e) strengthen the comprehension of fundamentals and concepts; and (f) lower learner reliance on the teacher (Fauville et al., 2014).

The increasing incorporation of AI in classrooms has transformed learning, teaching, and assessment methods, especially through interactive, real-time feedback mechanisms. With the urgency to personalise learning and meet diverse student needs, formative assessment offers an ideal lens for understanding AI's potential impact. Rushton (2005) defines feedback as information used to close the gap between what is actually achieved and the benchmark level of performance. Whereas, Havnes et al. (2012) defines formative feedback as knowledge given to the student that is intended to change his or her perspective in order to enhance the learning process.

This paper examines the effectiveness of integrating AI into formative assessment strategies within secondary education and explores how digital assessment tools can enhance student learning outcomes. The main objective is to evaluate whether AI-supported formative assessments improve learning engagement and performance compared to traditional methods.

Purpose of the Study

The research aims to evaluate the efficacy of AI-based formative assessments in promoting student learning outcomes and engagement in secondary education. The study aims to compare AI-based assessments with traditional assessment methods, focusing on key aspects such as the quality of feedback and progress tracking. Through this evaluation, the study seeks to identify the benefits and challenges of implementing AI tools in formative assessments, providing insights that can inform educational practices and support the integration of technology in classrooms to improve learning processes and teaching.

Comparing AI-based assessments to traditional methods would give an understanding of whether AI tools genuinely add value. By examining student feedback and progress tracking, it would become possible to determine tangible outcomes in learning addressing the core aim of evaluating AI's impact. Educators and policymakers need concrete evidence on whether AI-based formative assessments offer measurable benefits over traditional methods. This study would provide relevant findings for practical application in classrooms, guiding decision-making on whether to adopt AI tools for assessment.

Research Questions

1. How does using AI in formative assessment impact student learning outcomes and engagement in secondary education?
2. How does AI-based formative assessment compare to traditional assessment methods in terms of student feedback and progress tracking?

LITERATURE REVIEW

Theoretical framework

Constructivist Learning Theory (Vygotsky & Piaget)

Constructivist learning theory suggests that learners construct knowledge through experience and interaction with their environment rather than passively receiving information (Kaufman, 2004). Constructivist principles underscore the importance of formative feedback in helping students refine their knowledge structures, a core feature of AI-based assessments.

Vygotsky's Social Constructivism

Emphasising the social context of learning and the need of cooperation and interaction, Vygotsky's (1978) approach strengthens constructivism. Vygotsky noted that students can perform tasks with the help of a more experienced person such as a teacher or peer. By offering timely feedback and customised support, AI tools such as interactive quizzes or online learning platforms (Jannah, 2024) can scaffold students' learning and hence enable development within their ZPD (Vygotsky, 1978).

Real-time assessment technologies, for example, allows students to get quick direction and feedback, therefore encouraging learning just beyond their current capacity.

According to Vygotsky, social connection is absolutely vital for learning. Though over-reliance on technology may lower critical thinking and social connection (Parsons & Taylor, 2011), collaborative learning environments where students interact with peers and instructors to improve their knowledge could be facilitated by AI-based evaluations, thereby offering engaged discussions and problem-solving opportunities. AI-based formative assessments offer scaffolded support such as suggestions, tutorials, or peer collaboration features that enable students to complete activities they could not accomplish independently but could achieve with direction. This reflects ZPD developed by Vygotsky. By means of features like discussion boards, group projects, or interactive challenges, many AI applications facilitate peer cooperation and hence promote a shared learning environment that encourages collective knowledge construction. With the help of others or tools, (e.g. AI-based assessments) that offer just the right amount of challenge and support, Vygotsky contends that students can achieve more.

Piaget's Cognitive Development Theory

Piaget (1972) suggested that cognitive development occurs in phases, each reflecting a distinct perspective on and interaction with the environment. Piaget (1972) highlighted how students actively create knowledge by means of inquiry and problem-solving. Piaget's focus on phases of cognitive development emphasises the importance of learning opportunities appropriate for the developmental stage of the student. By providing tools that adjust to the learner's degree of cognitive growth, AI-based formative assessments can accommodate these different stages. Adaptive learning technology, for example, can show students' assignments or questions suitable for their cognitive level, therefore ensuring that tests are neither simple nor difficult (Mukazi, 2022). By motivating students to participate in hands-on learning experiences that support critical thinking and applying concepts, AI-based formative assessments such as simulations, problem-solving activities, and interactive tools align with this principle (Jannah, 2024).

Feedback Theory

According to their 2007 model of feedback, Hattie and Timperley argue that relevant feedback focuses on three main questions: Where am I going? (clearing objectives) How am I going? (tracking progress) and where to go next? (recommending strategies for improvement). They noted that feedback should be immediate, specific, and beneficial, allowing students comprehend their current performance and how they could improve.

This view stresses the need of timely, practical feedback for improving the impact on learning (Wisniewski et al., 2020). Feedback given in AI-based formative assessments is instantaneous and customised to the particular learner, therefore enabling them to grasp their current abilities and areas for improvement (Smit et al., 2023). Formative assessments allow AI tools including automated quizzes, LMS, and online rubrics to provide constant, actionable feedback, a crucial component in raising learning outcomes (Lim et al., 2023). The Feedback Theory provides the theoretical lens for analysing the quality and impact of feedback from AI-based formative assessments compared to traditional methods, focusing on how feedback can improve student performance and engagement.

Context of the Study

Formative assessments are important for providing feedback, tracking progress and supporting students in secondary education (Kaur, 2023). Traditional methods of giving feedback to students usually lack the capacity to give personalised feedback on time and adapt to the diverse needs of the students (Bhagat et al., 2019). AI-based formative assessments have emerged as a potential solution to address these problems with the increasing integration of AI in education. Despite its continuous usage in schools, there is little research on how it can enhance learning outcomes as compared to traditional methods. Furthermore, teachers need more training, and students have diverse access to technology (Mohammed & Almekhlafi, 2017), all of which might hinder the implementation of AI-based assessments.

Focusing on their impact on feedback quality, progress tracking, and general learning outcomes, this study highlights the necessity to critically review the efficacy of AI-based formative assessments. Examining the benefits and challenges of using AI in formative assessments would assist this study to provide insightful analysis of how teaching and learning strategies in secondary education could be improved. The study is informed by practical questions arising from a private secondary school located in the United Arab Emirates but the analysis draws on secondary evidence from published studies and reports and not primary data.

Review of Literature

The literature is reviewed under five main themes and the below three themes are interconnected, creating a cohesive narrative for the study:

Figure 1. Interconnected themes - These three themes form the narrative for the study

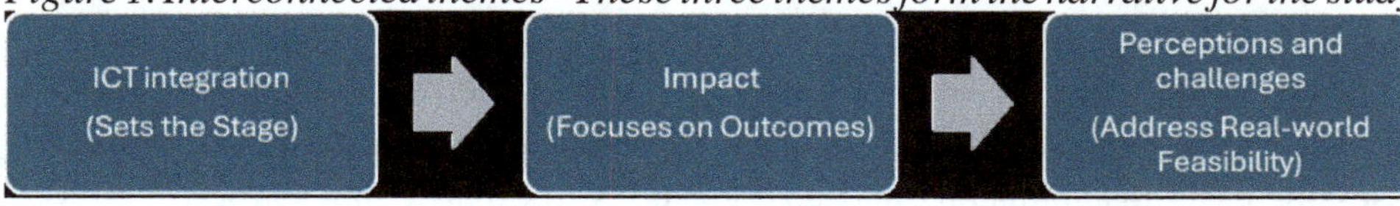

Technology and AI Integration in Education

From initial uses like radio and movies to current adaptive learning tools based on AI, AI's incorporation in education has changed dramatically. Early hope for AI's transformative power in education (Fauville et al., 2014) collided with the slower-than-expected acceptance in classrooms (Mirzajani et al., 2016). While Mirzajani et al. (2016) noted difficulties, such educator stress and lack of resources, Lawrence and Tar (2018) underlined the importance of AI in teaching twenty-century skills. Suryani (2010) advised against the superficial use of AI, claiming that its effectiveness depended on complete integration into educational methods, therefore undermining these optimistic views. These points of view align with research demonstrating how well AI adoption works depending on focused training and adaptability to culture (Mirzajani et al., 2016; Suryani, 2010).

Studies demonstrating benefits include improved motivation (Msafiri et al., 2023) and personalised learning experiences using adaptive systems (Jannah, 2024), thereby clearly demonstrating how technology encourages higher involvement. Jain and Alam (2022) stress how critical AI is for instruction and self-learning, hence improving access and quality in education. Moreover, research shows that AI might support secondary school students' academic performance, implying that integration is vital for promoting academic success (Adeloye et al., 2023).

Parsons and Taylor (2011) pointed out the changing emphasis on involvement, including emotional and cognitive aspects. Critics such as Parsons and Taylor (2011) advised against depending too much on technology, meanwhile pointing out declines in critical thinking and social contact. These issues highlight the need to use strategies to balance. On the other hand, using AI technologies still presents difficulties. García Gómez et al. (2022) address the fast transition to online learning during the epidemic, exposing notable teacher preparedness gaps and requiring a pedagogical paradigm unique from traditional face-to-face teaching. Obstacles to efficient AI integration, a lack of teacher training and support also reflects this (Koryuhina & Shamshina, 2018). Therefore, even while the possible advantages of AI in education are well-documented, applying this technology sometimes encounters major challenges.

The major advantages of flipped learning (FL) and gamification have been enhanced student self-efficacy and critical thinking (Seitan et al., 2020). Still, obstacles include student opposition and boring online resources (Seitan et al., 2020). The FL model's compatibility with constructivist ideas (Piaget, 1972; Vygotsky, 1978) promotes its efficiency in promoting student-centered learning.

According to Ghavifekr et al. (2014), AI is changing educational institutions by introducing course contents based on practical problems, giving learners and instructors more chances for feedback and reflection, and providing scaffolds to improve learning.

Formative Assessment and Feedback

Because it offers ongoing feedback and promotes adaptive teaching practices, formative evaluation is essential for student learning (Havnes et al., 2012). Stiggins and DuFour (2009) emphasised how it might inspire self-control and increase student confidence. Effective formative comments should, according to research, be timely, tailored, and actionable (Bhagat et al., 2019). This is consistent with the results of Kithungu et al. (2021) who claims that maximising the advantages of formative assessments depends on teachers' pedagogical abilities in AI integration. More effective learning experiences can result from traditional tests lacking the immediacy and adaptability AI-based exams provide (Bhagat et al., 2019). Some research found limited efficacy because of insufficient formative assessment systems (Havnes et al., 2012). These results demand improved matching of formative approaches with institutional objectives. Good feedback should be immediate, practical, and catered to personal requirements (Hattie & Timperley, 2007). According to research by Bhagat et al. (2019), tailored feedback made possible by AI technologies might support performance and motivation.

Real-time and adaptive feedback are some of the features that AI-based tests offer that conventional approaches sometimes lack. Bhagat et al. (2019) noted that students who used digital tools performed higher than others assessed traditionally. On the other hand, Wang and Dostal (2017) advised against possible over-reliance on technology but encouraged complementary use alongside traditional methods.

There are various perceptions on the effectiveness of traditional as compared to AI-based formative evaluation systems, with some studies stressing the need of balancing new and traditional evaluation techniques. Some argue for AI tools' increased engagement and feedback capabilities, while others warn against over-reliance on technology (Oborah, 2022).

Impact of AI-Based Formative Assessments on Learning Outcomes

Formative assessment is considered to be mostly composed of feedback, which is also one of the elements influencing learning most strongly (Havnes et al., 2012). Many studies have examined the effects of AI-based formative assessments on learning outcomes. Using AI tools appears to result in notable gains in student performance and retention rates (Msafiri et al., 2023). For example, research by Bedin et al. (2023) shows how students' impressions and participation improved when technology was included in chemistry education during remote learning. Likewise, the results of the systematic review confirm that AI tools increase students' motivation and skill development, thereby increasing the general learning outcomes (Msafiri et al., 2023).

In three areas; motivation to study, awareness student's own learning and the consequences on learning, in terms of both processes and results make formative assessments a valuable instrument for students' learning (Weurlander et al., 2012).

By constantly using the AI-based formative assessment in the classroom, a teacher can demonstrate to students their strengths, mistakes, and qualities; he will also be able to change his teaching and evaluation methods by thus promoting values such as respect, solidarity, and accountability (Menéndez et al., 2019). From the student standpoint, AI-based formative assessment should be a tool for enhancing performance and supporting development as self-directed and motivated students (Wood, 2018).

Bhagat et al. (2019) used a web-based assessment tool called Siette in a course. This method gave extensive immediate feedback, meaning they immediately got the right response along with thorough justification for the incorrect responses. Students who used Siette performed better than those using a conventional formative evaluation technique. More remarkably, instantaneous feedback improved students' performance, something not achievable without the use of technologies (Bhagat et al., 2019). AI tools help students perform better by encouraging cooperation, creativity, and self-directed learning. Though low or infrequent use had little impact, intensive, deliberate use of AI was connected to higher outcomes.

Opposing research claim that too much AI use especially unrelated to academics may harm performance (Ben Youssef et al., 2022). These results underline the need to use AI deliberately and for education. Nonetheless, the efficacy of these technologies depends on several elements, including the infrastructure accessible in educational institutions and the teachers' technological competency. This suggests that even if AI has the ability to change the results of education, its effectiveness depends on the larger educational environment and the preparedness of instructors and students to accept these instruments.

Teacher Perceptions and Challenges

On one hand, the instructor is the one who would implement AI and is vital in merging AI with education. Their attitude toward AI determines the main factor influencing the infusion of AI into educational practice. Should teachers have a bad attitude toward AI, the incorporation of it into classroom instruction will be useless (Wang & Dostál, 2017).

The way AI-based formative assessments are used in the classroom is influenced by educators' views. While uncertainty or lack of confidence impedes implementation, positive opinions correspond with more excellent adoption rates (Mohammed & Almekhlafi, 2017). A number of educators admit the benefits of AI but also express concerns regarding their own readiness and the challenges with technology integration (Hossein-Mohand et al., 2021). Hossein-Mohand et al. (2021) highlights how understanding AI technology determines how teachers accept and incorporate it into their courses. This is supported by the findings of Khan and Markauskaite (2018), who emphasised several concepts of AI-enhanced education among educators. Many teachers acknowledge the advantages of AI but also express worries about their own preparation and the difficulties with technological integration (Hossein-Mohand et al., 2022). Hossein-Mohand et al. (2022) highlighted how teachers adopt and apply AI depending on their knowledge of it. Similarly, Khan and Markauskaite (2018) underlined the need to use several concepts of AI-enhanced education among teachers.

Kaur (2023) claims that the obstacles to the use of computers and AI in educational institutions are as follows: lack of software problem, insufficient training, inadequate learning equipment and resources, teachers' reluctance, time limits, lack of confidence, and lack of knowledge.

Using AI tools has various challenges, including inadequate infrastructure, pedagogical restrictions, and inadequate training (Handayani, 2024). Nur et al. (2021) stress how important it is for teachers to effectively implement AI in their classrooms with enough training and support. Strategies to overcome these challenges are programs for professional development and institutional support for AI infrastructure. Solving these problems is, therefore, crucial to establishing a setting suitable for AI integration in the classroom.

These challenges could be overcome by means of role models, encouragement of leadership, targeted professional development and resource investments to provide fair access to technology (Akram et al., 2022; Buabeng-Andoh, 2012; Goktas et al., 2009).

Progress Tracking and Data Analytics

Especially in the field of education, it is almost impossible to apply teaching strategies without using (AI). LMS including Moodle (Zhang et al., 2020) among are routinely applied in different educational environments. Real-time tracking of student development made possible by AI tools helps formative assessments to be improved. Data analytics in education helps teachers to adopt more informed teaching strategies and tailor their approaches depending on unique student needs (Khan & Markauskaitė, 2018; Msafiri et al., 2023). Studies reveal that while AI-based tracking systems offer instant feedback that might be utilised to modify teaching tactics, they are typically more efficient than traditional methods (Khan & Markauskaitė, 2018; Msafiri et al., 2023). Moodle and Kahoot AI tools enable personalised interventions through real-time tracking and data visualisation, hence facilitating these systems (Diahyleva et al., 2024). These systems improve teaching plans and help to assist wise decision-making. LMS provides a fast and accurate analysis of training statistics. Additionally, with Google Classroom, instructors can monitor student conversations and development. (Sakthivel, 2021).

Data analytics lets educators spot trends and focus on solutions (Admiraal et al., 2020). Dashboards and other tools offer practical information that helps to drive ongoing teaching practice development. Research on AI-based approaches demonstrates that they measure efficiency and involvement better than conventional ones (Fannakhosrow et al., 2022). AI-based instruction might support academic results by lowering test anxiety and encouraging intrinsic drive. Over time, teachers can track individual development, identify trends or patterns, and keep an eye on their student's performance. Graphs, charts, or dashboards help teachers visualise this data so they may better spot every student's areas of strength and weakness (Abduxalilova et al., 2023).

Still, the success of these tracking systems depends on the teachers' capacity for accurate data interpretation and application. Studies indicate that although AI tools can improve tracking efficiency, the successful application of data analytics in formative assessments requires a strong knowledge of the technology and educational practices (Bedin et al., 2023; Khan & Markauskaite, 2018). Thus, maximising the advantages of AI in tracking student growth depends on constant training and assistance for teachers.

METHODOLOGY

This research follows a qualitative approach, utilising secondary data from case studies and recent studies that have examined AI use in formative assessments in secondary education settings. By focusing on secondary data, the study avoids ethical concerns associated with primary data collection, especially concerning minors. The selected case studies primarily draw from developed educational contexts, offering insights into the infrastructure, teacher preparedness, and student response to AI-based assessments.

This alignment with the constructivist and feedback theories supports exploring how digital assessments allow student-centred learning, collaboration, and active feedback loops. Thematic analysis is used to interpret the data, focusing on key themes such as feedback quality, progress tracking, and learning outcomes

Thematic analysis is the chosen method for analysis in this evaluative case study. This qualitative method is well-suited to examining patterns and insights within secondary data, enabling the researchers to focus on specific themes related to the effectiveness and impact of AI-based formative assessments.

Procedure

Data Collection

This study employs secondary data collection as the main source of data. This entails searching for, reading and assessing reports on AI-based formative assessments in secondary schools, case studies and current research papers. The paper focuses on the secondary school settings in which the AI technologies have been integrated with the formative assessment techniques. The data for the study were obtained from peer-reviewed academic publications, government and institutional records and instructional sites that recorded the use of AI in assessment strategies.

Data Analysis

The qualitative research design involved the use of a thematic analysis in the organisation of the data collection process. All data acquired were categorised according to the research questions that is, feedback quality, progress tracking, student involvement, and learning outcomes. First, all of the data were collated and coded; then, they were regularly arranged among investigations. Naeem et al. (2023) presents a methodical six-step approach for doing thematic analysis including keyword selection, coding, and theme development with regard to in qualitative research, these methodologies improve the rigour and openness of the analysis, hence enabling replicability and trustworthiness (Nowell et al., 2017). These tests were evaluated in line with conventional methods including formative evaluations grounded on AI. The main emphasis was on how AI tools influence progress tracking, engagement methods, and feedback mechanisms. Constructivist learning and feedback theories were used as a lens to understand how AI tools support active learning, scaffold knowledge production, and timely feedback.

DISCUSSION

By providing opportunities for individualised learning, more participation, and efficient development tracking, AI technologies have reshaped education. Nevertheless, the results show how effectively AI integration is integrated into instructional strategies, thereby establishing its importance. Research (Jannah, 2024; Msafiri et al., 2023) suggest that particularly when integrated with adaptive learning systems, AI-based formative assessment tools could increase motivation and engagement. Constructivist concepts reinforce these conclusions by underlining how AI tools allow students to create knowledge using inquiry and interaction, supporting active learning. Gamified tests and interactive quizzes let students negotiate their ZPD by aligning with Piaget's and Vygotsky's ideas of hands-on problem-solving and scaffolding. To maximise the possibilities of AI-based formative assessments, issues including inadequate infrastructure and teacher preparedness should be addressed, and the need for institutional support and focused professional development should be called to.

Formative assessments depend on feedback, and AI tools provide benefits over traditional approaches (Abduxalilova et al., 2023). Platforms like Siette provide instantaneous, detailed, and relevant feedback that helps learners find and fill in knowledge gaps (Bhagat et al., 2019). This corresponds with the feedback model of Hattie and Timperley (2007), stressing the need to respond to the three feedback questions: Where am I going? How am I doing? Where to go from here? Underpinned by the constructivist theory, AI-based formative evaluations help to scaffold by offering tailored support and timely feedback. According to Vygotsky's (1978) theory, which emphasises the need for group settings, AI tools sometimes produce these via interactive learning platforms and peer review. Though over-reliance on technology may lower critical thinking and social connection, these characteristics may improve outcomes and simplify knowledge (Parsons & Taylor, 2011).

There is much evidence that AI-based formative assessment technologies could improve learning results. According to research, AI-based evaluations improve student performance, motivation, and retention rates by means of real-time, adaptive feedback (Bedin et al., 2023). These results are supported by the constructivist perspective since adaptive technologies challenge students' cognitive development levels, therefore encouraging more critical thinking and deeper involvement. However, these advantages depend on the regular, intentional use of AI technologies. Ben Youssef et al. (2022) noted that, too high or poor integration of AI use can lower academic achievement. To maximise learning results, teachers must carefully balance AI integration with conventional approaches, ensuring that technology is used as an additional method rather than a replacement (Handayani, 2024).

Effective application of AI-based formative assessments depends much on teacher attitudes and readiness. While teachers agree that AI-based formative assessments have advantages, studies show that effective adoption is hampered by inadequate infrastructure, poor training, and time limits (Handayani, 2024; Kaur, 2023). The constructivist theory supports teacher preparedness since ZPD ideas and scaffolding mainly depend on the capacity of the teacher to lead and assist in the development. To remove these obstacles, professional development initiatives stressing technical competency and pedagogical integration are vital (Johnson et al., 2016). Further guarantees that teachers can boldly apply AI tools to improve formative assessments include institutional support, including investments in infrastructure and resource accessibility (Akram et al., 2022).

AI technologies shine in tracking student development and providing real-time data analytics to enable individualised education and informed decision-making (Mukazi, 2022). Gamification tools such as Kahoot give teachers practical knowledge that will help them modify their approaches depending on student performance patterns (Diahyleva et al., 2024). This fits the constructivist focus on active feedback loops and customised learning paths. While these tools improve accuracy and efficiency, their effectiveness relies on teachers' capacity to understand and apply data. The possibility of AI-based progress tracking to enhance learning outcomes stays underused without appropriate training (Khan & Markauskaite, 2018). Therefore, the maximum benefits of AI technologies depend on continuous teacher training in data literacy.

CONCLUSION

Based on both Constructivist Learning Theory and Feedback Theory, this paper emphasises the transforming power of AI-based formative assessments in secondary education. AI tools enable individualised, group, and scaffolded learning environments consistent with active knowledge building. These instruments solve significant shortcomings of conventional assessment techniques, such as delayed replies and lack of personalisation, by allowing instantaneous and adaptable feedback.

To break down the fundamental feedback questions: Where am I going? How am I going? and Where to go next? The Feedback Theory of Hattie and Timperley presents a lens through which one could observe how student achievements are impacted by AI-based formative assessments. Among other AI tools, interactive assessments and LMS offer quick, focused, actionable feedback that supports self-regulation and guides students towards meeting their learning goals. This type of feedback supports students going through their ZPD and is in line with Vygotsky's idea of scaffolding.

However, there are challenges that come with the use of AI-based formative assessment, which has the potential of causing problems if not handled properly. These include differences in the preparedness of the teachers, the inequality in access to the technology and the possible disadvantages of relying on the digital tools rather than traditional approaches. Combining AI tools with traditional approaches can maximise their advantages and minimise their negative effects.

Educational institutions should therefore, focus on teacher professional development, enhancement of infrastructure and equity in the distribution of resources to ensure that AI-based formative assessment is fully realised. Additionally, the use of AI technologies should enhance traditional methods so that individualised feedback and comprehensive learning experiences are given more emphasis. The AI-based formative assessments based on the Constructivist Learning and Feedback Theories have the potential to change teaching and learning environments. Through these initiatives, AI tools can act as a stimulant for inclusive, efficient, student-centered education.

Limitations

The study mostly depends on secondary data, which could restrain its capacity to provide complex, context-specific insights or solve differences in AI deployment among several educational institutions. Many of the studies centre on particular geographic or socioeconomic settings. Therefore, the results could not be completely relevant to institutions with different degrees of infrastructure, teacher preparation, or student population. The speed of AI tool creation might surpass some results when more recent technologies arrive with improved means of student involvement and feedback.

Recommendations

Programs for teacher development emphasising both technological and pedagogical competencies should be a top priority in institutions. Particularly in data interpretation and actionable feedback, educators need help properly implementing AI-based formative assessments in their classes. To guarantee that teachers and students can access and use AI resources efficiently, schools must invest in robust AI infrastructure comprising dependable internet, devices, and LMS. Although formative assessments based on AI have special advantages, they should enhance rather than replace conventional evaluation techniques. Combining both strategies guarantees students get individualised comments while honing social skills and critical thinking. It also helps to maximise the qualities of each. To conform with constructivist ideas of shared knowledge building, schools should promote using AI tools that support peer cooperation, such as group projects and discussion forums. Administrators and teachers should use data analytics from AI tools to routinely review formative assessment performance. These studies can provide insights that direct changes in technology integration and instructional approaches.

Particularly in various educational environments, future studies should look at the long-term implications of AI-based formative assessments on student performance, involvement, and skill development. Further research might look at how AI-based formative assessments might be successfully applied in low-resource environments, addressing issues including inequities in access and infrastructure.

REFERENCES

Abduxalilova, S., Tilovxo'jayeva, A., & Abdug'afforova, N. (2023). Data Analysis in English Language Teaching and Using it for Feedback and Progress Monitoring. *Modern Science and Research, 2*(10), 202–207. DOI: 10.5281/zenodo.10205650

Adeloye, A., Kayode, T., Ariyo, E., & Jeje, O. (2023). The impact of Artificial Intelligence on the academic achievement of creative Art students in secondary schools. *NIU Journal of Humanities, 8*(4), 163–169. DOI: 10.58709/niujhu.v8i4.1740

Admiraal, W., Vermeulen, J., & Bulterman-Bos, J. (2020). Teaching with learning analytics: How to connect computer-based assessment data with classroom instruction? *Technology, Pedagogy and Education, 29*(5), 577–591. DOI: 10.1080/1475939X.2020.1825992

Akram, H., Abdelrady, A. H., Al-Adwan, A. S., & Ramzan, M. (2022). Teachers' perceptions of technology integration in teaching-learning practices: A systematic review. *Frontiers in Psychology, 13*, 1–9. DOI: 10.3389/fpsyg.2022.920317 PMID: 35734463

Bedin, E., S Marques, M., & das Graças Cleophas, M. (2023). Research on the content, technological, and pedagogical knowledge (TPACK) of chemistry teachers during remote teaching in the pandemic in the light of students' perceptions. *Journal of Information Technology Education Research, 22*, 001–024. DOI: 10.28945/5063

Ben Youssef, A., Dahmani, M., & Ragni, L. (2022). ICT use, digital skills and students' academic performance: Exploring the digital divide. *Information (Basel), 13*(3), 129. DOI: 10.3390/info13030129

Bhagat, K. K., Liou, W. K., Michael Spector, J., & Chang, C. Y. (2019). To use augmented reality or not in formative assessment: A comparative study. *Interactive Learning Environments, 27*(5-6), 830–840. DOI: 10.1080/10494820.2018.1489857

Buabeng-Andoh, C. (2012). Factors influencing teachersâ adoption and integration of Artificial Intelligenceinto teaching: A review of the literature. *International Journal of Education and Development using AI, 8*(1), 136-155. https://www.learntechlib.org/p/188018/

Diahyleva, O., Leshchenko, A., Paziak, A., & Yurzhenko, A. (2024). Kahoot! as a tool to gamify learning process at maritime higher education. [ITE]. *Journal of Information Technology Education, 1*(55), 25–34. DOI: 10.14308/ite000777

Fannakhosrow, M., Nourabadi, S., Ngoc Huy, D. T., Dinh Trung, N., & Tashtoush, M. A. (2022). A Comparative Study of Artificial Intelligence (AI)-Based and Conventional Methods of Instruction on Learners' Academic Enthusiasm for L2 Learning. *Education Research International, 2022*(1), 5478088. DOI: 10.1155/2022/5478088

Fauville, G., Lantz-Andersson, A., & Säljö, R. (2014). AI tools in environmental education: Reviewing two newcomers to schools. *Environmental Education Research, 20*(2), 248–283. DOI: 10.1080/13504622.2013.775220

García Gómez, B., Coca, J. R., & Mesquita, C. (2022). Teacher's perspective in a challenging pandemic scenario. *Aula abierta, 51*(2), 181-190. DOI: 10.17811/rifie.52.2.2022.181-190

Ghavifekr, S., Razak, A. Z. A., Ghani, M. F. A., Ran, N. Y., Meixi, Y., & Tengyue, Z. (2014). AI integration in education: Incorporation for teaching & learning improvement. *Malaysian Online Journal of Educational Technology, 2*(2), 24-45. https://files.eric.ed.gov/fulltext/EJ1086419.pdf

Goktas, Y., Yildirim, S., & Yildirim, Z. (2009). Main barriers and possible enablers of AIs integration into pre-service teacher education programs. *Journal of Educational Technology & Society, 12*(1), 193–204. https://www.jstor.org/stable/jeductechsoci.12.1.193

Handayani, F. (2024). The Role of Technology in Enhancing English Language Learning: A Study of Digital Tools and Their Impact on Student Engagement. *Berajah Journal, 4*(6), 1257–1266. DOI: 10.47353/bj.v4i6.430

Hattie, J., & Timperley, H. (2007). The power of feedback. *Review of Educational Research, 77*(1), 81–112. DOI: 10.3102/003465430298487

Havnes, A., Smith, K., Dysthe, O., & Ludvigsen, K. (2012). Formative assessment and feedback: Making learning visible. *Studies in Educational Evaluation, 38*(1), 21–27. DOI: 10.1016/j.stueduc.2012.04.001

Hossein-Mohand, H., Trujillo-Torres, J. M., Gómez-García, M., Hossein-Mohand, H., & Campos-Soto, A. (2021). Analysis of the use and integration of the flipped learning model, project-based learning, and gamification methodologies by secondary school mathematics teachers. *Sustainability (Basel), 13*(5), 2606. DOI: 10.3390/su13052606

Jain, S., & Alam, M. A. (2022). Review of forthcoming AI-enabled applications promoting learning in higher education. In *AI with Intelligent Applications* (pp. 613–621). Springer Singapore. DOI: 10.1007/978-981-16-4177-0_61

Jannah, M. (2024). Analysing the Impact of Technology Integration on Student Engagement and Learning Outcomes in K-12 Education: A Systematic Literature Review. [INJOE]. *Indonesian Journal of Education*, *4*(3), 969–980. https://www.injoe.org/index.php/INJOE/article/view/170

Johnson, A. M., Jacovina, M. E., Russell, D. G., & Soto, C. M. (2016). Challenges and solutions when using technologies in the classroom. In *Adaptive educational technologies for literacy instruction* (pp. 13–30). Routledge. DOI: 10.4324/9781315647500-2

Kaufman, D. (2004). 14. Constructivist issues in language learning and teaching. *Annual Review of Applied Linguistics*, *24*, 303–319. DOI: 10.1017/S0267190504000121

Kaur, K. (2023). Teaching and Learning with AI Tools: Issues and Challenges. *International Journal on Cybernetics & Informatics*, *12*(3), 16–22. DOI: 10.5121/ijci.2023.120302

Khan, M. S. H., & Markauskaite, L. (2018). Technical and Vocational Teachers' Conceptions of AI in the Workplace: Bridging the gap between teaching and professional practice. *Journal of Educational Computing Research*, *56*(7), 1099–1128. DOI: 10.1177/0735633117740396

Kithungu, R. M., Gakunga, D. K., & Nungu, M. (2021). Influence of AI integration on content delivery by AI and Non-AI trained teachers in secondary schools in Machakos County, Kenya. *Kenya. Journal of Studies in Education*, *11*(1).

Koryuhina, C., & Shamshina, T. (2018, April 26-27). Challenges of AI in education. In *The 16th international scientific conference information technologies and management*. ISMA University., https://ismaitm.lv/wp-content/uploads/theses_2018.pdf#page=142

Lawrence, J. E., & Tar, U. A. (2018). Factors that influence teachers' adoption and integration of AI in teaching/learning process. *Educational Media International*, *55*(1), 79–105. DOI: 10.1080/09523987.2018.1439712

Lim, N. T., Lee, Y., & Lee, P. P. F. (2023). What types of feedback do undergraduate chemistry students give each other? a case study from singapore. *International Journal of Innovation in Science and Mathematics Education*, *31*(2). Advance online publication. DOI: 10.30722/IJISME.31.02.003

Menéndez, I. Y. C., Napa, M. A. C., Moreira, M. L. M., & Zambrano, G. G. V. (2019). The importance of formative assessment in the learning teaching process. *International Journal of Social Science and Humanity*, *3*(2), 238–249. DOI: 10.29332/ijssh.v3n2.322

Mirzajani, H., Mahmud, R., Fauzi Mohd Ayub, A., & Wong, S. L. (2016). Teachers' acceptance of AI and its integration in the classroom. *Quality Assurance in Education, 24*(1), 26–40. DOI: 10.1108/QAE-06-2014-0025

Mohammed, A. H. H., & Almekhlafi, A. G.Ali Hussein H. MohammedAbdurrahman Ghaleb Almekhlafi. (2017). English language teachers' perceptions of using AI in teaching in cycle three in the United Arab Emirates. *US-China Foreign Language, 15*(6), 349–366. DOI: 10.17265/1539-8080/2017.06.001

Msafiri, M. M., Kangwa, D., & Cai, L. (2023). A systematic literature review of AI integration in secondary education: What works, what does not, and what next? *Discover Education, 2*(1), 44. DOI: 10.1007/s44217-023-00070-x

Mukazi, F. M. (2022). Digital-based formative assessments in higher education institutions. In *Handbook of Research on Digital-Based Assessment and Innovative Practices in Education* (pp. 247–264). IGI Global., DOI: 10.4018/978-1-6684-2468-1.ch013

Naeem, M., Ozuem, W., Howell, K., & Ranfagni, S. (2023). A step-by-step process of thematic analysis to develop a conceptual model in qualitative research. *International Journal of Qualitative Methods, 22*, 16094069231205789. Advance online publication. DOI: 10.1177/16094069231205789

Nowell, L. S., Norris, J. M., White, D. E., & Moules, N. J. (2017). Thematic analysis: Striving to meet the trustworthiness criteria. *International Journal of Qualitative Methods, 16*(1), 160940691773384. DOI: 10.1177/1609406917733847

Nur, S. A. A., Muliati, M., & Munir, M. (2021). English Teacher's Attitudes and Practices of AI Adoption in English Language Classrooms. *Celebes Journal of Language Studies, 1*(2), 210–218. DOI: 10.51629/cjls.v1i2.63

Oborah, J. O. (2022). Effectiveness of the infusion teaching approach for the development of general AI skills in Nigerian tertiary education. *Journal of Research in Innovative Teaching & Learning, 15*(2), 245–258. DOI: 10.1108/JRIT-11-2021-0076

Parsons, J., & Taylor, L. (2011). Improving Student Engagement. *Current Issues in Education (Tempe, Ariz.), 14*(1). https://cie.asu.edu/ojs/index.php/cieatasu/article/view/745

Piaget, J. (1972). *The principles of genetic epistemology*. Routledge and Kegan Paul.

Rushton, A. (2005). Formative assessment: A key to deep learning? *Medical Teacher, 27*(6), 509–513. DOI: 10.1080/01421590500129159 PMID: 16199357

Sakthivel, D. (2021). AI Tools for Modern Education. *International Journal of Multidisciplinary Research and Explorer*, *1*(9), 22–27. https://doie.org/10.280229/IJMRE.20211932685958

Seitan, W. I., Ajlouni, A. O., & Al-Shra'h, N. D. (2020). The Impact of Integrating Flipped Learning and Artificial Intelligenceon the Secondary School Students' Academic Achievement and Their Attitudes towards It. *International Education Studies*, *13*(2), 1–10. DOI: 10.5539/ies.v13n2p1

Smit, R., Bachmann, P., Dober, H., & Hess, K. (2023). Feedback levels and their interaction with the mathematical reasoning process. *Curriculum Journal*, *35*(2), 184–202. DOI: 10.1002/curj.221

Stiggins, R., & DuFour, R. (2009). Maximizing the power of formative assessments. *Phi Delta Kappan*, *90*(9), 640–644. DOI: 10.1177/003172170909000907

Suryani, A. (2010). ICT in education: Its benefits, difficulties, and organizational development issues. [JSH]. *Jurnal Sosial Humaniora*, *3*(1), 13–33. DOI: 10.12962/j24433527.v3i1.651

Vygotsky, L. S. (1978). *Mind in society: The development of higher psychological processes* (Vol. 86). Harvard university press.

Wang, X., & Dostál, J. (2017). An Analysis of the Integration of AI in Education from the Perspective of Teachers'Attitudes. In *Edulearn17 Proceedings* (pp. 8156–8162). IATED., DOI: 10.21125/edulearn.2017.0507

Weurlander, M., Söderberg, M., Scheja, M., Hult, H., & Wernerson, A. (2012). Exploring formative assessment as a tool for learning: Students' experiences of different methods of formative assessment. *Assessment & Evaluation in Higher Education*, *37*(6), 747–760. DOI: 10.1080/02602938.2011.572153

Wisniewski, B., Zierer, K., & Hattie, J. (2020). The power of feedback revisited: A meta-analysis of educational feedback research. *Frontiers in Psychology*, *10*, 1–14. DOI: 10.3389/fpsyg.2019.03087 PMID: 32038429

Wood, D. F. (2018). Formative assessment: Assessment for learning. *Understanding medical education: Evidence, theory, and practice*, 361-373. DOI: 10.1002/9781119373780.ch25

Zhang, Y., Ghandour, A., & Shestak, V. (2020). Using learning analytics to predAI students performance in moodle LMS. *International Journal of Emerging Technologies in Learning*, *15*(20), 102. DOI: 10.3991/ijet.v15i20.15915

Chapter 8
Rethinking Student Assessment in the Age of AI:
Insights and Framework Proposals From a Gulf-Based Educational Program

Wafaa Elsawah
http://orcid.org/0000-0002-9538-4697
British University in Dubai, UAE

ABSTRACT

As generative AI tools become more embedded in education, their impact on assessment raises urgent ethical and pedagogical questions. This qualitative study, based on observations from a Gulf-based, high-stakes professional program, explores how AI detection tools, institutional policies, and student behaviors intersect where assessments influence employment. Grounded in Constructivist and Academic Integrity theories, the research analyzes the use of tools due to compliance. Findings reveal inconsistent detection outputs, limited student preparedness, and institutional uncertainty. In response, the study proposes a four-pillar framework: early AI orientation, AI-resistant assessment designs, diagnostic—not punitive—use of detection tools, and AI-aware rubrics. Strategies such as oral exams, staged submissions, and project-based tasks are recommended to ensure authenticity. This work offers practical guidance for institutions striving to promote fairness, originality, and trust in an AI-driven educational landscape.

DOI: 10.4018/979-8-2600-0328-2.ch008

INTRODUCTION

Study Background and Significance

The rapid integration of generative AI tools into academic environments is reshaping the way students learn, write and interact with information. Many existing applications like ChatGPT, Grammarly, QuillBot and other AI-enhanced platforms are no longer optional tools; they are becoming routine or standard parts of students' daily academic workflow. These tools offer significant advantages in terms of efficiency, access, and support for language improvement, especially for multilingual learners or those lacking confidence in their writing skills (Yan et al., 2024). AI tools can scaffold learning, help students organise their thoughts, and scaffold learning when used properly and transparently.

However, this technological shift also brings some difficult questions about academic authorship and originality, and what the true purpose of assessment should be. As Weng and Fu (2024) note, the presence of AI increases the bluring line between a learner's own thinking and the forms of assistance available through technology. In high-stakes educational contexts such as professional training programs or degree pathways which directly influence employment prospects these blurred boundaries become more troubling. Assessments, after all, are more than just tools for measuring content knowledge; they act as gateways to real-world opportunities and professional advancement. For this reason, it is crucial that assessment practices maintain both fairness and academic rigor while still capturing genuine learning and the individual effort of each student.

As AI tools continue to evolve, they are capable of generating not just grammatically correct text, but also convincing arguments, summaries, and even critical reflections, which seems true core components of many academic tasks. This places educators in a difficult position: how they can evaluate a student's cognitive development in a fair way if large parts of the work may have been shaped, prompted, or entirely generated by artificial intelligence? The concern isn't just about plagiarism in the traditional sense. It is about the growing potential for students to outsource thinking tasks to machines. In essence, unfortunately these tasks meant to develop higher level skills like critical thinking, synthesis, and original argumentation (Balalle & Pannilage, 2025; Zaibout & Madrane, 2024).

In response, many institutions have turned to AI detection tools to govern this new landscape. Yet the growing body of research into these tools raises serious concerns. While they may serve as a first line of inquiry, their reliability is questionable. Studies have documented how detection algorithms produce false positives, especially for students whose writing does not align with native speaker norms or standardized academic discourse (Lee & Low, 2024). Others have shown how simple tactics such as rephrasing, using hybrid human-AI drafting methods, or pasting content into a different editor can easily evade detection (Ateeq et al., 2024). This seems especially a true paradox. Those attempting to "cheat smartly" can often bypass detection, while honest students risk being wrongly accused based on flawed algorithmic judgments.

The ethical implications of relying too heavily on these tools are substantial. In academic settings where grades often open or close doors to future jobs and qualifications, even a single false accusation or lingering doubt can have real consequences for a student's life. When AI detection software starts acting as the final judge of honesty, it pulls authority away from teachers and chips away at the trust that should sit at the center of the student–teacher relationship. As Gonsalves (2025) and Premat and Farazouli (2025) point out, academic judgment is ultimately a human duty. These tools might help as part of a diagnostic process, but they shouldn't be used to punish especially when the results are uncertain or when the work involves creativity, reflection, or open-ended thinking.

This study matters on both a practical and an academic level. On a day-to-day level, it draws on direct experience from a nine-month professional program in the Gulf region, where assessment outcomes directly affected participants' job placements. Seen through that lens, the research offers a grounded look at how students, teachers, and institutions are all learning to deal with AI in real educational contexts. It doesn't just describe the technical issues; it also explores the human ones, the ethical, social, and procedural struggles that are emerging as people try to balance fairness, innovation, and trust in an age shaped by artificial intelligence.

Scholarly, the study contributes to a fast-growing academic conversation about the future of assessment in the age of artificial intelligence. While much recent literature has focused on detection and enforcement, this research takes a different route. It advocates for constructive and trust-based solutions by proposing a framework that includes early AI orientation, AI-resistant assessment design, diagnostic use of detection tools, and rubrics that account for AI-related input. The aim is to move beyond reactive policies toward proactive, pedagogically sound strategies that can withstand both current and future challenges.

In doing so, this study hopes to offer a practical model not just a case study for educators, administrators, and policymakers. As institutions worldwide wrestle with similar issues, there is an urgent need for assessment practices that preserve integrity without rejecting innovation. By grounding its recommendations in both real experiences and ethical reflection, this work seeks to support the development of fairer, more transparent, and future-ready assessment systems that honour student effort and uphold academic trust.

Research Purpose

This research seeks to explore, reflect upon, and critically analyze the real-world complexities of implementing AI detection tools in open-ended student assessments. It aims to examine how these technologies are currently used, additionally how they shape perceptions of fairness, authorship, and creativity within academic contexts. The goal is to develop a pragmatic framework that upholds academic integrity while allowing room for innovation, independent thought, and authentic expression. By doing this, the study recognizes the conflict between maintaining rigorous standards and encouraging the kind of exploratory thinking that higher education is meant to foster.

Research Questions

This research is structured around a series of key questions that drive both inquiry and reflection:

1. How do students perceive and respond to AI usage limits in critical, open-ended assessments?
2. What institutional challenges emerge when attempting to implement AI tools in education programs?
3. How can educators balance ethics, pedagogy, and practicality when grading work influenced by generative AI?

LITERATURE REVIEW

Theoretical Framework

Constructivist Learning Theory

Piaget's constructivist theory (Piaget, 2005) underpins this study. It claims that learning is an active process shaped by the learner's environment, resources and social context. From this viewpoint, knowledge is constructed by the learner through engagement with their work, relationships with others and the growing impact of technology. In this framework, AI tools may be considered as active learning facilitators rather than impartial tools. They affect how students do cognitive tasks, especially those open-ended questions that need them to think critically and analyze new ideas.

In the context of the project management and data science modules examined in this research, constructivist principles place a strong emphasis on creativity, originality, and the authentic application of conceptual knowledge to real-world scenarios. When used appropriately, AI can assist students by supporting problem-solving and expanding their analytical capacity. However, when misused, these same tools may undermine the constructivist process. As noted in recent studies (Shah, 2024; Żammit, 2025), an overreliance on generative AI often leads students to engage only superficially with course material, producing polished yet shallow responses that reflect minimal cognitive effort. Such outcomes reveal a key tension: while AI can enrich learning when used critically and intentionally, it can also dilute the very essence of education if it replaces rather than supports independent reasoning. Therefore, AI detection acts as diagnostic tools to assist teachers in determining whether a student's submission is the result of automated generation or an actual engagement with the content. When used appropriately, these tools can help preserve the integrity of constructivist learning environments, guaranteeing that the main objective of education is still to assist students in creating and expressing their own ideas rather than replicating what machines can produce for them.

Academic Integrity Theory

The Theory of Academic Integrity frames integrity as a web of interconnected values: honesty, trust, fairness, respect, and responsibility that form the moral foundation of educational practice together (Fishman, 2014). These are working principles that should shape every layer of an academic institution, from policy development to classroom interaction and the design of assessment itself. True integrity, in this sense, is something lived and practiced rather than merely declared.

Recent scholarship has underscored that technological solutions alone are not enough to preserve these values. Eze (2024) cautions that an excessive dependence on AI detection tools can shift the emphasis from fostering genuine ethical awareness to enforcing rule-based compliance. Students may feel less in control of their education and less accountable for the authenticity of their work if integrity is reduced to a surveillance issue rather than a shared understanding. Similarly, Pellerin and Ogandaga (2024) argue that academic integrity must be cultivated through open dialogue and reflective pedagogy, not through punitive measures. Their work challenges educators to reconsider how they respond to AI-related misconduct, encouraging approaches that teach ethical engagement rather than simply punish violations.

When the detection tools themselves have flaws or operate in an opaque manner, this problem becomes even more critical. Gonsalves (2025), for instance, demonstrates how uncertain or contradictory AI detection outcomes can lead to unfair judgments, especially when such results are used to penalize or discredit student work. Rather than promoting fairness, unreliable technology can actually undermine it, creating a climate of suspicion and anxiety that runs counter to the spirit of integrity it claims to defend. In the case examined within this study, Grammarly, a tool formally approved for use, often produced inconsistent and unreliable detection results, casting doubt on its effectiveness as a measure of originality. Premat and Farazouli (2025) therefore stress that AI systems should function as supportive instruments within ethical learning environments, not as replacements for human discernment. Upholding integrity, they argue, requires educators to remain the final arbiters of judgment, using technology as a complement to, not a substitute for, professional and moral responsibility.Taken together, these studies underscore the importance of using Academic Integrity Theory not just as a reactive framework to address misconduct, but also as a proactive guide for designing fair, transparent, and educationally meaningful policies for AI use in assessment.

Context of the study

Although AI tools are increasingly being used to assist both instruction and assessment, there is still no shared or context-sensitive framework to guide their ethical and effective use. This absence becomes especially noticeable in open-ended assessments, those that rely heavily on creativity, critical analysis, and real-world application, where rigid rules often fail to capture the nuance of learning. In the Gulf-based professional program explored in this study, the situation was even more complex. Due to the lack of legally recognized or officially approved AI technologies, educators were often forced to decide on an individual basis what kinds of AI support were appropriate. In practice, this meant long discussions among faculty, occasional confusion among students, and inconsistent decisions across courses.

For instance, Grammarly was widely used and legally permitted, but when applied to actual submissions, its integrated AI detection feature frequently yielded inconsistent or unreliable results. Educators found that even when institutional policies attempted to define thresholds for acceptable AI use, students quickly discovered workarounds and alternative tools. These inconsistencies revealed a deeper and systemic issue. Institutions run the danger of misinterpreting student work, reducing trust, and in some cases imposing penalties that are not fully justified in the absence of clear and well-communicated norms. What seems especially true is that effective AI governance in education requires a clear policy, also ongoing dialogue, professional judgment and a willingness to adapt as technology evolves.

Review of Literature

AI Tools in Student Assessment

The growing presence of AI tools in education has significantly altered how students engage with writing, feedback, and evaluation. Platforms such as Grammarly, QuillBot, ChatGPT, and a range of other AI-powered systems have become embedded in everyday academic practice; they are now used not only for grammar correction and stylistic refinement but also for more complex forms of text generation and enhancement designed to improve overall academic performance (Żammit, 2025). For many students, these tools act as valuable companions that offer a lot of features such as instant feedback, reducing anxiety around writing and providing linguistic support that might otherwise take hours of instructor attention. In this way, AI technologies have made some parts of academic support more democratic and made it easier to edit and revise your own work.

Yet, these same technologies have also introduced new complexities into the assessment process especially in assignments that demand independent reasoning and creativity or reflective insight. Many academics have drawn attention to the dual nature of AI in education, pointing out that while it promotes inclusivity and productivity, if applied carelessly, it also runs the risk of weakening deep learning. According to Triantafyllidis and Leftheriotis (2024), such tools provide real pedagogical benefits, particularly for students who struggle with structure, grammar, or language proficiency. However, when they are overused or misused, they can lead to a lack of engagement and conflict with the development of education. Shah (2024) observes that AI assistance often bypasses the student's internal problem-solving process, effectively turning writing tasks into mechanical submissions empty of original thought. This concern is especially visible in open-ended assessments like those explored in this study, where success depends less on linguistic accuracy and more on conceptual depth, synthesis, and argumentation.

At the same time, educators and institutions are increasingly turning to AI detection systems as a means of safeguarding academic integrity. While these tools may appear to offer a solution, their reliability is far from assured. As Gonsalves (2025) and Rodrigues et al. (2025) demonstrate, most detection platforms are plagued by technical inconsistencies that complicate fair evaluation. False positives, ambiguous probability scores and over-sensitivity to paraphrased or formulaic content are common issues especially in writing produced by non native English speakers (Giray, 2024; Wee & Reimer, 2023). It's even more worrying that these systems have a hard time telling the difference between text written by people and text written by AI. This problem has only gotten worse as models like GPT-4 have become more advanced (Elkhatat et al., 2023).

In the context of this study, Grammarly was the only officially approved detection tool, yet it repeatedly proved unreliable in producing consistent or transparent results (Abubakari, 2025). These inconsistencies raise both ethical and operational concerns, especially when educators are expected to make high-stakes decisions based on uncertain data. Relying too heavily on such tools risks compromising fairness and undermining trust between instructors and students. When combined, these results highlight the necessity of a well-rounded strategy, stress the importance of human judgement in assessments of academic integrity, and highlight the need for caution when utilising AI detection tools to evaluate students.

Academic Integrity in the AI Era

As artificial intelligence becomes more deeply embedded in higher education, the definition of academic misconduct is undergoing profound and sometimes confusing change (Nwozor, 2025). Acts that were once clearly understood, copying, plagiarism, or unauthorized collaboration, have become far more complex in a digital environment where generative AI can produce, refine, or even simulate original academic work. What was once an issue of "who wrote this sentence" has evolved into questions about how the writing was produced, what kind of intellectual contribution it represents, and whether the student can still be said to be the author of their own ideas. The distinction between acceptable academic support and unethical substitution has become more hazy due to the growing sophistication of AI systems, especially those that can write entire essays or construct arguments. Scholars such as Song (2024) note that plagiarism and forms of academic dishonesty have risen markedly since the widespread introduction of these tools, this underscores the urgent need for institutions to adopt thoughtful and adaptive implementation strategies.

One of the most challenging aspects of this shift is that AI-generated writing often appears original. AI output is created entirely from scratch, leaving no recognizable trace, in contrast to traditional plagiarism, where text can be linked to a specific source. (Hutson, 2024; Ogwueleka, 2025). This complicates how educators and administrators conceptualize ownership, authorship, and intellectual property (Premat & Farazouli, 2025). It also raises philosophical questions about what counts as "student work" when a significant portion of the content or phrasing may have been shaped by an algorithm. Integrity in the era of artificial intelligence must therefore take into consideration the genuineness of cognitive engagement in addition to the absence of copied content. The Theory of Academic Integrity, as articulated by Fishman (2014), provides an essential framework for navigating this shift. According to the theory, integrity is situated within a constellation of interrelated, operationally as well as aspirational values, including honesty, trust, fairness, respect, and responsibility.They are intended to be implemented in classroom procedures, assessment design, and institutional policies. But no matter how sophisticated, automated systems are unable to comprehend and apply these values in a contextual way like humans can (Khamassi et al., 2024), which is precisely where their limitations become most apparent.

Eze (2024) warns that excessive dependence on AI detection software risks transforming education into a culture of surveillance rather than learning. When students feel watched rather than trusted, they are more likely to comply out of fear than out of a genuine ethical conviction. Long-term effects on how students view authorship and accountability may result from this motivational shift from internalized values to external enforcement. A student who views integrity as a set of rules to avoid punishment, rather than as a moral framework guiding intellectual honesty, may produce compliant but disengaged work (Dahl & Waltzer, 2024). In support of this claim, Pellerin and Ogandaga (2024) advocate for a teaching strategy that incorporates discussion, introspection, and moral reasoning into the educational process. They found that when teachers openly discuss the purpose of integrity policies and set an example of moral academic conduct, students are more likely to internalise integrity values. In other words, dialogue and mentoring, not policing, are the best ways to teach integrity.

Further highlighting the need for integrity frameworks to develop in step with technological advancements are complementary studies by Wang and Cornely (2023). They argue that policies created without student input or a pedagogical foundation frequently fall flat with students, resulting in miscommunication and inadvertent behaviour violations. Co-developing integrity policies with students through workshops, reflective activities, or participatory codes of conduct can foster mutual ownership and shared accountability. By doing this, educational institutions shift from a punitive approach to one that recognizes technology's potential as a valid teaching tool and promotes its responsible use. This collaborative approach becomes especially important as AI continues to reshape the nature of assessment, writing, and intellectual effort.

Nevertheless, notable policy disparities still exist between institutions despite the implementation of such frameworks. These gaps are concerning in high-stakes educational contexts such as the Gulf-based program examined in this study, where assessment outcomes have a direct influence on students' employment opportunities and career progression. In such settings, uncertainty about acceptable AI use can have severe consequences (Zhang & Reusch, 2025). Students and teachers must negotiate ethical ambiguity on their own because many institutions lack explicit policies outlining the boundaries between "assistance" and "misconduct." Lack of clear guidelines also leads to different interpretations by instructors or departments, which can lead to uneven enforcement and unfairness perceptions.

Gonsalves (2025) identifies this inconsistency as a fundamental breach of the fairness principle that underpins Academic Integrity Theory. AI detection results run the risk of skewing the evaluation process and infringing on students' right to due consideration when they are regarded as authoritative in spite of their known limitations. False positives, vague classifications, and algorithmic bias can all lead to situations where honest students are penalized for using permissible tools or even for exhibiting writing styles that the software misinterprets as “AI-like.” The consequences are not merely academic, they can affect confidence, motivation, and trust in the educational system itself. Ambiguous or misaligned policies may thus punish students not for dishonesty, but for their attempts to operate within an unclear and shifting technological landscape (Gonsalves, 2025).

The wider implication is that upholding academic integrity in the AI era necessitates institutional flexibility and ethical sensitivity in addition to technical solutions (Gulumbe et al., 2025). Human judgment remains essential for interpreting both the intent and the context of student work. Detection tools can play a supportive and diagnostic role, but they must never replace the reflective evaluation of experienced educators (Khlaif et al., 2025). Educational institutions must create policies that are both adaptable enough to take advantage of new technologies and strict enough to uphold the enduring principles of integrity and respect that define genuine scholarship.

Ethical and Pedagogical Frameworks for AI Use

A growing number of academics are advocating for integrated frameworks that are simultaneously ethical, pedagogical, and practical in scope, given the shortcomings of both unrestricted AI use and the blind reliance on detection software. These frameworks acknowledge that academic integrity cannot be protected solely by technology; rather, integrity must be cultivated through intentional teaching design, transparent communication, and institutional accountability (Pant, 2025). Bretag (2013) argues that academic integrity should be ingrained in all phases of the learning process, from the early stages of assessment design and classroom instruction to the later phases of feedback, reflection, and policy enforcement. It is not a singular event or policy. When assessments are designed to elicit critical reasoning, self-reflection, and personal insight, students are far less likely to misuse AI tools from the outset (Campbell et al., 2024). A well-designed task leaves little space for misconduct because it invites engagement and demands intellectual ownership.

At the institutional level, policy clarity and legal compliance play an equally complex role. On one hand, clearly articulated regulations provide structure and protect academic standards. On the other, as Gheda et al. (2024) point out, universities often struggle to create policies that balance legal obligations, educational objectives, and the fast-changing nature of AI technology. Rodrigues et al. (2025)

refer to this tension as the "compliance paradox", a situation where institutions judge tools more by their ability to meet legal documentation standards than by their actual pedagogical value. Innovation suffers when avoiding risk takes precedence over other motivations. As a result, teachers might be compelled to use strict systems that adhere to rules but don't improve student learning. This dynamic reflects a deeper question about priorities: should academic institutions lead the conversation on how AI reshapes learning, or merely react to legal and reputational pressures that frame it as a problem to control?

Fair and ethical grading practices therefore require a far more nuanced approach (Fagbohun et al., 2024), one that incorporates student voice, educator judgement and contextual understanding in addition to mechanical detection. Premat and Farazouli (2025) stress that AI detection systems ought to be diagnostic tools that support fruitful communication between educators and students rather than being used as tools of punishment. Their argument aligns with a growing movement to reimagine assessment as a collaborative and reflective process rather than a purely evaluative one. Within this discussion, several scholars propose frameworks for responsible AI integration. An adaptable method for incorporating generative AI into learning tasks is provided by one such model, the Artificial Intelligence Assessment Scale (AIAS). Developed to support both accountability and creativity, it emphasizes areas where human insight and critical reasoning remain irreplaceable (Perkins et al., 2024; Furze et al., 2024). For example, under this framework, AI might assist in brainstorming or linguistic correction but would not replace human analysis, evaluation, or argument development.

Implementing these principles in real educational settings has shown encouraging results. Studies indicate that when students are explicitly taught how to use AI responsibly, instances of misconduct tend to decline, and engagement with coursework increases (Furze et al., 2024). Rather than viewing AI as a threat to integrity, students begin to perceive it as a legitimate learning partner, one that demands ethical awareness and critical thinking. However, as Kizilcec et al. (2024) note, this shift depends heavily on institutional willingness to adapt assessment practices. Frameworks such as AIAS work best when they are backed by systems that prioritize formative feedback over punitive measures, clear communication about acceptable AI use, and continual professional development for educators.

Ultimately, the emerging literature converges on a shared conclusion: the future of academic integrity in the age of generative AI lies not in restriction but in thoughtful integration (Koop & Gröblinger, 2024; Nagpal, 2024; Pellerin & Ogandaga, 2024). Institutions must move toward assessment designs that recognize the capabilities of AI while reaffirming the central role of human cognition and moral reasoning. When AI is positioned as a complement to, rather than a replacement for human thought, the result is a learning environment that promotes both ethical responsibility and intellectual independence. In this sense, academic integrity becomes not merely a matter of compliance, but a living practice, continuously negotiated between human judgment, technological potential, and the evolving purposes of education itself.

METHODOLOGY

Study Design

This study adopts a qualitative, observational case study design to explore how AI detection tools are implemented in open-ended and critically oriented student assessments within a professional education program. The focus on a single, bounded case allows for a detailed exploration of a real-world educational setting in which AI policy, assessment design, and student behavior converge in intricate and sometimes unpredictable ways. A case study approach was chosen precisely because it enables the researcher to capture the contextual complexity that would likely be lost in broader quantitative investigations. Through this lens, the study aims to understand how institutional rules and personal choices interact in the everyday practice of teaching and assessment rather than simply measuring the frequency or outcomes of AI use.

A rich and interpretive analysis that emphasizes the lived experiences of participants is supported by the qualitative nature of this study. Through the observation and interpretation of how educators and students deal with the existence of AI detection tools in their academic setting, the study aims to identify not only technical or procedural issues but also the ethical and emotional aspects of this process. The study's conceptual underpinnings are the Theory of Academic Integrity and constructivist learning theory, both of which are strongly supported by this interpretive position.

In this context, the observational case study seeks to explain why and how these interactions transpire in the way that they do, rather than just recording what happens, it offers a framework for comprehending the dynamic interplay between technological systems, institutional policy and human judgement. This study aspires to produce both descriptive and reflective insights that can guide pedagogical and ethical practices in other educational contexts dealing with comparable AI integration challenges.

Context of the Study

The case under investigation is part of a nine-month professional education program that is offered to a very selective group of Gulf students. The program was created with the specific and audacious goal of preparing 163 participants for professional placements in a renowned national institution that acts as a training ground and a gateway to competitive positions in the public sector. Admission to the program is selective reflecting not only the academic caliber of its participants, but also the expectation that graduates will transition directly into positions of responsibility upon completion. Because of this, the stakes for assessment results are very high, and grades have effects that go far beyond the classroom.

While the curriculum spans several disciplinary areas, this research focuses specifically on the project management and data science modules. These were chosen because they rely heavily on open-ended written assessments designed to test the students' ability to think critically, solve complex problems and apply theoretical knowledge to practical and real-world contexts. Such assessments require interpretation, synthesis and creativity; skills that are particularly vulnerable to distortion when generative AI is used inappropriately. Because student work frequently involves original reasoning and applied analysis that are difficult to distil into formulaic responses, the nature of these tasks also makes them perfect for investigating how AI detection tools function in real-world scenarios.

In this environment, the dual identity of the participants, as both students and potential employees, adds another layer of complexity. Each written submission is not only an academic exercise but also a reflection of the student's professional readiness. Educators therefore carry dual responsibility: to uphold academic integrity while also ensuring that assessments remain valid indicators of job-related competencies. The use of AI tools whether for assistance or generation, introduces tension into this process by blurring the boundaries between authentic learning and technological mediation; consequently, this setting provides a rich and relevant context for investigating how AI detection tools are implemented, interpreted, and experienced within high-stakes, real-world educational environments.

Researcher Role and Positionality

Within the context of this study, the researcher occupied several interrelated roles: subject matter expert (SME), module manager, facilitator, and assessor; each carrying distinct responsibilities but also overlapping in ways that provided a uniquely comprehensive perspective on the program. This multifaceted position granted sustained access to diverse dimensions of the educational process, including the development and evaluation of assessment methods, the implementation of institutional governance structures, and the collection of both formal and informal student feedback. The proximity afforded by these roles allowed for an exceptionally nuanced understanding of how AI detection tools were interpreted and applied in practice, also how students and educators negotiated their presence within the learning environment.

However, this closeness also required deliberate reflexivity and critical self-awareness. Being simultaneously an insider and an observer presented both opportunities and risks. While it enabled the researcher to gather rich, authentic insights, it also increased the possibility of bias and interpretive subjectivity. Recognizing this tension, the researcher adopted a reflective stance throughout the research process, documenting observations, emotions, and decisions through field notes and reflective memos. This practice helped to maintain analytical distance while preserving the depth of insight that comes from embedded observation.

This approach was based on being aware of ethics. The researcher consistently scrutinized their impact on classroom dynamics, student perceptions and data interpretation to ensure that professional authority did not hinder participants' readiness to convey candid opinions. The ethical guidelines of the host institution and general qualitative research standards were strictly adhered to, with transparency and confidentiality as the main goals. In this context, reflexivity served as a methodological safeguard and ethical obligation to maintain integrity, honor participant autonomy and remain critically cognizant of how positionality influences both the creation and interpretation of knowledge.

Data Collection Procedures

Observations were conducted in May 2025, following the completion of phase 1 and phase 2 modules of the program, which lasted for six months. After the assessments and based on the results, the students are classified into different specializations in phase three, which leads them to the final hiring process. During these observations, the researcher monitored trends in student engagement and submission, as well as observable behaviors that indicated reliance on AI or uncertainty regarding institutional policies. Data was collected using two primary methods:

Grading logs: which recorded recurring patterns in student submissions, indicators of AI usage, and responses to detection outcomes.

Personal reflection notes: derived from both experiential engagement and documentary evidence, including grading outcomes, email correspondence regarding tool approvals, and internal communications concerning policy enforcement. These reflections were composed contemporaneously and served to document ethical tensions, procedural ambiguities, and contextual factors that influence educator judgement.

Ethical Considerations

All data in this study are anonymised. Neither the organisation delivering the programme nor the institutional client is identified by name. No student names, identifiers, or personal information are disclosed, and all observations were drawn from professional interactions and grading data within the researcher's official role. As this study does not involve interviews or direct participant involvement, formal consent procedures were not applicable; however, the research design adheres to ethical standards of transparency, privacy, and non-maleficence.

Limitations

This study is limited by its single-site scope and the researcher's insider status, which, while enabling deep access, may also introduce subjectivity. The absence of student interviews or survey data means the findings are based solely on observed behaviors and institutional processes. Additionally, the dependence on three tools, Gemini, Grammarly and QuillBot, limits their generalizability to other AI platforms.

RESULTS

This section presents key patterns and insights derived from observational data collected during the assessment, grading, and institutional decision-making phases of a Gulf-based graduate development program. Academic Integrity and Constructivist Learning Theory served as theoretical frameworks that were used to analyze the data. Out of this, three main themes emerged: (1) Institutional challenges in tool approval; (2) student engagement and workarounds; and (3) accuracy and reliability of AI detection tools.

Institutional Challenges in Tool Approval

One of the earliest and most visible challenges observed in this study was the institutional complexity of approving and deploying AI detection tools. Despite the institutional initiative to explore Gemini's capabilities because it is already pre-approved for internal use, the tool was found inadequate for assessment needs, as it lacked the capacity to quantify AI-generated content in a meaningful way. Then, the next proposed solution, QuillBot, demonstrated high functional accuracy based on the researcher's prior experience and independent evaluations (Gewirtz, 2025).

However, the tool could not pass the organisation's legal and compliance approval process.

The compliance and security teams required specific documentation: server location for input data, completion of a vendor risk questionnaire, and details on internal security protocols. QuillBot's responses were noncommittal and generic, pointing only to public privacy documentation without providing custom responses or formal agreements. Consequently, they rejected the tool. This situation revealed a bigger problem in the rules we follow: the "compliance paradox" (Rodrigues et al., 2025), where useful educational tools are ignored because of unclear laws, even when they are needed right away for teaching.

Grammarly was subsequently proposed as an alternative and received approval, although with mandatory restrictions. These restrictions included the removal of all personal data from uploaded documents and the issuance of a clear privacy notice to students prior to the assessment. However, there was a very short notice period because the approval was only given ten days prior to the assessments. This experience shows that logistical barriers, rather than pedagogical priorities, frequently influence the adoption of technology in institutional settings. While Grammarly met the formal requirements, it was chosen more for compliance purposes than for its proven effectiveness in AI detection.

Student Engagement and Workarounds

The students were informed about AI detection policies in advance, as the organising team had communicated these to them on short notice prior to the assessments. Each assessment (Project Management and Data Science) lasted three hours and was conducted under strict proctoring conditions: students were not allowed to access phones, use generative AI tools, or leave the room in groups. In theory, these constraints aimed to minimise misconduct. However, practical enforcement revealed gaps in behavior management and student maturity.

Despite knowing that AI detection and cheating reports would be attached to their grades, many students attempted various forms of academic misconduct, from whispering and copying to attempting to bypass network restrictions by switching to personal hotspots. Several students admitted in prior informal conversations that they intended to use AI regardless of institutional limitations. This behavior was also evident in the uniformity and surface-level content of many submissions, despite the detection tool returning low or negligible AI usage scores.

This reveals the tension between policy design and actual student behavior. The announcement of AI usage penalties was intended as a deterrent. The penalties are as follows: up to 4 marks deducted for content showing >80% AI generation; 3 marks deducted for content showing from 50 to 80 AI generation; 2 marks deducted for content showing from 25 to 49% AI generation; 0 deduction for content showing less than 25% AI generation. However, in the absence of a reliable enforcement mechanism, the effectiveness of this deterrent function was markedly diminished. The constructivist ideal that students should engage in original thought was, in many instances, compromised by their efforts to exploit the system.

Accuracy and Reliability of AI Detection Tools

The most significant concern identified was the inaccuracy of AI detection results, especially when compared to educators' expectations and direct observations. Despite Grammarly being legally approved, it often struggled to recognise clear instances of AI-generated content. Several students submitted work that bore a strong resemblance to output from recognised AI platforms in terms of style and structure, a conclusion supported by the researcher's familiarity with the students' previous performance and language proficiency. However, since Grammarly identified this type of work as having little to no AI involvement, no penalties have been applied.

This inconsistency between the outputs of the tool and the judgements of educators presents both ethical and operational risks. In a programme where assessment outcomes directly impact hiring decisions and departmental placements, reliance on flawed AI tools can result in profoundly unjust consequences. Those who successfully evade detection may penalise or outperform honest students. Furthermore, educators are placed in a conflicted position: either override the tool's report and risk procedural challenge or accept an evidently inaccurate assessment as valid.

These findings reinforce claims in the literature that AI detection tools should augment, not replace, human academic judgement (Gonsalves, 2025; Eze, 2024). The evidence from this case indicates that, despite having official approval and regulations in place, the tools are insufficiently reliable for making important decisions, particularly in open-ended assessments that demand deep thinking and originality.

DISCUSSION

The findings of the study provide valuable insights into the complex dynamics involved in incorporating AI detection tools within educational assessments. Although the primary aim of this implementation is to uphold academic integrity, the results indicate notable tensions among the policy's objectives, the limitations of technology, and established pedagogical principles. The ethical, cognitive, and procedural issues that emerged are most effectively analyzed through the dual perspectives of Academic Integrity Theory and Constructivist Learning Theory.

Piaget's constructivist framework emphasizes that learners build knowledge actively through engagement, reflection, and contextual problem-solving. In the context of the assessments examined, this principle was undermined in two significant ways. Firstly, numerous students opted to evade the intellectual challenge presented by open-ended tasks by utilizing AI tools to shortcut the cognitive process. Secondly, the detection technology designed to protect constructivist learning frequently failed to identify these shortcuts, permitting superficial, AI-generated work to go unchallenged.

These observations resonate with the concerns expressed by Shah (2024) and Żammit (2025), who contend that an overreliance on generative AI tools diminishes deep thinking in favor of automated synthesis. This issue is particularly significant in assessments intended to evaluate real-world application and originality, as seen in the project management and data science modules examined. If students can easily conceal their use of AI and still attain full marks, it fundamentally undermines the essence of constructivist assessment.

As for Fishman's Academic Integrity Theory, it emphasizes values such as honesty, fairness, and responsibility. The findings of this study indicate that technological detection tools alone cannot guarantee the upholding of these values, especially when they are either inaccurate or lack transparency. The approval of Grammarly was based on legal compliance rather than pedagogical suitability, whereas QuillBot was excluded due to gaps in corporate transparency, despite its reported accuracy. This scenario demonstrates how institutional priorities can redirect attention from ethical considerations to risk management, consequently sidelining pedagogical concerns.

A deeper concern emerges from the lack of prior student orientation. In this program, learners were only informed near the assessment that their assessments would be reviewed using AI detection tools. While the policy applied specific mark deductions based on detected AI percentage, this reactive enforcement contradicts the pedagogical principles of fairness and transparency. Rather than fostering ethical engagement, such surprise enforcement risks creating confusion and resentment. Students must first be educated on the ethical, creative, and cognitive risks of AI misuse before being penalized for its detection. This aligns with calls by Pellerin and Ogandaga (2024) and Wang & Cornely (2023) to treat integrity as an educative process, not a punitive one.

The most problematic aspect was the inaccuracy and inconsistency of AI detection tools. The researcher, possessing considerable expertise in AI tools and firsthand understanding of the students' capabilities, discerned numerous occurrences where evidently AI-generated work went unnoticed or received low evaluations. These instances resulted in a divergence between policy and practice, wherein students who exploited the system encountered no repercussions, while others were misclassified or subjected to arbitrary evaluation.

Recent comparative analyses substantiate the variability of detection outputs among tools. For example, a study by Elkhatat et al. (2023) revealed that detection tools such as GPTZero, Turnitin, and Grammarly yielded inconsistent outcomes, particularly with hybrid or paraphrased material. Giray (2024) cautions about the widespread occurrence of false positives and inadequate accuracy in critical environments, especially for non-native English writers. These findings are consistent with the researcher's personal trials and institutional observations, adding weight to the claim that such tools are not reliable enough to justify penalizing students.

AI will not disappear from education; it is here to stay. Therefore, it is no longer pedagogically viable to prohibit its use entirely. Instead of discouraging AI utilization, institutions should transition to creating assessment tasks that encourage transparent and ethical interaction with AI, while allowing educators to evaluate original thinking. This includes formats such as reflective essays on AI-supported work, oral justifications of written assignments, and multi-step projects with process tracking.

RECOMMENDATIONS AND FRAMEWORK DESIGN

The challenges identified in this study, ranging from inaccurate detection tools to policy misalignment and pedagogical contradictions, highlight a critical need for a principled yet pragmatic framework for managing AI in student assessment. This section suggests a four-pillar framework designed to support academic integrity, support learner development, and ensure institutional compliance, without stifling innovation or unfairly penalizing students.

Pedagogical Transparency and Early AI Orientation

The AI policies must be introduced to students at the beginning of the program, rather than during the assessment. In this study, informing students about detection thresholds late in the process introduced unnecessary stress and undermined trust.

Recommendations:

- Include an AI literacy orientation session at the start of the program.
- Share detailed policies on allowed AI usage, ethical risks, and consequences for misuse.
- Encourage open discussion on how to use tools like Grammarly or ChatGPT ethically for idea generation, not substitution.

This aligns with Academic Integrity Theory's emphasis on trust, fairness, and shared responsibility (Fishman, 2014).

AI-Resistant Assessment Strategies

To maintain the integrity of open-ended assessments in an AI-integrated environment, institutions must reconsider not only the content of assessments but also the methods used. While AI detection tools are still unreliable, educators can create assessment experiences that are challenging to delegate to machines and that encourage genuine engagement.

Below are seven AI-resistant assessment strategies, each aligned with the principles of constructivist learning and academic integrity:

Table 1. AI-resistant assessment strategies

Strategy	Why It Works	AI-Proofing Benefit
Oral Presentations or Viva Voce	Real-time explanation of understanding; allows probing.	It is difficult for students to rely on AI when speaking live.
In-Class Reflections or Timed Essays	Promotes spontaneous thinking and authentic writing.	Reduces the ability for AI use due to monitored conditions.
Group Problem-Solving or Debates	Fosters evidence-based reasoning and live collaboration.	Unscripted nature neutralizes AI's usefulness.
Project-Based Learning	Emphasizes developmental thinking and iteration.	Allows educators to track progression and detect sudden AI use.
Multimedia or Creative Work + Justification	Encourages diverse output and metacognitive reasoning.	Combination of media + reflection is difficult to fake.
Peer Teaching or Student-Led Sessions	Forces real comprehension through instruction.	Live demonstration of knowledge confirms originality.
Staged Assessments (Draft → Feedback → Final)	Makes the learning journey visible; reduces opportunity for outsourcing.	Draft tracking helps identify suspicious leaps in quality or voice.

This addresses constructivist principles by reinforcing knowledge construction over reproduction (Piaget, 2005).

Detection Tools as Diagnostic Aids, Not Gatekeepers

The findings confirm that AI detectors, especially those like Grammarly can be misleading or inconsistent. While such tools may offer supporting evidence, they should never be used as the sole basis for penalizing students.

Recommendations:

- Use AI detectors only to flag work for further review, not to assign marks.
- Require that educators triangulate AI results with rubrics and academic judgment.
- Avoid assigning numeric penalties based on AI-use percentages without human verification.

As Gonsalves (2025) and Giray (2024) suggest, tools must inform, not replace, educator discretion.

AI-Aware Rubrics and Feedback Models

Grading rubrics should reflect the realities of AI-generated work by differentiating between acceptable support such as grammar checks, and problematic substitution such as full-text generation. Educators should offer feedback that promotes ethical use of AI rather than solely penalizing its presence.

Recommendations:

- Develop AI rubrics that encompass criteria for originality, analysis, and critical engagement.
- Train graders to recognize patterns indicative of AI-influenced writing and address ambiguities in a constructive manner.
- Utilize resources such as the AI Assessment Scale (AIAS) (Furze et al., 2024) as a reference for the development of these rubrics.

CONCLUSION

This study provides a timely, practice-informed exploration of how generative AI is transforming the landscape of student assessment in professional education settings. Drawing on direct observations from a significant program in the Gulf Region, it examines both the potential benefits, and the challenges associated with AI-assisted learning and AI detection tools in education. The analysis highlighted significant gaps, including the slow dissemination of AI policies, the inconsistency of detection tools, and the unclear repercussions for students navigating the ambiguous boundaries of acceptable use.

The findings also highlighted a broader issue: AI is not merely a technological tool but a significant pedagogical and ethical disruptor. While tools such as Grammarly and QuillBot can be beneficial in certain contexts, they present risks when utilised for grading decisions without adequate human oversight. Moreover, when institutional policies fail to clearly differentiate between acceptable and problematic uses of AI, or neglect to involve students in discussions regarding ethical implications, both trust and fairness within the educational environment are undermined.

To address these concerns, the study suggests a four-pillar framework that is consistent with academic integrity theory and constructivist learning theory. This framework is not just theoretical; it is based on real challenges and practical solutions that educators and institutions can implement.

By emphasizing early orientation, ethical assessment design, detection as a diagnostic tool (not a gatekeeper), and AI-aware rubrics, this model empowers institutions to uphold integrity without resorting to punitive or surveillance-based approaches. Importantly, it repositions the educator, not the algorithm, as the ultimate arbiter of academic quality.

The path forward does not lie in banning AI, but in building systems of trust, reflection, and pedagogical resilience. As AI continues to evolve, so must our methods for helping learners build and demonstrate knowledge, honestly, creatively, and responsibly.

Table 2. Framework Summary Table

Pillar	Focus	Key Actions
1. Pedagogical Transparency and Early AI Orientation	Introduce AI policies from the start of the program.	Host AI ethics sessions early Share acceptable use examples Foster open discussion on AI use
2. AI-Resistant Assessment Strategies	Redesign tasks to be process-driven and hard to automate.	Viva voce, debates, handwritten essays Project-based and staged submissions Peer teaching, multimedia justifications
3. Detection Tools as Diagnostic Aids	Use AI detectors as support tools, not grading authorities.	Never assign marks based on detection alone Triangulate AI flags with rubric evaluation
4. AI-Aware Rubrics and Feedback Models	Develop rubrics that distinguish between assistance and substitution.	Use AI Assessment Scale (AIAS) Include originality and critical thinking indicators Train graders to spot AI patterns

LIMITATIONS

This study is subject to several limitations that might constrain the generalizability and depth of its findings despite its valuable insights. First, the study is limited to a single-site case study within a gulf-based professional education program, restricting its relevance to various institutional, cultural, or disciplinary contexts. Additionally, the distinctive characteristics of this program, particularly its significant connection to employment, may not accurately reflect broader educational settings.

Second, the researcher's double role as both an observer and an assessor could lead to positional bias, even though they tried to be reflexive. This positioning facilitated access to profound, contextual observations. However, it may have also impacted on student behavior or distorted the interpretation of assessment results.

Third, the absence of direct student voice is a critical methodological constraint. The study cannot completely capture the motivations, interpretations, or emotional responses of students interacting with AI policies and detection systems without interviews, focus groups, or surveys. Observations and grading logs only show a little bit about how engaged and interested students are.

Furthermore, the dependence on three AI-related tools "Grammarly, Gemini, and QuillBot", with only one (Grammarly) being institutionally approved, limits the study's technological scope. This means that what we learn about how well AI can find things may not be true for other detection tools like Turnitin, GPTZero, or originality.ai.

Lastly, the study took place during a time when AI policy was still being put into place, which meant that there were still some problems with communication, enforcement and the availability of tools. The changing nature of institutional policies, student comprehension and AI capabilities constrains the enduring stability of the study's findings.

FUTURE RECOMMENDATIONS

In light of the challenges and insights identified, several actionable recommendations are proposed to guide future research, policy, and pedagogical practices:

Incorporate Student Perspectives through Mixed Methods

Future research should incorporate student perspectives through interviews, focus groups, or reflective journals. Comprehending student perspectives on AI ethics, policy transparency, and their personal usage practices can enhance institutional responses and alleviate deficiencies in engagement or compliance.

Expand Cross-Institutional and Cross-Disciplinary Research

More extensive comparative research across various institutions and disciplines is essential to assess the universality of identified challenges. Humanities, sciences, and applied technologies may show different ways that AI is used and misused that need more research.

Evaluate a Broader Range of AI Detection Tools

Future evaluations should include newer and more diverse AI detection platforms to compare reliability, false-positive rates, and usability. Independent benchmarking under different assessment types (e.g., essays, coding tasks, oral responses) would enhance validity.

Longitudinal Tracking of Policy Impact

Research should follow the long-term impact of AI policies on student behavior, academic performance, and perceptions of integrity. This would allow institutions to assess whether early orientation, rubric redesign, or AI literacy interventions produce sustained ethical outcomes.

Involve Students in Co-Creation of AI Guidelines

According to Wang & Cornely (2023), involving students in the creation of policies could promote clarity and a sense of ownership. Participatory models for policy development that strike a balance between institutional expectations and student realities should be investigated in future research.

Pilot Alternative Assessment Models at Scale

Institutions are encouraged to pilot alternative assessment strategies—such as oral defenses, peer instruction, or iterative drafts—across larger cohorts to test scalability, equity, and faculty workload implications.

Institutional Professional Development for Educators

To interpret AI detection reports, create AI-resistant tasks, and mentor students in the ethical use of tools, educators must receive ongoing training. Future studies could assess how well such professional development affects the enforcement of integrity and instructional quality.

Test and Refine AI-Aware Rubrics Across Contexts

The proposed rubric adjustments that account for AI-supported writing (e.g., grammar checks vs. full text generation) should be field-tested across different levels of education to determine their fairness, transparency, and pedagogical effectiveness.

By addressing these future directions, educators and researchers can develop more equitable, flexible, and transparent assessment ecosystems that acknowledge the presence of AI without compromising core academic values.

REFERENCES

Abubakari, M. S. (2025). Overviewing the Maze of Research Integrity and False Positives Within AI-Enabled Detectors: Grammarly Dilemma in Academic Writing. In *Impacts of Generative AI on the Future of Research and Education* (pp. 335-366). IGI Global.

Ateeq, A., Alzoraiki, M., Milhem, M., & Ateeq, R. A. (2024, October). Artificial intelligence in education: Implications for academic integrity and the shift toward holistic assessment. [). Frontiers Media SA.]. *Frontiers in Education*, *9*, 1470979. DOI: 10.3389/feduc.2024.1470979

Balalle, H., & Pannilage, S. (2025). Reassessing academic integrity in the age of AI: A systematic literature review on AI and academic integrity. *Social Sciences & Humanities Open*, *11*, 101299. DOI: 10.1016/j.ssaho.2025.101299

Bretag, T. (2013). Challenges in addressing plagiarism in education. *PLoS Medicine*, *10*(12), e1001574. DOI: 10.1371/journal.pmed.1001574 PMID: 24391477

Campbell, C., Townsend, T., & Harman, J. (2024). Addressing GenAI use through transparency in teaching and learning in a Master of Cyber Security program. *ASCILITE Publications*, 664-668.

Dahl, A., & Waltzer, T. (2024). A canary alive: What cheating reveals about morality and its development. *Human Development*, *68*(1), 6–25. DOI: 10.1159/000534638

Elkhatat, A. M., Elsaid, K., & Almeer, S. (2023). Evaluating the efficacy of AI content detection tools in differentiating between human and AI-generated text. *International Journal for Educational Integrity*, *19*(1), 17. DOI: 10.1007/s40979-023-00140-5

Eze, C. A. (2024). The role of educators in upholding academic integrity in an ai-driven era. *AI and ethics, academic integrity and the future of quality assurance in higher education.*

Fagbohun, O., Iduwe, N. P., Abdullahi, M., Ifaturoti, A., & Nwanna, O. M. (2024). Beyond traditional assessment: Exploring the impact of large language models on grading practices. *Journal of Artificial Intelligence. Machine Learning and Data Science*, *2*(1), 1–8.

Fishman, T. (2014). *The fundamental values of academic integrity*. International Center for Academic Integrity, Clemson University.

Furze, L., Perkins, M., Roe, J., & MacVaugh, J. (2024). The AI Assessment Scale (AIAS) in action: A pilot implementation of GenAI-supported assessment. *Australasian Journal of Educational Technology*, *40*(4), 38–55. DOI: 10.14742/ajet.9434

Gewirtz, D. (2025, April 30). *I tested 10 AI content detectors, and these 5 correctly identified AI text every time*. ZDNet. https://www.zdnet.com/article/i-tested-10-ai-content-detectors-and-these-5-correctly-identified-ai-text-every-time/

Gheda, M. L. M., Hamid, S. A., Syed, S. R., Latif, A., & Nusran, N. F. M. (2024). *Optimising AI for developing reliable academic assessment design. Asian Journal of Open and Distance Learning*.

Giray, L. (2024). The Problem with False Positives: AI Detection Unfairly Accuses Scholars of AI Plagiarism. *The Serials Librarian*, *85*(5-6), 181–189. DOI: 10.1080/0361526X.2024.2433256

Gonsalves, C. (2025). Addressing student non-compliance in AI use declarations: Implications for academic integrity and assessment in higher education. *Assessment & Evaluation in Higher Education*, *50*(4), 592–606. DOI: 10.1080/02602938.2024.2415654

Gulumbe, B. H., Audu, S. M., & Hashim, A. M. (2025). Balancing AI and academic integrity: What are the positions of academic publishers and universities? *AI & Society*, *40*(3), 1775–1784. DOI: 10.1007/s00146-024-01946-8

Hutson, J. (2024). Rethinking plagiarism in the era of generative AI. *Journal of International Communication*, *4*(1).

Khamassi, M., Nahon, M., & Chatila, R. (2024). Strong and weak alignment of large language models with human values. *Scientific Reports*, *14*(1), 19399. DOI: 10.1038/s41598-024-70031-3 PMID: 39169090

Khlaif, Z. N., Alkouk, W. A., Salama, N., & Abu Eideh, B. (2025). Redesigning assessments for AI-enhanced learning: A framework for educators in the generative AI era. *Education Sciences*, *15*(2), 174. DOI: 10.3390/educsci15020174

Kizilcec, R. F., Huber, E., Papanastasiou, E. C., Cram, A., Makridis, C. A., Smolansky, A., Zeivots, S., & Raduescu, C. (2024). Perceived impact of generative AI on assessments: Comparing educator and student perspectives in Australia, Cyprus, and the United States. *Computers and Education: Artificial Intelligence*, *7*, 100269. DOI: 10.1016/j.caeai.2024.100269

Koop, M., & Gröblinger, O. (2024). Generative AI and academic integrity-a contradiction. In *European Association of Distance Teaching Universities.(2024, November 25). Leading the Future of Learning. Proceedings of the Innovating Higher Education Conference* (pp. 101-114).

Lee, C. C., & Low, M. Y. H. (2024). Using genAI in education: The case for critical thinking. *Frontiers in Artificial Intelligence*, *7*, 1452131. DOI: 10.3389/frai.2024.1452131 PMID: 39554991

Nagpal, H. (2024). *Policies, procedures, and guidelines: are universities effectively ensuring AI (academic integrity) in the era of generative AI?* (Doctoral dissertation).

Nwozor, A. (2025). Artificial intelligence (AI) and academic honesty-dishonesty nexus: Trends and preventive measures. *AI and Ethics, Academic Integrity and the Future of Quality Assurance in Higher Education, 27.*

Ogwueleka, F. N. (2025). Plagiarism Detection in the age of artificial intelligence: current technologies and future directions. *AI and ethics, academic integrity and the future of quality assurance in higher education, 10.*

Pant, P. (2025). Upholding Ethical Standards: Governance, Transparency, and Integrity in Higher Education Administration. In *Challenges of Public Administration Management for Higher Education* (pp. 195-208). IGI Global.

Pellerin, M., & Ogandaga, M. (2024). *Rethinking Academic Integrity and Plagiarism in the Age of AI.*

Perkins, M., Furze, L., Roe, J., & MacVaugh, J. (2024). The Artificial Intelligence Assessment Scale (AIAS): A framework for ethical integration of generative AI in educational assessment. *Journal of University Teaching & Learning Practice*, *21*(6), 49–66. DOI: 10.53761/q3azde36

Piaget, J. (2005). *The psychology of intelligence*. Routledge. DOI: 10.4324/9780203981528

Premat, C., & Farazouli, A. (2025). Academic Integrity vs. Artificial Intelligence: A tale of two AIs. *Praxis Educativa (Santa Rosa)*, (20), 23.

Rodrigues, M., Silva, R., Borges, A. P., Franco, M., & Oliveira, C. (2025). Artificial intelligence: Threat or asset to academic integrity? A bibliometric analysis. *Kybernetes*, *54*(5), 2939–2970. DOI: 10.1108/K-09-2023-1666

Song, N. (2024). Higher education crisis: Academic misconduct with generative AI. *Journal of Contingencies and Crisis Management*, *32*(1), e12532. DOI: 10.1111/1468-5973.12532

Triantafyllidis, A., Leftheriotis, K., Kotsovoulou, M., Cirstea, T., & Vranopoulos, G. (2024). INTRODUCING AI IN FLIPPED CLASSROOM. A PRELIMINARY STUDY. In *EDULEARN24 Proceedings* (pp. 8828-8835). IATED.

Wang, J., & Cornely, P. R. (2023, November). Addressing academic misconduct in the age of ChatGPT: Strategies and solutions. In *Proceedings of the 2023 7th International Conference on Education and E-Learning* (pp. 19-25). DOI: 10.1145/3637989.3638014

Wee, H. B., & Reimer, J. D. (2023). Non-English academics face inequality via AI-generated essays and countermeasure tools. *Bioscience*, *73*(7), 476–478. DOI: 10.1093/biosci/biad034

Yan, L., Greiff, S., Teuber, Z., & Gašević, D. (2024). Promises and challenges of generative artificial intelligence for human learning. *Nature Human Behaviour*, *8*(10), 1839–1850. DOI: 10.1038/s41562-024-02004-5 PMID: 39438686

Zaibout, N., & Madrane, M. (2024). Optimizing Academic Assessment: The Impact of AI on Student Integrity, Creativity, and Achievement. *International Journal of Engineering Trends and Technology*, *72*(11), 357–370. DOI: 10.14445/22315381/IJETT-V72I11P134

Żammit, J. (2025). Secondary School Teachers' Experiences with Generative AI in Maltese Language Teaching. *Technology, Knowledge and Learning*, 1-19.

Zhang, Y., & Reusch, P. (2025, April). Trust in and Adoption of Generative AI in University Education: Opportunities, Challenges, and Implications. In *2025 IEEE Global Engineering Education Conference (EDUCON)* (pp. 1-10). IEEE. DOI: 10.1109/EDUCON62633.2025.11016490

Compilation of References

Abbas, M., Jam, F. A., & Khan, T. I. (2024). Is it harmful or helpful? Examining the causes and consequences of generative AI usage among university students. *International Journal of Educational Technology in Higher Education*, *21*, 10. Advance online publication. DOI: 10.1186/s41239-024-00444-7

Abbas, S., Al-Barhamtoshy, H., & Alotaibi, F. (2021). Towards an Arabic Sign Language (ArSL) corpus for deaf drivers. *PeerJ. Computer Science*, *7*, e741. DOI: 10.7717/peerj-cs.741

Abdelghani, N. (2022). Artificial intelligence and Arabic language processing: Opportunities and challenges. *Journal of Arabic Linguistics*, *56*(2), 145–162.

Abdulhadi, S. (2024). Uprooted but Unbroken: Exploring the Experiences of Yemeni Students at Yemeni Schools in Cairo.

Abduxalilova, S., Tilovxo'jayeva, A., & Abdug'afforova, N. (2023). Data Analysis in English Language Teaching and Using it for Feedback and Progress Monitoring. *Modern Science and Research*, *2*(10), 202–207. DOI: 10.5281/zenodo.10205650

Abubakari, M. S. (2025). Overviewing the Maze of Research Integrity and False Positives Within AI-Enabled Detectors: Grammarly Dilemma in Academic Writing. In *Impacts of Generative AI on the Future of Research and Education* (pp. 335-366). IGI Global.

Adeloye, A., Kayode, T., Ariyo, E., & Jeje, O. (2023). The impact of Artificial Intelligence on the academic achievement of creative Art students in secondary schools. *NIU Journal of Humanities*, *8*(4), 163–169. DOI: 10.58709/niujhu.v8i4.1740

Admiraal, W., Vermeulen, J., & Bulterman-Bos, J. (2020). Teaching with learning analytics: How to connect computer-based assessment data with classroom instruction? *Technology, Pedagogy and Education*, *29*(5), 577–591. DOI: 10.1080/1475939X.2020.1825992

Ahmed, H. (2024). Institutional integration of artificial intelligence in higher education: The moderation effect of ethical consideration. *International Journal of Educational Reform*. Online publication. DOI: 10.1177/10567879241247551

Ajuwon, O. A., Animashaun, E. S., & Chiekezie, N. R. (2024). Integrating AI and technology in educational administration: Improving efficiency and educational quality. *Open Access Research Journal of Science and Technology*, *11*(2), 116–127. DOI: 10.53022/oarjst.2024.11.2.0102

Akacem, M., Faulkner, J. L., & Miller, D. D. (2023). Oil MENA's Challenges and the Policy Response: Addressing the Institutional and Trust Deficits. *Journal of South Asian and Middle Eastern Studies*, *46*(4), 1–32. DOI: 10.1353/jsa.2023.a899953

Akbar, M. S. (2025). Beyond Detection: Designing AI-Resilient Assessments with Automated Feedback Tool to Foster Critical Thinking. arXiv preprint arXiv:2503.23622.

Akbarighatar, P. (2024). Operationalizing responsible AI principles through responsible AI capabilities. *AI and Ethics*, *5*(2), 1787–1801. DOI: 10.1007/s43681-024-00524-4

Akgun, S., & Greenhow, C. (2021). Artificial intelligence in education: Addressing ethical challenges in K-12 settings. *AI and Ethics*, *2*(3), 431–440. DOI: 10.1007/s43681-021-00096-7 PMID: 34790956

Akram, H., Abdelrady, A. H., Al-Adwan, A. S., & Ramzan, M. (2022). Teachers' perceptions of technology integration in teaching-learning practices: A systematic review. *Frontiers in Psychology*, *13*, 1–9. DOI: 10.3389/fpsyg.2022.920317 PMID: 35734463

Al Karam, A. (2021). Quality assurance and academic integrity in UAE higher education. *Journal of Higher Education Policy and Leadership Studies*, *2*(1), 49–62.

Alabbas, A., & Alomar, K. (2024). Tayseer: A novel AI-powered Arabic chatbot framework for technical and vocational student helpdesk services and enhancing student interactions. *Applied Sciences (Basel, Switzerland)*, *14*(5), 2547. DOI: 10.3390/app14062547

Al-Abdullatif, A., & Gameel, B. (2023). Artificial intelligence–driven decision-making in higher education: Emerging practices and ethical concerns. *Education and Information Technologies*, *28*(4), 5231–5252.

AlAfnan, M. A. (2024). Artificial Intelligence and Language: Bridging Arabic and English with Technology. *Journal of Ecohumanism*, *3*(8). Advance online publication. DOI: 10.62754/joe.v3i8.4961

Alameddine, M., Sabra, N., El Amaout, N., El Dakkoudi, A., El Jaouni, M. B., Hamadeh, R., Shanaa, A., & Saleh, S. (2025). Utilizing gamification, artificial intelligence, and mHealth for the professional development of maternal care providers: Exploratory pilot cross-sectional study assessing providers' satisfaction in primary health care centers in Lebanon. *JMIR Serious Games, 13*, e53735. DOI: 10.2196/53735 PMID: 40929508

Alamgir, A., Roy, P., & Taverna, F. (2024). Levels of engagement of South Asian participants in health research: Effectiveness of community-based research (CBR) framework. *Journal of Scientific Research and Reports*, *30*(9), 880–897. DOI: 10.9734/jsrr/2024/v30i92415

Alam, S., Usama, M., Alam, M. M., Jabeen, I., & Ahmad, F. (2023). Artificial Intelligence in Global World: A case study of Grammarly as e-Tool on ESL Learners' writing of Darul Uloom Nadwa. *International Journal of Information and Education Technology (IJIET)*, *13*(11), 1741–1747. DOI: 10.18178/ijiet.2023.13.11.1984

Albariqi, Z. (2024). A systematic review exploring the use of artificial intelligence in developing writing skills. *Journal of Critical Studies in Language and Literature*, *5*(6), 59–64. DOI: 10.46809/jcsll.v5i6.308

Al-Ghadhban, D., & Al-Twairesh, N. (2020). Nabiha: An Arabic dialect chatbot. *International Journal of Advanced Computer Science and Applications*, *11*(3). Advance online publication. DOI: 10.14569/IJACSA.2020.0110357

Alhassan, N. A., Albarrak, A. S., Bhatia, S., & Agarwal, P. (2022). A novel framework for Arabic dialect chatbot using machine learning. *Computational Intelligence and Neuroscience*, *1844051*, 1–11. DOI: 10.1155/2022/1844051 PMID: 35310584

Al-Kendi, R., & Al-Mehairi, S. (2022). The adoption of artificial intelligence in universities across the United Arab Emirates. *International Journal of Educational Technology in Higher Education*, *19*, 38.

Al-Khalifa, S., Alhumaidhi, F., Alotaibi, H., & Al-Khalifa, H. S. (2023). ChatGPT across Arabic Twitter: A study of topics, sentiments, and sarcasm. *Data 8(11),* 171, 1-19.

Almahasees, Z., Al Awabdeh, A., & Mahmoud, S. (2024). ChatGPT and higher education: A pathway to unprecedented progress. *Journal of Higher Education Theory and Practice*, *24*(5). Advance online publication. DOI: 10.33423/jhetp.v24i5.7004

Almassaad, A., Alajlan, H., & Alebaikan, R. (2024). Student perceptions of generative artificial intelligence: Investigating utilization, benefits, and challenges in higher education. *Systems*, *12*(10), 385. DOI: 10.3390/systems12100385

Almelhes, S. A. (2024). Gamification for teaching the Arabic language to non-native speakers: A systematic literature review. *Frontiers in Education*, *9*, 1371955. DOI: 10.3389/feduc.2024.1371955

Alsheddi, A. S., & Alhenaki, L. S. (2022). English and Arabic chatbots: A systematic literature review. *International Journal of Advanced Computer Science and Applications*, *13*(8), 662–675. DOI: 10.14569/IJACSA.2022.0130876

Alshumaimeri, Y. A., & Alshememry, A. K. (2023). The extent of AI applications in EFL learning and teaching. *IEEE Transactions on Learning Technologies*, *17*, 653–663. DOI: 10.1109/TLT.2023.3322128

Al-Zahrani, A. M., & Alasmari, T. M. (2024). Exploring the impact of artificial intelligence on higher education: The dynamics of ethical, social, and educational implications. *Humanities & Social Sciences Communications*, *11*(1), 912. DOI: 10.1057/s41599-024-03432-4

Ansari, A. N., Ahmad, S., & Bhutta, S. (2023). Mapping the global evidence around the use of ChatGPT in higher education: A systematic scoping review. *Education and Information Technologies*, *29*(9), 1–41. DOI: 10.1007/s10639-023-12223-4

Ansari, S. R., & Qamari, I. N. (2025). Artificial intelligence and students' cognitive learning outcomes with bibliometric and content analysis for future research agenda. *Discover Education*, *4*(1), 441. Advance online publication. DOI: 10.1007/s44217-025-00865-0

Antia, B. E. (2021). Multilingual examinations: Towards a schema of politicization of language in end of high school examinations in sub-Saharan Africa. *International Journal of Bilingual Education and Bilingualism*, *24*(1), 138–153. DOI: 10.1080/13670050.2018.1450354

Arabisard. (n.d.). Title of page. https://www.arabisard.com/site

Ateeq, A., Alzoraiki, M., Milhem, M., & Ateeq, R. A. (2024, October). Artificial intelligence in education: Implications for academic integrity and the shift toward holistic assessment. []. Frontiers Media SA.]. *Frontiers in Education*, *9*, 1470979. DOI: 10.3389/feduc.2024.1470979

Avsheniuk, N., Seminikhyna, N., Ruban, L., & Sviatiuk, Y. (2025). Exploring overreliance on AI tools in English for specific purposes Courses: Challenges and implications for learning and academic integrity. *Arab World English Journal*, *1*(1), 3–20. DOI: 10.24093/awej/AI.1

Badrasawi, K., Zaki, W., & Mustafa, F. (2021). Understanding research identities among faculty in Gulf universities. *International Journal of Research in Education and Science*, *7*(4), 1043–1062.

Balaji, M. T. M., & Balajiraja, N. UMA, M. P., & Nair, M. S. P. (2025). Generative AI Tools: Concepts, Applications, and Innovations. Academic Guru Publishing House.

Balalle, H., & Pannilage, S. (2025). Reassessing academic integrity in the age of AI: A systematic literature review on AI and academic integrity. *Social Sciences & Humanities Open*, *11*, 101299. DOI: 10.1016/j.ssaho.2025.101299

Bannister, P., Alcalde Peñalver, E., & Santamaría Urbieta, A. (2023). Transnational higher education cultures and generative AI: A nominal group study for policy development in English medium instruction. *Journal for Multicultural Education*, *18*(4). Advance online publication. DOI: 10.1108/JME-10-2023-0102

Barnes, E., & Huston, J. (2024). Strategic integration of AI in higher education and industry: The AI8-point model. *Advances in Social Sciences and Management*, *2*(6), 39–52. DOI: 10.63002/assm.26.520

Barnes, E., & Hutson, J. (2024). Navigating the ethical terrain of AI in higher education: Strategies for mitigating bias and promoting fairness. *Forum for Education Studies.*, *2*(2), 1229. DOI: 10.59400/fes.v2i2.1229

Beale, R. (2025). The Revolution Has Arrived: What the Current State of Large Language Models in Education Implies for the Future. arXiv preprint arXiv:2507.02180.

Becheru, A., Calota, A., & Popescu, E. (2018). Analyzing students' collaboration patterns in a social learning environment using StudentViz platform. *Smart Learn. Environ.*, *5*(18), 1–18. DOI: 10.1186/s40561-018-0063-0

Bedin, E., S Marques, M., & das Graças Cleophas, M. (2023). Research on the content, technological, and pedagogical knowledge (TPACK) of chemistry teachers during remote teaching in the pandemic in the light of students' perceptions. *Journal of Information Technology Education Research, 22*, 001–024. DOI: 10.28945/5063

Belaid, L., & Ma a, L. (2024). Revolutionizing AI in education: A review of ethical challenges and frontiers. *Journal of Innovation in Psychology. Education and Didactics*, *28*(2), 165–174.

Ben Youssef, A., Dahmani, M., & Ragni, L. (2022). ICT use, digital skills and students' academic performance: Exploring the digital divide. *Information (Basel)*, *13*(3), 129. DOI: 10.3390/info13030129

Betz, H. C. (2025). AI and Writing: Where Are We Now? (Doctoral dissertation, The Florida State University).

Bhagat, K. K., Liou, W. K., Michael Spector, J., & Chang, C. Y. (2019). To use augmented reality or not in formative assessment: A comparative study. *Interactive Learning Environments*, *27*(5-6), 830–840. DOI: 10.1080/10494820.2018.1489857

Bonthu, C., & Goel, G. (2025). Autonomous Supplier Evaluation and Data Stewardship with AI: Building Transparent and Resilient Supply Chains. *International Journal of Computational and Experimental Science and Engineering*, *11*(3). Advance online publication. DOI: 10.22399/ijcesen.3854

Borenstein, J., & Howard, A. (2020). Emerging challenges in AI and the need for AI ethics education. *AI and Ethics*, *1*(1), 61–65. DOI: 10.1007/s43681-020-00002-7 PMID: 38624388

Borge, M., Smith, B. K., & Aldemir, T. (2024). Using generative ai as a simulation to support higher-order thinking. *International Journal of Computer-Supported Collaborative Learning*, *19*(4), 479–532. DOI: 10.1007/s11412-024-09437-0

Boscardin, C. K., Gin, B., Golde, P. B., & Hauer, K. E. (2023). ChatGPT and Generative Artificial Intelligence for Medical Education: Potential Impact and Opportunity. *Academic Medicine*, *99*(1), 22–27. DOI: 10.1097/ACM.0000000000005439 PMID: 37651677

Boudihaj, A., & Sahli, M. (2022). Education in the MENA Region. In World Education Patterns in the Global South: The Ebb of Global Forces and the Flow of Contextual Imperatives (pp. 19-41). Emerald Publishing Limited. DOI: 10.1108/S1479-36792022000043B002

Braun, V., & Clarke, V. (2006). Using thematic analysis in psychology. *Qualitative Research in Psychology*, *3*(2), 77–101. DOI: 10.1191/1478088706qp063oa

Bretag, T. (2013). Challenges in addressing plagiarism in education. *PLoS Medicine*, *10*(12), e1001574. DOI: 10.1371/journal.pmed.1001574 PMID: 24391477

Buabeng-Andoh, C. (2012). Factors influencing teachersâ adoption and integration of Artificial Intelligenceinto teaching: A review of the literature. *International Journal of Education and Development using AI, 8*(1), 136-155. https://www.learntechlib.org/p/188018/

Bulut, O., Beiting-Parrish, M., Casabianca, J. M., Slater, S. C., Jiao, H., Song, D., Ormerod, C. M., Fabiyi, D. G., Ivan, R., Walsh, C., Rios, O., Wilson, J., Yildirim-Erbasli, S. N., Wongvorachan, T., Liu, J. X., Tan, B., & Morilova, P. (2024). The rise of artificial intelligence in educational measurement: opportunities and ethical challenges. *arXiv (Cornell University)*. https://doi.org//arxiv.2406.18900DOI: 10.48550

Cabrera, I., Vilca, J., Oliva, E., García, K., Rojas, R., Casaverde, M., & Colonia, C. U. (2024). *Artificial intelligence in the ethics of education*. Editorial Mar Caribe. DOI: 10.70288/emc.9789915970646

Campbell, C., Townsend, T., & Harman, J. (2024). Addressing GenAI use through transparency in teaching and learning in a Master of Cyber Security program. *ASCILITE Publications*, 664-668.

Casebourne, I., Shi, S., Hogan, M., Holmes, W., Hoel, T., Wegerif, R., & Yuan, L. (2025). Using AI to Support Education for Collective Intelligence. *International Journal of Artificial Intelligence in Education*, *35*(11), 1597–1629. DOI: 10.1007/s40593-024-00437-7

Centennial Vision, U. A. E. 2071. (2017). *Centennial 2071 strategic document*. UAE Government.

Chan, C. K. Y., & Colloton, T. (2024). *Generative AI in higher education*. https://doi.org/DOI: 10.4324/9781003459026

Chan, C. K. Y. (2023). A comprehensive AI policy education framework for university teaching and learning. *International Journal of Educational Technology in Higher Education*, *20*(1), 38. Advance online publication. DOI: 10.1186/s41239-023-00408-3

Chang, D. H., Lin, M. P., Hajian, S., & Wang, Q. Q. (2023). Educational design principles of using AI chatbot that supports Self-Regulated learning in education: Goal setting, feedback, and personalization. *Sustainability (Basel)*, *15*(17), 12921. DOI: 10.3390/su151712921

Chatzichristofis, S. A., Tsopozidis, A., Kyriakidou-Zacharoudiou, A., Evripidou, S., & Amanatiadis, A. (2025). Designing an AI-supported framework for literary text adaptation in primary classrooms. *AI*, *6*(7), 150. DOI: 10.3390/ai6070150

Chaudhry, M. A., Cukurova, M., & Luckin, R. (2022). A Transparency Index Framework for AI in education. *arXiv (Cornell University)*. https://doi.org//arxiv.2206.03220DOI: 10.1007/978-3-031-11647-6_33

Chen, W., Chen, R., & Lin, Y. (2020). Artificial intelligence in higher education: A systematic review. *Journal of Educational Technology & Society*, *23*(2), 103–118.

Chen, Y., Ahn, M. J., & Wang, Y. (2023). Artificial intelligence and Public Values: Value impacts and governance in the public sector. *Sustainability (Basel)*, *15*(6), 4796. DOI: 10.3390/su15064796

Christensen Hughes, J. (2022). Academic integrity across time and place: Higher education's questionable moral calling. In *Academic integrity in Canada: An enduring and essential challenge* (pp. 25–59). Springer International Publishing. DOI: 10.1007/978-3-030-83255-1_2

Commission for Academic Accreditation (UAE Ministry of Education). (2019). *Standards for institutional licensure and program accreditation*. Ministry of Education.

Cotton, D. R. E., Cotton, P. A., & Shipway, J. (2023). ChatGPT, assessment, and academic integrity: Student and staff perspectives. *Innovations in Education and Teaching International*, *60*(4), 1–12.

Cotton, D. R. E., Cotton, P. A., & Shipway, J. R. (2024). Chatting and cheating: Ensuring academic integrity in the era of ChatGPT. *Innovations in Education and Teaching International*, *61*(2), 228–239. DOI: 10.1080/14703297.2023.2190148

Crawford, J., Allen, K. A., Pani, B., & Cowling, M. (2024). When artificial intelligence substitutes humans in higher education: The cost of loneliness, student success, and retention. *Studies in Higher Education*, *49*(5), 883–897. DOI: 10.1080/03075079.2024.2326956

Creswell, J. W., & Poth, C. (2018). *Qualitative inquiry and research design: Choosing among five approaches* (4th ed.). SAGE.

Crompton, H., Edmett, A., Ichaporia, N., & Burke, D. (2024). AI and English language teaching: Affordances and challenges. *British Journal of Educational Technology*, *55*(6), 2503–2529. DOI: 10.1111/bjet.13460

Daher, R. (2025). Integrating AI literacy into teacher education: A critical perspective paper. *Discover Artificial Intelligence*, *5*(1), 217. Advance online publication. DOI: 10.1007/s44163-025-00475-7

Dahl, A., & Waltzer, T. (2024). A canary alive: What cheating reveals about morality and its development. *Human Development*, *68*(1), 6–25. DOI: 10.1159/000534638

Daou, L., & El Hajj, C. (2023). Challenges and Opportunities Faced by the Students and Faculty Members. Governance in Higher Education: Global Reform and Trends in the MENA Region, 89-105.

David, J. O. (2025, May). Redefining assessment for sustainability: A reflective approach to curriculum transformation in environmental education. []. Frontiers Media SA.]. *Frontiers in Education, 10*, 1553999. DOI: 10.3389/feduc.2025.1553999

Davis, A. (2023). Academic integrity in the time of contradictions. *Cogent Education, 10*(2), 2289307. DOI: 10.1080/2331186X.2023.2289307

Dawson, P., ChatGPT Detection Working Group, & Sutherland, K. (2023). Rethinking assessment in the age of generative AI. *Assessment & Evaluation in Higher Education, 48*(7), 1–15.

Deepshikha, D. (2025). A comprehensive review of AI-powered grading and tailored feedback in universities. *Discover Artificial Intelligence, 5*(1), 251. Advance online publication. DOI: 10.1007/s44163-025-00517-0

Deutschmann, M., & Vu, M. T. (2015). Computer assisted language learning in language education: an overview of theories, methods, and current practices. In Lindgren, E., & Enever, J. (Eds.), *Språkdidaktik: researching language teaching and learning* (pp. 43–60). Department of Language Studies, Umeå University., http://urn.kb.se/resolve?urn=urn:nbn:se:umu:diva-106898

Devasena, R. (2024). Artificial intelligence in Education: An alternative to Traditional learning. *Journal of English Language Teaching, 66*(1), 13–14. DOI: 10.66121/45wnfw13

Diahyleva, O., Leshchenko, A., Paziak, A., & Yurzhenko, A. (2024). Kahoot! as a tool to gamify learning process at maritime higher education. [ITE]. *Journal of Information Technology Education, 1*(55), 25–34. DOI: 10.14308/ite000777

Dieterle, E., Becker, S., & Williams, C. (2024). Ethical AI in education: Balancing innovation and equity. *Computers & Education, 192*, 104629.

Diglossia. (n.d.). Mubakkir. https://www.diglossia.net/mubakkir/

Dinnar, S. M., Dede, C., Johnson Dorley, E., Straub, C., & Korjus, K. (2021). Artificial intelligence and technology in teaching negotiation. *Negotiation Journal, 37*(2), 65–82. DOI: 10.1111/nejo.12351

Du, K., Geiger, J., Killen, T., Porta, A. E., & O'Brien, T. (2024). The Paradigm Shift in education in Big Data Era: Exploring the intersection of historical assessment frameworks and AI-Powered assessment methods in education. *Journal of Education and Training Studies, 12*(2), 22. DOI: 10.11114/jets.v12i2.6582

Edwards, J., Nguyen, A., Lämsä, J., Sobocinski, M., Whitehead, R., Dang, B., Roberts, A.-S., & Järvelä, S. (2024). Human–AI collaboration: Designing artificial agents to facilitate socially shared regulation among learners. *British Journal of Educational Technology*, *56*(2), 712–733. Advance online publication. DOI: 10.1111/bjet.13534

Elkhatat, A. M., Elsaid, K., & Almeer, S. (2023). Evaluating the efficacy of AI content detection tools in differentiating between human and AI-generated text. *International Journal for Educational Integrity*, *19*(1), 17. DOI: 10.1007/s40979-023-00140-5

ElSayary, A. (2023). An Investigation of Teachers' Perceptions of Using ChatGPT as a Supporting Tool for Teaching and Learning in the Digital Era. *Journal of Computer Assisted Learning*, •••, 1–15. DOI: 10.1111/jcal.12926

Elsayed, Y., Nabil, E., Torki, M., Faizullah, S., & Khalafallah, A. (2025). ZaQQ: A new Arabic dataset for automatic essay scoring via a novel human–AI collaborative framework. *Data, 10(9),* 148, 1–31.

Engelmann, S., Choksi, M. Z., Wang, A., & Fiesler, C. (2024). *Visions of a Discipline: Analyzing Introductory AI Courses on YouTube. FAccT '24: Proceedings of the 2024 ACM Conference on Fairness, Accountability, and Transparency*. https://doi.org/DOI: 10.1145/3630106.3659045

Essel, H. B., Vlachopoulos, D., Essuman, A. B., & Amankwa, J. O. (2023). ChatGPT effects on cognitive skills of undergraduate students: Receiving instant responses from AI-based conversational large language models. *Computers and Education: Artificial Intelligence*, *6*(1), 100198. DOI: 10.1016/j.caeai.2023.100198

Eze, C. A. (2024). The role of educators in upholding academic integrity in an ai-driven era. *AI and ethics, academic integrity and the future of quality assurance in higher education.*

Fagbohun, O., Iduwe, N. P., Abdullahi, M., Ifaturoti, A., & Nwanna, O. M. (2024). Beyond traditional assessment: Exploring the impact of large language models on grading practices. *Journal of Artificial Intelligence. Machine Learning and Data Science*, *2*(1), 1–8.

Falebita, O. S., & Kok, P. J. (2024). Strategic goals for artificial intelligence integration among STEM academics and undergraduates in African higher education: A systematic review. *Discover Education*, *3*, 151. Advance online publication. DOI: 10.1007/s44217-024-00252-1

Fannakhosrow, M., Nourabadi, S., Ngoc Huy, D. T., Dinh Trung, N., & Tashtoush, M. A. (2022). A Comparative Study of Artificial Intelligence (AI)-Based and Conventional Methods of Instruction on Learners' Academic Enthusiasm for L2 Learning. *Education Research International*, *2022*(1), 5478088. DOI: 10.1155/2022/5478088

Farrow, R. (2023). The possibilities and limits of XAI in education: A socio-technical perspective. *Learning, Media and Technology*, *48*(2), 266–279. DOI: 10.1080/17439884.2023.2185630

Fauville, G., Lantz-Andersson, A., & Säljö, R. (2014). AI tools in environmental education: Reviewing two newcomers to schools. *Environmental Education Research*, *20*(2), 248–283. DOI: 10.1080/13504622.2013.775220

Fernández-Herrero, J. (2024). Evaluating recent advances in affective intelligent tutoring systems: A scoping review of educational impacts and future prospects. *Education Sciences*, *14*(8), 839. DOI: 10.3390/educsci14080839

Ferrara, E. (2023). Fairness and Bias in Artificial intelligence: A brief survey of sources, impacts, and mitigation strategies. *Sci*, *6*(1), 3. DOI: 10.3390/sci6010003

Fischer, C., Davis, L., & Dougherty, S. (2023). Educators as ethical leaders in AI-rich classrooms. *Computers & Education. Artificial Intelligence*, *4*, 100143.

Fishman, T. (2014). *The fundamental values of academic integrity*. International Center for Academic Integrity, Clemson University.

Fitas, R. (2025). Inclusive education with AI: Supporting special needs and tackling language barriers. *AI and Ethics*, *5*(6), 5729–5757. DOI: 10.1007/s43681-025-00824-3

Fitria, T. N. (2021). THE USE TECHNOLOGY BASED ON ARTIFICIAL INTELLIGENCE IN ENGLISH TEACHING AND LEARNING). *ELT Echo the Journal of English Language Teaching in Foreign Language Context*, *6*(2). Advance online publication. DOI: 10.24235/eltecho.v6i2.9299

Foung, D., Lin, L., & Chen, J. (2024). Reinventing assessments with ChatGPT and other online tools: Opportunities for GenAI-empowered assessment practices. *Computers and Education: Artificial Intelligence*, *6*, 100250. DOI: 10.1016/j.caeai.2024.100250

Fraidan, A. A. (2024). Anticipatory Thinking and AI-Driven Assessments: A Balanced Approach to AI Integration in Education Aligned with Saudi Vision 2030. *African Journal of Biomedical Research*, •••, 619–628. DOI: 10.53555/AJBR.v27i3.2560

Furze, L., Perkins, M., Roe, J., & MacVaugh, J. (2024). The AI Assessment Scale (AIAS) in action: A pilot implementation of GenAI-supported assessment. *Australasian Journal of Educational Technology*, *40*(4), 38–55. DOI: 10.14742/ajet.9434

Gao, R. (2025). The Erosion and Reconstruction of Teachers' Authority in the Context of Artificial Intelligence. *Journal of Theory and Practice in Education and Innovation*, *2*(2), 26–33.

García Gómez, B., Coca, J. R., & Mesquita, C. (2022). Teacher's perspective in a challenging pandemic scenario. *Aula abierta, 51*(2), 181-190. DOI: 10.17811/rifie.52.2.2022.181-190

García-López, I. M., & Trujillo-Liñán, L. (2025). Ethical and regulatory challenges of Generative AI in education: A systematic review. *Frontiers in Education, 10*, 1565938. Advance online publication. DOI: 10.3389/feduc.2025.1565938

Garcia, M. B. (2025). The paradox of artificial creativity: Challenges and opportunities of generative AI artistry. *Creativity Research Journal*, *37*(4), 755–768. DOI: 10.1080/10400419.2024.2354622

Gascon, G. M., Wallman, K. K., Ravula, S., Cappelleri, J., Lee, J., Lum, K., Nagaraja, C. H., Paul, S., Roy, D., & Wu, E. (2023). DSLA 2023: Facing the dangers of data illiteracy. *Significance*, *20*(5), 26–29. DOI: 10.1093/jrssig/qmad077

Gay, G. (2018). *Culturally responsive teaching: Theory, research, and practice* (3rd ed.). Teachers College Press.

Gewirtz, D. (2025, April 30). *I tested 10 AI content detectors, and these 5 correctly identified AI text every time*. ZDNet. https://www.zdnet.com/article/i-tested-10-ai-content-detectors-and-these-5-correctly-identified-ai-text-every-time/

Ghavifekr, S., Razak, A. Z. A., Ghani, M. F. A., Ran, N. Y., Meixi, Y., & Tengyue, Z. (2014). AI integration in education: Incorporation for teaching & learning improvement. *Malaysian Online Journal of Educational Technology, 2*(2), 24-45. https://files.eric.ed.gov/fulltext/EJ1086419.pdf

Gheda, M. L. M., Hamid, S. A., Syed, S. R., Latif, A., & Nusran, N. F. M. (2024). *Optimising AI for developing reliable academic assessment design. Asian Journal of Open and Distance Learning*.

Gini, F., Bassanelli, S., Bonetti, F., Mogavi, R. H., Bucchiarone, A., & Marconi, A. (2025). The role and scope of gamification in education: A scientometric literature review. *Acta Psychologica*, *259*, 105418. DOI: 10.1016/j.actpsy.2025.105418 PMID: 40850223

Giray, L. (2024). The Problem with False Positives: AI Detection Unfairly Accuses Scholars of AI Plagiarism. *The Serials Librarian*, *85*(5-6), 181–189. DOI: 10.1080/0361526X.2024.2433256

Goktas, Y., Yildirim, S., & Yildirim, Z. (2009). Main barriers and possible enablers of AIs integration into pre-service teacher education programs. *Journal of Educational Technology & Society*, *12*(1), 193–204. https://www.jstor.org/stable/jeductechsoci.12.1.193

Gonsalves, C. (2025). Addressing student non-compliance in AI use declarations: Implications for academic integrity and assessment in higher education. *Assessment & Evaluation in Higher Education*, *50*(4), 592–606. DOI: 10.1080/02602938.2024.2415654

Gulumbe, B. H., Audu, S. M., & Hashim, A. M. (2025). Balancing AI and academic integrity: What are the positions of academic publishers and universities? *AI & Society*, *40*(3), 1775–1784. DOI: 10.1007/s00146-024-01946-8

Hakim, A., & Wahyuni, S. Postgraduate of State Institute of Islamic Studies of Kediri, Indonesia, & Postgraduate of State Institute of Islamic Studies of Kediri, Indonesia. (2024). A Critical review: Technology as Learning Media in Teaching Reading. *J-SHMIC : Journal of English for Academic, 11*(1). https://journal.uir.ac.id/index.php/jshmic

Hanandeh, A., Ayasrah, S., Kofahi, I., & Qudah, S. (2024). Artificial Intelligence in Arabic Linguistic Landscape: Opportunities, Challenges, and Future Directions. *TEM Journal*, *13*(4), 3137–3145. DOI: 10.18421/TEM134-48

Han, B., Coghlan, S., Buchanan, G., & McKay, D. (2025). Who is Helping Whom? Student Concerns about AI-Teacher Collaboration in Higher Education Classrooms. *Proceedings of the ACM on Human-Computer Interaction*, *9*(2), 1–32. DOI: 10.1145/3711104

Handayani, F. (2024). The Role of Technology in Enhancing English Language Learning: A Study of Digital Tools and Their Impact on Student Engagement. *Berajah Journal*, *4*(6), 1257–1266. DOI: 10.47353/bj.v4i6.430

Harding, S., & Smith, L. M. (2022). Freedom through constraint: Young women's embodiment, space and wellbeing during lockdown. *Wellbeing, Space and Society*, *3*, 100101. DOI: 10.1016/j.wss.2022.100101 PMID: 35990881

Haristiani, N. (2019). Artificial Intelligence (AI) Chatbot as Language Learning Medium: An inquiry. *Journal of Physics: Conference Series*, *1387*(1), 012020. DOI: 10.1088/1742-6596/1387/1/012020

Hattie, J., & Timperley, H. (2007). The power of feedback. *Review of Educational Research*, *77*(1), 81–112. DOI: 10.3102/003465430298487

Havnes, A., Smith, K., Dysthe, O., & Ludvigsen, K. (2012). Formative assessment and feedback: Making learning visible. *Studies in Educational Evaluation*, *38*(1), 21–27. DOI: 10.1016/j.stueduc.2012.04.001

Helsper, E. (2021). The digital disconnect: The social causes and consequences of digital inequalities.

Henriksen, D., Creely, E., Gruber, N., & Leahy, S. (2025). Social-emotional learning and generative AI: A critical literature review and framework for teacher education. *Journal of Teacher Education*, *76*(3), 312–328. DOI: 10.1177/00224871251325058

Holmes, W., Anastopoulou, S., Schafer, B., Payne, A., Smith, M., & Gray, E. (2022). AI in higher education: Risks, opportunities, and future directions. *British Journal of Educational Technology*, *53*(6), 1355–1373.

Holmes, W., Bialik, M., & Fadel, C. (2019). *Artificial intelligence in education: Promises and implications for teaching and learning*. Center for Curriculum Redesign.

Holmes, W., Porayska-Pomsta, K., Holstein, K., Sutherland, E., Baker, T., Shum, S. B., Santos, O. C., Rodrigo, M. T., Cukurova, M., Bittencourt, I. I., & Koedinger, K. R. (2021). Ethics of AI in Education: Towards a Community-Wide framework. *International Journal of Artificial Intelligence in Education*, *32*(3), 504–526. DOI: 10.1007/s40593-021-00239-1

Hossein-Mohand, H., Trujillo-Torres, J. M., Gómez-García, M., Hossein-Mohand, H., & Campos-Soto, A. (2021). Analysis of the use and integration of the flipped learning model, project-based learning, and gamification methodologies by secondary school mathematics teachers. *Sustainability (Basel)*, *13*(5), 2606. DOI: 10.3390/su13052606

Huang, L. (2023). Ethics of Artificial intelligence in Education: Student privacy and data protection. *Science Insights Education Frontiers*, *16*(2), 2577–2587. DOI: 10.15354/sief.23.re202

Huang, W., Hew, K. F., & Fryer, L. K. (2021). Chatbots for language learning—Are they really useful? A systematic review of chatbot-supported language learning. *Journal of Computer Assisted Learning*, *38*(1), 237–257. DOI: 10.1111/jcal.12610

Hubert, K. F., Awa, K. N., & Zabelina, D. L. (2024). The current state of artificial intelligence generative language models is more creative than humans on divergent thinking tasks. *Scientific Reports*, *14*(1), 3440. Advance online publication. DOI: 10.1038/s41598-024-53303-w PMID: 38341459

Hutson, J. (2024). Rethinking plagiarism in the era of generative AI. *Journal of International Communication, 4*(1).

Ibitoye, A. O., Nkwo, M. S., & Orji, R. (2025). Rethinking responsible AI from ethical pillars to sociotechnical practice. *AI and Ethics, 5*(6), 6207–6223. DOI: 10.1007/s43681-025-00809-2

Ibrahim, M. B., Dadeh, T., & Rola, F. (2022). Student Activities in Organizing, Learning Motivation and Self-Adjustment (Case Study In Ptkin Students). *Edukasi Islami Jurnal Pendidikan Islam, 11*(4), 417. DOI: 10.30868/ei.v11i4.3271

Ifenthaler, D. (2024). Digital transformation and AI adoption in universities: A global overview. *Technology. Knowledge and Learning, 29*(3), 677–694.

Ifenthaler, D., Majumdar, R., Gorissen, P., Judge, M., Mishra, S., Raffaghelli, J., & Shimada, A. (2024). Artificial intelligence in Education: Implications for policymakers, researchers, and practitioners. *Technology Knowledge and Learning, 29*(4), 1693–1710. DOI: 10.1007/s10758-024-09747-0

Islam, A., & Arifeen, S. H. (2024). Empowering virtual collaboration: Harnessing AI for enhanced teamwork in higher education. *Educational Technology Quarterly, 2024*(3), 337–359. DOI: 10.55056/etq.746

Jain, S., & Alam, M. A. (2022). Review of forthcoming AI-enabled applications promoting learning in higher education. In *AI with Intelligent Applications* (pp. 613–621). Springer Singapore. DOI: 10.1007/978-981-16-4177-0_61

Jannah, M. (2024). Analysing the Impact of Technology Integration on Student Engagement and Learning Outcomes in K-12 Education: A Systematic Literature Review. [INJOE]. *Indonesian Journal of Education, 4*(3), 969–980. https://www.injoe.org/index.php/INJOE/article/view/170

Jendia, J., & Ismail, H. H. (2023). Developing personalised reading materials for Malaysian primary school pupils using ChatGPT: A review. *International Journal of Academic Research in Business & Social Sciences, 13*(12). Advance online publication. DOI: 10.6007/IJARBSS/v13-i12/20172

Johnson, A. M., Jacovina, M. E., Russell, D. G., & Soto, C. M. (2016). Challenges and solutions when using technologies in the classroom. In *Adaptive educational technologies for literacy instruction* (pp. 13–30). Routledge. DOI: 10.4324/9781315647500-2

Johnson, C. (2023). *Understanding academic integrity and plagiarism in the digital age: can digital forensics techniques help prevent and detect academic misconduct?* University of South Wales.

Jordan, M. I., & Mitchell, T. (2020). Artificial intelligence: Evolution, opportunities, and challenges. *Science*, *349*(6245), 255–260. DOI: 10.1126/science.aaa8415 PMID: 26185243

Kallio, H., Pietilä, A., Johnson, M., & Kangasniemi, M. (2016). Systematic methodological review: Developing semi-structured interviews. *Journal of Advanced Nursing*, *72*(12), 2954–2965. DOI: 10.1111/jan.13031 PMID: 27221824

Kannan, J., & Munday, P. (2018). New Trends in Second Language Learning and Teaching through the lens of ICT, Networked Learning, and Artificial Intelligence. *Círculo de Lingüística Aplicada a la Comunicación*, *76*, 13–30. DOI: 10.5209/CLAC.62495

Karimi, H., & Khawaja, S. (2023). The impact of artificial intelligence on higher education in England. *Creative Education*, *14*(12), 2405–2415. DOI: 10.4236/ce.2023.1412154

Kasztelnik, K. (2024). Artificial Intelligence-Assisted Curriculum Development: Innovations in designing educational content for the 21st century learner. *Journal of Higher Education Theory and Practice*, *24*(11). Advance online publication. DOI: 10.33423/jhetp.v24i11.7367

Katsamakas, E., Pavlov, O. V., & Saklad, R. (2024). Artificial intelligence and the transformation of higher education institutions: A systems approach. *Sustainability*, *16*(14), 6118. DOI: 10.3390/su16146118

Kaufman, D. (2004). 14. Constructivist issues in language learning and teaching. *Annual Review of Applied Linguistics*, *24*, 303–319. DOI: 10.1017/S0267190504000121

Kaur, K. (2023). Teaching and Learning with AI Tools: Issues and Challenges. *International Journal on Cybernetics & Informatics*, *12*(3), 16–22. DOI: 10.5121/ijci.2023.120302

Kayyali, M. (2025 A). Ethical Implications of Generative AI in Education: Privacy, Bias, and Integrity. In Transformative AI Practices for Personalized Learning Strategies (pp. 185-218). IGI Global Scientific Publishing.

Kayyali, M. (2025 B). Generative AI and Education: Transforming Teaching and Learning Through Collaborative Intelligence. In Humans and Generative AI Tools for Collaborative Intelligence (pp. 25-52). IGI Global Scientific Publishing.

Kayyali, M. (2025). C). The Evolution of AI in Education From Concept to Classroom. In *Navigating Barriers to AI Implementation in the Classroom* (pp. 325–368). IGI Global Scientific Publishing. DOI: 10.4018/979-8-3373-1827-1.ch013

Kayyali, M. (2026). A). AI in higher education: The risk of excluding vulnerable learners. In *AI and New Forms of Exclusion* (pp. 57–82). IGI Global Scientific Publishing.

Khairullah, S. A., Harris, S., Hadi, H. J., Sandhu, R. A., Ahmad, N., & Alshara, M. A. (2025). Implementing artificial intelligence in academic and administrative processes through responsible strategic leadership in higher education institutions. *Frontiers in Education, 10*, 1548104. Advance online publication. DOI: 10.3389/feduc.2025.1548104

Khaleej Times. (2021). The UAE pushes forward as a global leader in artificial intelligence. https://www.khaleejtimes.com

Khalifa, M., & Albadawy, M. (2024). Using artificial intelligence in academic writing and research: An essential productivity tool. *Computer Methods and Programs in Biomedicine Update, 5*, 100145. DOI: 10.1016/j.cmpbup.2024.100145

Khamassi, M., Nahon, M., & Chatila, R. (2024). Strong and weak alignment of large language models with human values. *Scientific Reports, 14*(1), 19399. DOI: 10.1038/s41598-024-70031-3 PMID: 39169090

Khan, M. S. H., & Markauskaite, L. (2018). Technical and Vocational Teachers' Conceptions of AI in the Workplace: Bridging the gap between teaching and professional practice. *Journal of Educational Computing Research, 56*(7), 1099–1128. DOI: 10.1177/0735633117740396

Khlaif, Z. N., Alkouk, W. A., Salama, N., & Abu Eideh, B. (2025). Redesigning assessments for AI-enhanced learning: A framework for educators in the generative AI era. *Education Sciences, 15*(2), 174. DOI: 10.3390/educsci15020174

King, A., Fischer, C., & Johnson, W. (2022). Toward adaptive expertise: Rethinking faculty roles in AI-mediated learning environments. *Computers & Education, 185*, 104529.

King, D. (2024). *Legal & Humble AI: Addressing the Legal, Ethical, and Societal Dilemmas of Generative AI*. Ingene Publishers.

Kirby, N. (2022). Institutional integrity: Its meaning and value. *Ethical Theory and Moral Practice, 25*(5), 809–834. DOI: 10.1007/s10677-022-10330-8

Kithungu, R. M., Gakunga, D. K., & Nungu, M. (2021). Influence of AI integration on content delivery by AI and Non-AI trained teachers in secondary schools in Machakos County, Kenya. *Kenya. Journal of Studies in Education, 11*(1).

Kizilcec, R. F., Huber, E., Papanastasiou, E. C., Cram, A., Makridis, C. A., Smolansky, A., Zeivots, S., & Raduescu, C. (2024). Perceived impact of generative AI on assessments: Comparing educator and student perspectives in Australia, Cyprus, and the United States. *Computers and Education: Artificial Intelligence*, *7*, 100269. DOI: 10.1016/j.caeai.2024.100269

Klimova, B., & Pikhart, M. (2025). Exploring the effects of artificial intelligence on student and academic well-being in higher education: A mini-review. *Frontiers in Psychology*, *16*, 1498132. DOI: 10.3389/fpsyg.2025.1498132 PMID: 39963679

Klimova, B., Pikhart, M., Benites, A. D., Lehr, C., & Sanchez-Stockhammer, C. (2022). Neural machine translation in foreign language teaching and learning: A systematic review. *Education and Information Technologies*, *28*(1), 663–682. DOI: 10.1007/s10639-022-11194-2

Knox, J. (2023). AI, automation, and the academic self: Reframing digital labor. *Postdigital Science and Education*, *5*(1), 14–29.

Koehler, M. J., Mishra, P., Mishra, P., & Koehler, M. J. (2009). What is Technological Pedagogical Content Knowledge? In Judi Harris & Matt Koehler (Eds.), *Contemporary Issues in Technology and Teacher Education* (Vol. 9, Issue 1, pp. 60–70). https://www.citejournal.org/wp-content/uploads/2016/04/v9i1general1-1.pdf

Koop, M., & Gröblinger, O. (2024). Generative AI and academic integrity-a contradiction. In *European Association of Distance Teaching Universities.(2024, November 25). Leading the Future of Learning. Proceedings of the Innovating Higher Education Conference* (pp. 101-114).

Koryuhina, C., & Shamshina, T. (2018, April 26-27). Challenges of AI in education. In *The 16th international scientific conference information technologies and management*. ISMA University., https://ismaitm.lv/wp-content/uploads/theses_2018.pdf#page=142

Kosmützky, A., & Krücken, G. (2014). Transnational university rankings and the quest for legitimacy. *Higher Education*, *68*(3), 411–424.

Kovari, A. (2025). A systematic review of AI-powered collaborative learning in higher education: Trends and outcomes from the last decade. *Social Sciences & Humanities Open*, *11*, 101335. DOI: 10.1016/j.ssaho.2025.101335

Krange, I., Segaran, M., Gamlem, S., Moltudal, S., & Engeness, I. (2023). A triple challenge: Students' identification, interpretation, and use of individualized automated feedback in learning to write English as a foreign language. *Deleted Journal*, *59*(59), 37–61. DOI: 10.55612/s-5002-059-001

Kulesz, O. (2024). Artificial Intelligence and International Cultural Relations: Challenges and Opportunities for Cross-Sectoral Collaboration.

Laux, J. (2023). Institutionalised distrust and human oversight of artificial intelligence: Towards a democratic design of AI governance under the European Union AI Act. *AI & Society*, *39*(6), 2853–2866. DOI: 10.1007/s00146-023-01777-z PMID: 39640298

Lawrence, J. E., & Tar, U. A. (2018). Factors that influence teachers' adoption and integration of AI in teaching/learning process. *Educational Media International*, *55*(1), 79–105. DOI: 10.1080/09523987.2018.1439712

Lee, C. C., & Low, M. Y. H. (2024). Using genAI in education: The case for critical thinking. *Frontiers in Artificial Intelligence*, *7*, 1452131. DOI: 10.3389/frai.2024.1452131 PMID: 39554991

Lee, S. (2022). A social ladder or a glass floor? The role of higher education in intergenerational social mobility: Empirical evidence from South Korea. *Higher Education Policy*, *35*(4), 969–998. DOI: 10.1057/s41307-021-00241-1

Létourneau, A., Deslandes Martineau, M., Charland, P., Karran, J. A., Boasen, J., & Léger, P. M. (2025*). A systematic review of AI-driven intelligent tutoring systems (ITS) in K-12 education. npj Science of Learning, 10*, 29, 1-13.

Lim, N. T., Lee, Y., & Lee, P. P. F. (2023). What types of feedback do undergraduate chemistry students give each other? a case study from singapore. *International Journal of Innovation in Science and Mathematics Education*, *31*(2). Advance online publication. DOI: 10.30722/IJISME.31.02.003

Luckin, R., Holmes, W., Griffiths, M., & Forcier, L. B. (2016). *Intelligence unleashed: An argument for AI in education*. Pearson Education.

Luckin, R., Smith, M., Baines, L., & Dolan, R. (2022). AI readiness in universities: Frameworks for strategic decision-making. *International Journal of Artificial Intelligence in Education*, *32*(3), 771–792.

Mah, D.-K., & Groß, N. (2024). Artificial intelligence in higher education: Exploring faculty use, self-efficacy, distinct profiles, and professional development needs. *International Journal of Educational Technology in Higher Education*, *21*, 58. Advance online publication. DOI: 10.1186/s41239-024-00466-8

Marín, Y., Caro, O., Rituay, A., Llanos, K., Perez, D., Bardales, E., Tuesta, J., & Santos, R. (2025). Ethical Challenges Associated with the Use of Artificial Intelligence in University Education. *Journal of Academic Ethics*, *23*(4), 2443–2467. DOI: 10.1007/s10805-025-09660-w

Meddeb, O., Maraoui, M., & Zrigui, M. (2021). Personalized smart learning recommendation system for Arabic users in smart campus. *International Journal of Web-Based Learning and Teaching Technologies, 16*(6), 1–21. DOI: 10.4018/IJWLTT.20211101.oa9

Mello, R. F., Freitas, E., Pereira, F. D., Cabral, L., Tedesco, P., & Ramalho, G. (2023). Education in the age of Generative AI: Context and Recent Developments. *arXiv preprint arXiv:2309.12332.*

Menéndez, I. Y. C., Napa, M. A. C., Moreira, M. L. M., & Zambrano, G. G. V. (2019). The importance of formative assessment in the learning teaching process. *International Journal of Social Science and Humanity, 3*(2), 238–249. DOI: 10.29332/ijssh.v3n2.322

Merino-Campos, C. (2025). The Impact of Artificial Intelligence on Personalized Learning in Higher Education: A Systematic Review. *Trends in Higher Education, 4*(2), 17. DOI: 10.3390/higheredu4020017

Mezirow, J. (1991). *Transformative dimensions of adult learning*. Jossey-Bass.

Michaeli, T., Seegerer, S., & Romeike, R. (2023). What Students Can Learn About Artificial intelligence — Recommendations for K-12 Computing Education. *arXiv (Cornell University).* https://doi.org//arxiv.2305.06450DOI: 10.1007/978-3-031-43393-1_19

Mirzajani, H., Mahmud, R., Fauzi Mohd Ayub, A., & Wong, S. L. (2016). Teachers' acceptance of AI and its integration in the classroom. *Quality Assurance in Education, 24*(1), 26–40. DOI: 10.1108/QAE-06-2014-0025

Mishra, S. (2024). Revolutionizing Education: The impact of AI-Enhanced Teaching Strategies. *International Journal for Research in Applied Science and Engineering Technology, 12*(9), 9–32. DOI: 10.22214/ijraset.2024.64127

Mita, S. (2022). AI proctoring: Academic integrity vs. student rights. *The Hastings Law Journal, 74*, 1513.

Mohammadinejad, H., & Mohammadhoseini, F. (2020). Privacy protection in smart cities by a personal data management protocol in blockchain. *I.J. Computer Network and Information Security, 2020*(3), 44–52. DOI: 10.5815/ijcnis.2020.03.05

Mohammed, A. H. H., & Almekhlafi, A. G.Ali Hussein H. MohammedAbdurrahman Ghaleb Almekhlafi. (2017). English language teachers' perceptions of using AI in teaching in cycle three in the United Arab Emirates. *US-China Foreign Language, 15*(6), 349–366. DOI: 10.17265/1539-8080/2017.06.001

Mollick, E. R., & Mollick, L. (2023). Assigning AI: Seven Approaches for Students, with Prompts. SSRN *Electronic Journal*. https://doi.org/DOI: 10.2139/ssrn.4475995

Mouta, A., Pinto-Llorente, A. M., & Torrecilla-Sánchez, E. M. (2023). Uncovering Blind Spots in Education Ethics: Insights from a Systematic Literature Review on Artificial Intelligence in Education. *International Journal of Artificial Intelligence in Education*, *34*(3), 1166–1205. DOI: 10.1007/s40593-023-00384-9

Msafiri, M. M., Kangwa, D., & Cai, L. (2023). A systematic literature review of AI integration in secondary education: What works, what does not, and what next? *Discover Education*, *2*(1), 44. DOI: 10.1007/s44217-023-00070-x

Mukazi, F. M. (2022). Digital-based formative assessments in higher education institutions. In *Handbook of Research on Digital-Based Assessment and Innovative Practices in Education* (pp. 247–264). IGI Global., DOI: 10.4018/978-1-6684-2468-1.ch013

Mzwri, K., & Turcsányi-Szabó, M. (2025). The impact of prompt engineering and a generative AI-driven tool on autonomous learning: A case study. *Education Sciences*, *15*(2), 199. DOI: 10.3390/educsci15020199

Nabilla, C., Apriani, E., & Gusmuliana, P. (2024). Promoting Students' Writing Critical Thinking By Using Paragraph Writing Ai Technology (Doctoral dissertation, Institut agama islam negeri curup).

Naeem, M., Ozuem, W., Howell, K., & Ranfagni, S. (2023). A step-by-step process of thematic analysis to develop a conceptual model in qualitative research. *International Journal of Qualitative Methods*, *22*, 16094069231205789. Advance online publication. DOI: 10.1177/16094069231205789

Nagaraj, B. K., A, K., R, S. B., S, A., Sachdev, H. K., & N, S. K. (2023). The Emerging Role of Artificial intelligence in STEM Higher Education: A Critical review. *International Research Journal of Multidisciplinary Technovation*, 1–19. https://doi.org/DOI: 10.54392/irjmt2351

Nagpal, H. (2024). *Policies, procedures, and guidelines: are universities effectively ensuring AI (academic integrity) in the era of generative AI?* (Doctoral dissertation).

Nah, F. F.-H., Zheng, R., Cai, J., Siau, K., & Chen, L. (2023). Generative AI and ChatGPT: Applications, challenges, and AI-human collaboration. *Journal of Information Technology Case and Application Research*, *25*(3), 277–304. DOI: 10.1080/15228053.2023.2233814

Nayak, R., Yassin, H., Ramesh, G., & Godiishala, A. G. (2024). Inclusive learning and assessment in the era of AI. *SN Computer Science*, *5*(8), 975. Advance online publication. DOI: 10.1007/s42979-024-03346-7

Ng, D. T. K., Leung, J. K. L., Su, J., Ng, R. C. W., & Chu, S. K. W. (2023). Teachers' AI digital competencies and twenty-first century skills in the post-pandemic world. *Educational Technology Research and Development*, *71*(1), 137–161. DOI: 10.1007/s11423-023-10203-6 PMID: 36844361

Nguyen, A., Ngo, H. N., Hong, Y., Dang, B., & Nguyen, B. T. (2022). Ethical principles for artificial intelligence in education. *Education and Information Technologies*, *28*(4), 4221–4241. DOI: 10.1007/s10639-022-11316-w PMID: 36254344

Nowell, L. S., Norris, J. M., White, D. E., & Moules, N. J. (2017). Thematic analysis: Striving to meet the trustworthiness criteria. *International Journal of Qualitative Methods*, *16*(1), 160940691773384. DOI: 10.1177/1609406917733847

Nur, S. A. A., Muliati, M., & Munir, M. (2021). English Teacher's Attitudes and Practices of AI Adoption in English Language Classrooms. *Celebes Journal of Language Studies*, *1*(2), 210–218. DOI: 10.51629/cjls.v1i2.63

Nwozor, A. (2025). Artificial intelligence (AI) and academic honesty-dishonesty nexus: Trends and preventive measures. *AI and Ethics, Academic Integrity and the Future of Quality Assurance in Higher Education, 27.*

Oborah, J. O. (2022). Effectiveness of the infusion teaching approach for the development of general AI skills in Nigerian tertiary education. *Journal of Research in Innovative Teaching & Learning*, *15*(2), 245–258. DOI: 10.1108/JRIT-11-2021-0076

Ogwueleka, F. N. (2025). Plagiarism Detection in the age of artificial intelligence: current technologies and future directions. *AI and ethics, academic integrity and the future of quality assurance in higher education, 10.*

Omirali, A., Kozhakhmet, K., & Zhumaliyeva, R. (2025). Digital Trust in Transition: Student Perceptions of AI-Enhanced Learning for Sustainable Educational Futures. *Sustainability (Basel)*, *17*(17), 7567. DOI: 10.3390/su17177567

Opesemowo, O., & Adekomaya, V. (2024). Harnessing artificial intelligence for advancing sustainable development goals in South Africa's higher education system: A qualitative study. *International Journal of Learning. Teaching and Educational Research*, *23*(3), 67–86. DOI: 10.26803/ijlter.23.3.4

Outay, F., Jabeur, N., Bellalouna, F., & Al Hamzi, T. (2024). Multi-agent system-based framework for an intelligent management of competency building. *Smart Learn Environments*, *11*(41), 1–18. DOI: 10.1186/s40561-024-00328-3

Özer, M., Perc, M., & Suna, H. (2024). Participatory management can help AI ethics adhere to the social consensus. *İstanbul Üniversitesi Sosyoloji Dergisi / İstanbul University Journal of Sociology, 0*(0), 0. https://doi.org/DOI: 10.26650/SJ.2024.44.1.0001

Palinkas, L. A., Horwitz, S., Green, C. A., Wisdom, J., Duan, N., & Hoagwood, K. (2015). Purposeful sampling for qualitative data collection and analysis in mixed-method implementation research. *Administration and Policy in Mental Health, 42*(5), 533–544. DOI: 10.1007/s10488-013-0528-y PMID: 24193818

Panjaitan, A. O., Novelyn, S., & Angreni, F. (2024). The impact of proper citation on academic integrity and scholarship. *Asian Journal of Advanced Research and Reports, 18*(10), 192–201. DOI: 10.9734/ajarr/2024/v18i10766

Pant, P. (2025). Upholding Ethical Standards: Governance, Transparency, and Integrity in Higher Education Administration. In *Challenges of Public Administration Management for Higher Education* (pp. 195-208). IGI Global.

Parsons, J., & Taylor, L. (2011). Improving Student Engagement. *Current Issues in Education (Tempe, Ariz.), 14*(1). https://cie.asu.edu/ojs/index.php/cieatasu/article/view/745

Pellerin, M., & Ogandaga, M. (2024). *Rethinking Academic Integrity and Plagiarism in the Age of AI.*

Pérez-Jorge, D., González-Afonso, M. C., Santos-Álvarez, A. G., Plasencia-Carballo, Z., & Perdomo-López, C. A. (2025). The impact of AI-driven application programming interfaces (APIs) on educational information management. *Information, 16*(6), 540, 1-31.

Perkins, M., Furze, L., Roe, J., & MacVaugh, J. (2024). The Artificial Intelligence Assessment Scale (AIAS): A framework for ethical integration of generative AI in educational assessment. *Journal of University Teaching & Learning Practice, 21*(6), 49–66. DOI: 10.53761/q3azde36

Piaget, J. (1972). *The principles of genetic epistemology*. Routledge and Kegan Paul.

Piaget, J. (2005). *The psychology of intelligence*. Routledge. DOI: 10.4324/9780203981528

Prazeres, F. G., & Silva-Pina, A. (2024, October 30). *AI Integrated Learning for Higher Education Social Science Educators*. https://dergipark.org.tr/tr/pub/usdad/issue/86150/1529088

Premat, C., & Farazouli, A. (2025). Academic Integrity vs. Artificial Intelligence: A tale of two AIs. *Praxis Educativa (Santa Rosa)*, (20), 23.

Qedear, A., Almatrafy, A., Al-Sowat, A., Saigh, A., & Alayed, A. (2024). Real-time air-writing recognition for Arabic letters using deep learning. *Sensors, 24(18)*, 6098, 1-25.

Radanliev, P., Santos, O., Brandon-Jones, A., & Joinson, A. (2024). Ethics and responsible AI deployment. *Frontiers in Artificial Intelligence*, *7*, 1377011. DOI: 10.3389/frai.2024.1377011 PMID: 38601110

Rahimi, S., & Rezvani, R. Corresponding Author. (2024). Enhancing English instructors' TPACK through AI: Exploring its role in Language Education. *Iranian Journal of English for Academic Purposes, 13–3*, 76–97. https://journalscmu.sinaweb.net/article_212184.html

Ren, X., & Wu, M. L. (2025). Examining teaching competencies and challenges while integrating artificial intelligence in higher education. *TechTrends*, *69*(3), 519–538. DOI: 10.1007/s11528-025-01055-3

Resnick, M. (2024, March 27). *Generative AI and Creative Learning: Concerns, Opportunities, and Choices [Online forum post]*. An MIT Exploration of Generative AI. https://doi.org/DOI: 10.21428/e4baedd9.cf3e35e5

Rettberg, J. W. (2024). How generative AI endangers cultural narratives. *Issues in Science and Technology*, *40*(2), 76–79. DOI: 10.58875/TJOD6844

Riar, M., Morschheuser, B., Zarnekow, R., & Hamari, J. (2022). Gamification of cooperation: A framework, literature review and future research agenda. *International Journal of Information Management*, *67*, 102549. DOI: 10.1016/j.ijinfomgt.2022.102549

Ridge, N. (2014). *Education in the UAE: Drivers and challenges*. Dubai School of Government.

Rodrigues, M., Silva, R., Borges, A. P., Franco, M., & Oliveira, C. (2025). Artificial intelligence: Threat or asset to academic integrity? A bibliometric analysis. *Kybernetes*, *54*(5), 2939–2970. DOI: 10.1108/K-09-2023-1666

Rožman, M., Tominc, P., & Vrečko, I. (2023). Building skills for the future of work: Students' perspectives on emerging jobs in the Data and AI Cluster through artificial intelligence in education. *Environment and Social Psychology*, *8*(2). Advance online publication. DOI: 10.54517/esp.v8i2.1670

Rushton, A. (2005). Formative assessment: A key to deep learning? *Medical Teacher*, *27*(6), 509–513. DOI: 10.1080/01421590500129159 PMID: 16199357

Ryoo, J., & Winkelmann, K. (Eds.). (2021). Innovative Learning Environments in STEM Higher Education: Opportunities, challenges, and looking forward. In *SpringerBriefs in Statistics* [Book]. https://library.oapen.org/bitstream/handle/20.500.12657/47325/1/9783030589486.pdf#page=31

Sadigzade, Z. (2025). AI-Powered Feedback in ESL writing Classes: Pedagogical opportunities and ethical concerns. *Journal of Azerbaijan Language and Education Studies.*, *2*(4), 5–17. DOI: 10.69760/jales.2025004000

Sain, Z. H., Hina, S., & Serban, R. (2024). Implementing artificial intelligence in educational management systems: A comprehensive study of opportunities and challenges. *Asian Journal of Managerial Science*, *13*(1), 23–31. DOI: 10.70112/ajms-2024.13.1.4235

Sakthivel, D. (2021). AI Tools for Modern Education. *International Journal of Multidisciplinary Research and Explorer*, *1*(9), 22–27. https://doie.org/10.280229/IJMRE.20211932685958

Salla, S., Pasumarthy, A., Tadikonda, D., Parsha, T., & Mandal, S. K. (2024). Private AI in Education: Critical Challenges and Aspects of Enhancement Strategies. In Sustainable Development Using Private AI (pp. 109-131). CRC Press.

Salloum, S. A., Alomari, K. M., Alfaisal, A. M., Aljanada, R. A., & Basiouni, A. (2025). Emotion recognition for enhanced learning: Using AI to detect students' emotions and adjust teaching methods. *Smart Learning Environments*, *12*(21), 1–17. DOI: 10.1186/s40561-025-00374-5

Saltman, K. J. (2022). *The alienation of fact: Digital educational privatization, AI, and the false promise of bodies and numbers*. MIT Press. DOI: 10.7551/mitpress/14387.001.0001

Samin, S. M., & Osman, R. A. (2024). Integrating artificial intelligence into the Arabic language teaching plan at higher education. *SHS Web of Conferences, 202*, 06010, 1-9.

Schorske, C. E., & Bender, T. (2021). American academic culture in transformation: Fifty years, four disciplines.

Seitan, W. I., Ajlouni, A. O., & Al-Shra'h, N. D. (2020). The Impact of Integrating Flipped Learning and Artificial Intelligenceon the Secondary School Students' Academic Achievement and Their Attitudes towards It. *International Education Studies*, *13*(2), 1–10. DOI: 10.5539/ies.v13n2p1

Selwyn, N. (2024). *The future of AI in higher education: Critical questions and emerging tensions*. Polity Press.

Shadiev, R., & Liu, J. (2022). Review of research on applications of speech recognition technology to assist language learning. *ReCALL, 35*(1), 74–88. DOI: 10.1017/S095834402200012X

Shah, P. (2023). *AI and the Future of Education: Teaching in the Age of Artificial Intelligence*. John Wiley & Sons.

Sharadgah, T. A., & Sa'di, R. A. (2022). A systematic review of research on the use of artificial intelligence in English language teaching and learning (2015-2021): What are the current effects? *Journal of Information Technology Education, 21*, 337–377. DOI: 10.28945/4999

Shi, H. Yantai University, Chinese University of Hong Kong, Aryadoust, V., & National Institute of Education, Nanyang Technological University, Singapore. (2024). A systematic review of AI-based automated written feedback research. In *ReCALL* (Vols. 36–2, pp. 187–209). https://doi.org/DOI: 10.1017/S0958344023000265

Simbeck, K. (2023). They shall be fair, transparent, and robust: Auditing learning analytics systems. *AI and Ethics, 4*(2), 555–571. DOI: 10.1007/s43681-023-00292-7

Sitnicka, S., Mursalov, M., Mammadov, H., Babaiev, D., & Zhou, Y. (2025). Ethics, Institutions, Infrastructure, and Governance in AI National-Level Readiness: A Hidden driver of Banking transformation. *Business Ethics and Leadership, 9*(3), 290–304. DOI: 10.61093/bel.9(3).290-304.2025

Smit, R., Bachmann, P., Dober, H., & Hess, K. (2023). Feedback levels and their interaction with the mathematical reasoning process. *Curriculum Journal, 35*(2), 184–202. DOI: 10.1002/curj.221

Smutny, P., & Schreiberova, P. (2020). Chatbots for learning: A comprehensive review. *Computers & Education, 151*, 103862. DOI: 10.1016/j.compedu.2020.103862

Snoussi, T. (2024). LMS VS. SOCIAL MEDIA USE FOR LEARNING IN THE MENA REGION BEFORE THE COVID-19 PANDEMIC. Social Media, Youth, and the Global South: Comparative Perspectives, 169.

Solanki, P., Grundy, J., & Hussain, W. (2022). Operationalising ethics in artificial intelligence for healthcare: A framework for AI developers. *AI and Ethics, 3*(1), 223–240. DOI: 10.1007/s43681-022-00195-z

Song, N. (2024). Higher education crisis: Academic misconduct with generative AI. *Journal of Contingencies and Crisis Management*, *32*(1), e12532. DOI: 10.1111/1468-5973.12532

Srinivasan, V. (2022). AI & learning: A preferred future. *Computers and Education: Artificial Intelligence*, *3*, 100062.

Srivastava, S., & Kumar, M. A. S. M. V. (2025). *Unlocking Generative AI: A Beginner's Guide*. Perfect Writer Publishing.

Stade, E. C., Stirman, S. W., Ungar, L. H., Boland, C. L., Schwartz, H. A., Yaden, D. B., Sedoc, J., DeRubeis, R. J., Willer, R., & Eichstaedt, J. C. (2024). Large language models could change the future of behavioral healthcare: A proposal for responsible development and evaluation. *npj Mental Health Research, 3(1)*, 12, 1-12.

Stiggins, R., & DuFour, R. (2009). Maximizing the power of formative assessments. *Phi Delta Kappan*, *90*(9), 640–644. DOI: 10.1177/003172170909000907

Stitzlein, S. (2023). Teaching Honesty and Improving Democracy in the Post-Truth Era. *Educational Theory*, *73*(1), 51–73. DOI: 10.1111/edth.12565

Strzelecki, A. (2024). Students' acceptance of ChatGPT in higher education: An extended unified theory of acceptance and use of technology. *Innovative Higher Education*, *49*, 223–245. DOI: 10.1007/s10755-023-09686-1

Subhash, S., & Cudney, E. A. (2018). Gamified learning in higher education: A systematic review of the literature. *Computers in Human Behavior*, *87*, 192–206. DOI: 10.1016/j.chb.2018.05.028

Suryani, A. (2010). ICT in education: Its benefits, difficulties, and organizational development issues. [JSH]. *Jurnal Sosial Humaniora*, *3*(1), 13–33. DOI: 10.12962/j24433527.v3i1.651

Susnjak, T. (2023). Beyond predictive learning analytics modelling and onto explainable artificial intelligence with prescriptive analytics and ChatGPT. *International Journal of Artificial Intelligence in Education*, *34*(2), 452–482. DOI: 10.1007/s40593-023-00336-3

Swiecki, Z., Khosravi, H., Chen, G., Martinez-Maldonado, R., Lodge, J. M., Milligan, S., Selwyn, N., & Gašević, D. (2022). Assessment in the age of artificial intelligence. *Computers and Education Artificial Intelligence*, *3*, 100075. DOI: 10.1016/j.caeai.2022.100075

Tabuenca, B., Uche-Soria, M., Greller, W., Hernández-Leo, D., Balcells-Falgueras, P., Gloor, P., & Garbajosa, J. (2024). Greening smart learning environments with Artificial Intelligence of Things. *Internet of Things : Engineering Cyber Physical Human Systems*, *25*, 101051. DOI: 10.1016/j.iot.2023.101051

Tan, S. C., Lee, A. V. Y., & Lee, M. (2022). A systematic review of artificial intelligence techniques for collaborative learning over the past two decades. *Computers and Education: Artificial Intelligence*, *3*, 100097. DOI: 10.1016/j.caeai.2022.100097

Tan, S., Wong, L., & Ng, M. (2024). AI-enabled personalization in higher education. *Journal of Computer Assisted Learning*, *40*(1), 233–248.

Tolman, A. O., & Kremling, J. (Eds.). (2023). *Why students resist learning: A practical model for understanding and helping students*. Taylor & Francis.

Torraco, R. J. (2005). Human resource development transcends disciplinary boundaries. *Human Resource Development Review*, *4*(3), 251–253.

Torres-Toukoumidis, A., Merchan-Romero, J., Fernández, M. M., & Vega Ramírez, J. F. A. (2024). Gamification and artificial intelligence in the educational context: Analysis of scientific literature. *Lecture Notes in Computer Science*, •••, 349–354.

Triantafyllidis, A., Leftheriotis, K., Kotsovoulou, M., Cirstea, T., & Vranopoulos, G. (2024). INTRODUCING AI IN FLIPPED CLASSROOM. A PRELIMINARY STUDY. In *EDULEARN24 Proceedings* (pp. 8828-8835). IATED.

UAE Government Media Office. (2017). The UAE appoints the world's first minister of artificial intelligence. https://www.mediaoffice.ae

UAE Ministry of Cabinet Affairs. (2018). *UAE National Artificial Intelligence Strategy 2031*. UAE Government.

Unesco. (2023). Guidance for generative AI in education and research. In *UNESCO eBooks*. https://doi.org/DOI: 10.54675/EWZM9535

UNESCO. (2023). *Guidance for generative AI in education and research*. UNESCO Publishing.

van Dis, E. A. M., Bollen, J., Zuidema, W., van Rooij, R., & Littman, M. (2023). Large language models and the future of academic research. *Nature*, *620*, 115–118.

Viktorivna, K. L., Oleksandrovych, V. A., Oleksandrivna, K. I., & Oleksandrivna, K. N. (2022). Artificial Intelligence in Language Learning: What Are We Afraid of. *Arab World English Journal*, *8*(8), 262–273. DOI: 10.24093/awej/call8.18

Vygotsky, L. S. (1978). *Mind in society: The development of higher psychological processes* (Vol. 86). Harvard university press.

Wang, J., & Cornely, P. R. (2023, November). Addressing academic misconduct in the age of ChatGPT: Strategies and solutions. In *Proceedings of the 2023 7th International Conference on Education and E-Learning* (pp. 19-25). DOI: 10.1145/3637989.3638014

Wang, N., & Lester, J. (2023). K-12 Education in the Age of AI: A Call to Action for K-12 AI Literacy. *International Journal of Artificial Intelligence in Education, 33*(2), 228–232. DOI: 10.1007/s40593-023-00358-x

Wang, X., & Dostál, J. (2017). An Analysis of the Integration of AI in Education from the Perspective of Teachers'Attitudes. In *Edulearn17 Proceedings* (pp. 8156–8162). IATED., DOI: 10.21125/edulearn.2017.0507

Wee, H. B., & Reimer, J. D. (2023). Non-English academics face inequality via AI-generated essays and countermeasure tools. *Bioscience, 73*(7), 476–478. DOI: 10.1093/biosci/biad034

Wei, L. (2023). Artificial intelligence in language instruction: Impact on English learning achievement, L2 motivation, and self-regulated learning. *Frontiers in Psychology, 14*, 1261955. Advance online publication. DOI: 10.3389/fpsyg.2023.1261955 PMID: 38023040

Weurlander, M., Söderberg, M., Scheja, M., Hult, H., & Wernerson, A. (2012). Exploring formative assessment as a tool for learning: Students' experiences of different methods of formative assessment. *Assessment & Evaluation in Higher Education, 37*(6), 747–760. DOI: 10.1080/02602938.2011.572153

Wilkins, S. (2010). Higher education in the GCC: Accessibility, quality, and the role of private providers. *Journal of Higher Education Policy and Management, 32*(4), 401–414.

Williamson, B., & Eynon, R. (2020). Algorithmic decision-making in higher education. *Learning, Media and Technology, 45*(1), 87–106.

Williamson, B., & Molnar, A. (2022). The political economy of educational AI: Platforms, power, and policy. *Educational Theory, 72*(3), 323–342.

Wisniewski, B., Zierer, K., & Hattie, J. (2020). The power of feedback revisited: A meta-analysis of educational feedback research. *Frontiers in Psychology, 10*, 1–14. DOI: 10.3389/fpsyg.2019.03087 PMID: 32038429

Wood, D. F. (2018). Formative assessment: Assessment for learning. *Understanding medical education: Evidence, theory, and practice*, 361-373. DOI: 10.1002/9781119373780.ch25

Xiao, F., Zhu, S., & Wen, X. (2025). Exploring the landscape of generative AI (ChatGPT)-powered writing instruction in English as a foreign language education: A scoping review. *ECNU Review of Education*, 1-19.

Xu, X. (2023). AI optimization algorithms enhance higher education management and personalized teaching through empirical analysis. *Scientific Reports, 15(1)*, 51057, 1-19.

Yang, G. (2020). The application of Artificial intelligence in English teaching. *International Journal of Frontiers in Sociology*, *2*(3). Advance online publication. DOI: 10.25236/ijfs.2020.020309

Yan, L., Greiff, S., Teuber, Z., & Gašević, D. (2024). Promises and challenges of generative artificial intelligence for human learning. *Nature Human Behaviour*, *8*(10), 1839–1850. DOI: 10.1038/s41562-024-02004-5 PMID: 39438686

Yin, Z., Chinta, S. V., Wang, Z., Gonzalez, M., & Zhang, W. (2025). FairAIED: Navigating fairness, bias, and ethics in educational AI applications. arXiv, 1, 1-59.

Yin, R. K. (2018). *Case study research and applications: Design and methods* (6th ed.). SAGE.

Yusuf, A., Pervin, N., & Román-González, M. (2024). Generative AI and the future of higher education: A threat to academic integrity or reformation? Evidence from multicultural perspectives. *International Journal of Educational Technology in Higher Education*, *21*, 21. Advance online publication. DOI: 10.1186/s41239-024-00429-z

Yusuf, Z., Pervin, N., & Román-González, M. (2024). Scholarly responsibility in the age of AI: Rethinking authorship, rigor, and expertise. *Computers & Education. Artificial Intelligence*, *4*, 100152.

Zaibout, N., & Madrane, M. (2024). Optimizing Academic Assessment: The Impact of AI on Student Integrity, Creativity, and Achievement. *International Journal of Engineering Trends and Technology*, *72*(11), 357–370. DOI: 10.14445/22315381/IJETT-V72I11P134

ZAI–Zayed Artificial Intelligence Center. (n.d.). *ZAI Home*. https://www.zu.ac.ae/main/en/zai/index

Żammit, J. (2025). Secondary School Teachers' Experiences with Generative AI in Maltese Language Teaching. *Technology, Knowledge and Learning*, 1-19.

Zawacki-Richter, O., Kerres, M., Bedenlier, S., Bond, M., & Buntins, K. (2020). *Systematic reviews in educational research.* https://library.oapen.org/bitstream/handle/20.500.12657/23142/1007012.pdf?sequenc#page=22

Zawacki-Richter, O., Marín, V. I., Bond, M., & Gouverneur, F. (2019). Systematic review of research on artificial intelligence applications in higher education. *International Journal of Educational Technology in Higher Education, 16*(1), 39. DOI: 10.1186/s41239-019-0171-0

Zawya. (2025, March 10). Miqyas Al Dhad highlights role of Arabic reading scale in advancing literacy. https://www.zawya.com/en/press-release/companies-news/miqyas-al-dhad-highlights-role-of-arabic-reading-scale-in-advancing-literacy-nom82uft

Zekaj, R. (2023). AI language models as educational allies: Enhancing instructional support in higher education. *International Journal of Learning. Teaching and Educational Research, 22*(8), 120–134. DOI: 10.26803/ijlter.22.8.7

Zhai, Y., Nezakatgoo, B. (2025). Evaluating AI-Powered Applications for Enhancing Undergraduate Students' Metacognitive Strategies, Self-Determined Motivation, and Social Learning in English Language Education. *Sci Rep 15*, 35199 1-10.

Zhai, X., Chu, X., Chai, C. S., Jong, M. S. Y., Istenic, A., Spector, M., Liu, J.-B., Yuan, J., & Li, Y. (2021). A review of artificial intelligence (AI) in education from 2010 to 2020. *Education Research International, 2021*, 8812542.

Zhai, X., Chu, X., Chai, C. S., Jong, M. S. Y., Istenic, A., Spector, M., Liu, J., Yuan, J., & Li, Y. (2021). A Review of Artificial Intelligence (AI) in Education from 2010 to 2020. *Complexity, 2021*(1), 1–18. DOI: 10.1155/2021/8812542

Zhang, X., Ding, Y., Huang, X., Li, W., Long, L., & Ding, S. (2024). Smart classrooms: How sensors and AI are shaping educational paradigms. *Sensors (Basel), 24*(15), 5487. DOI: 10.3390/s24175487 PMID: 39275398

Zhang, Y., & Dong, C. (2024). Unveiling the dynamic mechanisms of generative AI in English language learning: A hybrid study based on fsQCA and system dynamics. *Behavioral Sciences (Basel, Switzerland), 14*(10), 1015. DOI: 10.3390/bs14111015 PMID: 39594315

Zhang, Y., Ghandour, A., & Shestak, V. (2020). Using learning analytics to predAI students performance in moodle LMS. *International Journal of Emerging Technologies in Learning, 15*(20), 102. DOI: 10.3991/ijet.v15i20.15915

Zhang, Y., & Reusch, P. (2025, April). Trust in and Adoption of Generative AI in University Education: Opportunities, Challenges, and Implications. In *2025 IEEE Global Engineering Education Conference (EDUCON)* (pp. 1-10). IEEE. DOI: 10.1109/EDUCON62633.2025.11016490

Zhou, W. (2020). Sociocultural Theory and its implications in college English teaching and learning in the age of artificial Intelligence. *Journal of Physics: Conference Series*, *1646*(1), 012142. DOI: 10.1088/1742-6596/1646/1/012142

Zhu, H., Sun, Y., & Yang, J. (2025). Towards responsible artificial intelligence in education: A systematic review on identifying and mitigating ethical risks. *Humanities & Social Sciences Communications*, *12*(1), 111. DOI: 10.1057/s41599-025-05252-6

Zhu, M., & Wang, C. (2014). A Systematic Review of Artificial Intelligence in Language Education from 2013 to 2023: Current Status and Future Implications. Available at *SSRN*: https://ssrn.com/abstract=4684304

About the Contributors

Tendai Charles Educated in Russell Group universities, Dr. Charles has a PhD in Education from the University of York, awarded in 2018. He joined the Faculty of Education at the British University in Dubai in 2019 as an Assistant Professor, was the inaugural Director of the Centre for Research in Digital Education. He is a post-positivist researcher with over 40 publications, who specialises in evidence-based education, technology-enhanced learning and second language acquisition. Dr. Charles is an Accredited Researcher with the UK Government's Office for National Statistics, and is a Fellow of the UK's Royal Statistical Society. To-date, he has supervised over 60 postgraduate theses/dissertations, and as a Fellow of the Higher Education Academy (FHEA), his excellence in teaching is internationally recognised.

Christopher Hill has worked in international higher education since 2008 and is an OBHE Associate, HEA Fellow, Specialist for the Hong Kong Council for Accreditation of Academic and Vocational Qualifications, an Adjunct Researcher for the Higher Evaluation and Accreditation Council of Taiwan and External Examiner for the University of Birmingham. Prof. Hill is currently Vice President of Research and Innovation at the Canadian University in Dubai. Prof. Hill's research interests include TNE and its impact on national systems; the role of online learning; and the development of international education and the student experience in the global arena. Prof. Hill is widely published, is a regular keynote speaker on the subject of international education, cultural teaching, TNE and institutional development, and a member of eight international journal editorial boards and a peer reviewer for a further ten journals. Prof. Hill hosts the Think Education podcast that provides a platform for reflection and discussion on research practice and teaching and learning within higher education.

Ibrahem Alamoush has over 20 years' experience in education. Previous to SEA, Dr. Alamoush served as an Educational Training Specialist in the Emirates

Schools Establishment. He has also served as an expert lecturer and adjunct faculty at various institutions in the UAE, Jordan, Oman, and Saudi Arabia, including Skyline University College Sharjah, the Queen Rania Teacher Academy, Al-Albayet University, King Saud University, among others. In his various roles, Dr. Alamoush has provided expertise on learning strategies, assessment and evaluation, and cognitive neuroscience for teachers. Research interests include learning and teaching strategies, Arabic language education, cognitive neuroscience, and its impact on reading comprehension. Dr. Alamoush also leads a research group focused on literacy for fluency and reading comprehension in the UAE. Expertise Language Education Literacy Cognitive Neuroscience Teacher Training Arabic Education

Kingsley Asante Dedicated and innovative educator with expertise in TESOL, Business, ICT integration, and academic leadership. Committed to advancing education through research, technology, and professional development. Recognised for excellence in student engagement, building positive relationships, giving outstanding feedback to students and fostering a culture of learning

Wafaa ElSawah is an educator, researcher, and instructional leader with over 13 years of experience in higher education, educational technology, and inclusive pedagogy. She is currently pursuing a Doctor of Education in Educational Technology at the British University in Dubai. Her research focuses on the ethical integration of generative AI, assessment design, and learner engagement in technology-enhanced environments. Wafaa has served as a lead instructor and senior manager in professional education programs across the UAE, designing and delivering training in AI, data analytics, and digital transformation. She has authored multiple peer-reviewed articles and book chapters on programming education, inclusive learning, and the use of assistive technologies. Passionate about equitable innovation, Wafaa's work bridges instructional design, academic integrity, and digital ethics in rapidly evolving educational landscapes. She is an active member of the AIEOU Research Hub at the University of Oxford and the Gulf Higher Education Network.

Areej ElSayary is an Associate Professor and Chair of the General Education department within the College of Interdisciplinary Studies. She previously served as the Graduate Program Coordinator within Zayed University's College of Education. She is a distinguished academic experienced in STE(A)M Education, curriculum design, teaching methodologies, assessment strategies, and school accreditation. Her knowledge and experience extend to her role as a certified associate of the Blackboard Academy, a recognized Fellow of the Higher Education Academy (FHEA), and a respected Editor and researcher. Dr. Areej has conducted numerous impactful teacher training programs across the United Arab Emirates, further elevating the region's education quality. Beyond academia, she is a Mental Health Ambassador at Zayed University, an ICF Coach Member, and a cyberpsychologist bringing her specialized expertise in positive psychology to promote holistic well-being. Her research interests encompass a wide spectrum, spanning cognitive development, cyberpsychology, human-computer interaction, entrepreneurship, innovation, design-thinking, interdisciplinary STE(A)M approaches, and advanced assessment methodologies.

Zeina Hojeij is a Professor in the College of Interdisciplinary Studies at Zayed University. She holds an EdD in Educational Leadership and Administration from Saint Louis University, USA. A certified peer reviewer for the UAE Commission for Academic Accreditation (CAA), Middle States Commission on Higher Education (MSCHE), and Quality Matters (QM), and Fellow of the Higher Education Academy (FHEA). Prof. Hojeij combines expertise in leadership and curriculum development with a strong research portfolio focusing on educational technology, leadership development, and teaching innovation. She has taught and coordinated undergraduate and graduate courses in Education and interdisciplinary studies while maintaining a ten-year commitment to teacher mentoring with the Al Jalila Foundation. Prof. Hojeij holds professional certifications, including Blackboard Certified Specialist, Accredited Facilitator, Certified Online Instructor, and CELTA & CELTYL qualifications. Fluent in English, Arabic, and French, Professor Hojeij brings a global perspective to advancing educational excellence through regular presentations at international conferences and publications in peer-reviewed journals.

Karim Ragab is a UAE-based school leader and STEM educator with 22 years' experience spanning teaching, curriculum development, and K–12 leadership. He is Vice Principal at Ittihad Private School–Mamzar, where he has led literacy/numeracy initiatives, strengthened instructional quality, and driven measurable gains. Previously, Karim served as Principal for the Applied Technology High Schools (Dubai and Umm Al Quwain). An active IEEE member, he previously developed national Applied Technology curricula and mentored students for Emirates/WorldSkills competitions. He represented the UAE as the CNC turning expert in the WorldSkills competitions (Leipzig 2013 and São Paulo 2015). Karim holds an MSc in Mechanical Engineering (American University of Sharjah) and a BSc from Alexandria University, and he is completing a PhD in Educational Technology (Universidad de Córdoba, expected Mar 2026). His recent publications focus on interactive technology in STEM education and energy efficiency in schools.

Index

A

C

www.ingramcontent.com/pod-product-compliance
Lightning Source LLC
LaVergne TN
LVHW081521300926
849161LV00006B/1256
9798260003282